EVENTIDE

Other books by Cindy Martinusen

The Salt Garden

Winter Passing

Blue Night

North of Tomorrow

PRAISE FOR CINDY MARTINUSEN'S NOVELS

"Compelling and poignant, Martinusen's *Eventide* will grip your heart and not let go! Another brilliant story by one of today's most riveting authors."

—SUSAN MAY WARREN,
award-winning author of *Flee the Night*

"Literary, heartfelt prose distinguishes this beautiful story."
—*Library Journal* review of *The Salt Garden*

"Martinusen's elegant prose creates memorable characters and evokes the sea's eternal power and mystery . . . readers of all ages will be transported into a tale of hope and renewed faith in the grace and sovereignty of God."

—*CBA Marketplace* review of *The Salt Garden*

"Combines elements from so many fine genres, reminiscent of so many fine secular authors."
—www.faithfulreader.com review of *The Salt Garden*

"Martinusen's language is almost poetic in its beauty."
—www.ChristianBookPreview.com review of *The Salt Garden*

"An author to contend with in the CBA market."
—*Publishers Weekly* review of *North of Tomorrow*

"Martinusen's gift for storytelling and passion for history add much to the world of Christian fiction."
—*Publishers Weekly* review of *Blue Night*

"Simply one of the strongest novels this year, this blends past, present, and future with compelling writing that captures the heart, imagination, and soul in one fell swoop."
—*Library Journal* review of *Winter Passing*

"*Winter Passing* is a tribute to mothers and daughters, and the love that binds them. It is testimony to the enduring nature of love."
—*Romantic Times*

EVENTIDE

CINDY MARTINUSEN

WestBow
PRESS
A Division of Thomas Nelson Publishers
Since 1798
www.thomasnelson.com

Mar

Published in Nashville, Tennessee, by WestBow Press, a division of Thomas Nelson, Inc.

WestBow Press books may be purchased in bulk for educational, business, fund-raising, or sales promotional use. For information, please e-mail SpecialMarkets@ThomasNelson.com.

Publisher's Note: This novel is a work of fiction. Names, characters, places, and incidents are either products of the author's imagination or used fictitiously. All characters are fictional, and any similarity to people living or dead is purely coincidental.

Library of Congress Cataloging-in-Publication Data

Martinusen, Cindy McCormick, 1970–
    Eventide / by Cindy Martinusen.
      p. cm.
    ISBN 1-59554-082-2 (trade pbk.)
    I. Title.
    PS3563.A737E94 2006
    813'.6—dc22

2005016964

Printed in the United States of America

06 07 08 09 10 RRD 5 4 3 2 1

for those
known and unknown
who kept me

Prologue

I t was momentary and often overlooked, though it happened every day.

A glance toward the eventide had stopped Carrie before, made her consider all the sunsets she'd missed, but never a pause with such foreboding. The sunset had been dramatic as Carrie, with Lauren and Graham, walked the cobblestone path along the village seashore. Now the light settled down, bringing a dark feeling of change. She quickly made a joke and laughed to avoid whatever warning this night attempted to bring.

"Beat you to the water," she said and started running.

Lauren raced after her until they reached the shore, where they kicked off their sandals to let the smooth Mediterranean waters cover their feet.

"I beat you," Carrie called, though Lauren had been ahead of her.

"Oh, no, you didn't," Lauren said, reaching down to splash water Carrie's way.

Graham approached more slowly, watching them as he came, the silent observer.

"We should swim," Carrie said, gazing farther out. Each wave slid softly over the pebbled shore to wrap around their feet. Behind them, strands of jazz played somewhere; the sounds of laughter and conversation in robust Italian tones filtered down from the village.

"It's nearly dark," Lauren said.

"Yes, it's nearly dark," Graham echoed as he came to Carrie's side. She laughed at his smile, remembering their night in this very place, swimming in streams of moonlight.

"And the Benders are expecting us for dinner," Lauren reminded.

Carrie sighed, thinking how perfect it'd be to swim in waves turning a deep chrome blue.

"Oh, it's the eventide," Carrie said, staring at the light on the horizon, the evidence of the sun's staged bow and exit into the sea.

Lauren unwound a string of seaweed from her feet.

Standing beside Carrie, Graham stared in silence at the liquid rhythms that met the last stretches of light on the horizon. His fingers wove through hers, and Carrie felt the electric tingles of his touch. She wondered if that sensation would ever subside—how she hoped it never would.

"Surely you have a poem or quote for this moment, Lauren," Carrie said.

Lauren splashed softly through the water to Carrie's other side. "Well, hmm, as Longfellow wrote, 'The day is done, and the darkness falls from the wings of Night.' I could go on."

"Yes, do," Graham said in an interested tone that pleased Carrie. Graham had tried to bridge the rift that had come at Lauren's arrival in Italy a few weeks earlier.

"'As a feather is wafted downward from an eagle in his flight.' That's enough," Lauren said firmly, though she smiled at them both.

"Lauren does this all the time—remembers the best quotes and says them at just the right moment. I wish I had such a memory." Carrie took Lauren's hand and pulled her closer. Now all three faced the darkening horizon.

Carrie knew the discomfort between Lauren and Graham would improve in time. It was her love for both of them that brought them together on this *bella noche*.

We each have our secrets. Is that what keeps Graham and Lauren at a distance? Perhaps soon we will give what we carry to one another, our burdens lightened at last.

"We should get back," Lauren said, then took a step away. "Or, I could go if you guys want . . . you know, some time alone. We only have a few more days left."

"Then back to America," Carrie whispered, wondering how to ever leave this perfect summer in Italy. Would it all disappear once the real world returned, become like a dream or a story once told?

"I really am American through and through," Lauren said. "And I'm so happy to be traveling home with an escort. The getting here alone nearly did me in."

Carrie laughed. "Well, next trip to Europe, you'll have to come for the entire vacation, not leave your best friend to jaunt around while you sit behind an office desk."

"Next trip to Europe, eh? Oh, to be back to Coke that tastes like Coke," Lauren said.

"Back to hamburgers and fries," Graham added.

"Back to jobs, responsibilities, and routines." Carrie frowned and was surprised by the warmth of Graham's kiss on her cheek.

"Always my free-spirited Carrie," Graham said softly near her ear.

Lauren stepped away. "It's getting dark. I'm going back to the *pensioni*."

Carrie turned to Graham and studied his face in the deepening night. Their eyes spoke of a deep longing and of summer days. "I guess we should go back too, not send her along alone."

"Yes, and we have a few more days together."

"And our entire future," Carrie said, then called to Lauren, "Wait, we'll come with you."

They turned from the sea, sand clinging to their wet feet. Shoes in hand, they climbed the steps back toward the promenade, back into the village lights, where Italians and tourists meandered along the narrow streets and village plaza. Carrie glanced back, then stopped. Lauren waited a few steps ahead with Graham beside her. Darkness had overcome the sea and sky except for a thin line of deep red that faded to a hazy blue and black. The stars were taking their places, shaking off sleep and tired eyes. Carrie thought how easy it was to miss the vast wonders within each day.

"Good night to the sea, to the sun and the day. We have plenty more together."

Carrie felt sudden meaning in how they all stood in this moment. An eventide foreboding. A time that was the end of something. What would they find in the time to come?

"That is a promise," Carrie said, then to Lauren and Graham, "Promise?"

"What are we promising?" Lauren asked.

"To be together always. No matter what the future holds, let's promise to stay close and never let life steal us away from moments like this. Moments together."

They both hesitated. Carrie met their eyes and sensed their unspoken commitments.

She wouldn't let worries or apprehension take over these final Italian days. Someday they'd look back at the years since this moment and tell the stories of this summer and of the time between. This night would be a marker in her life, the ending of one age and the beginning of another.

And anyway, that someday was surely a long way off.

TURN BACK

Time: every moment there has ever been or ever will be.

1

He'd been found again.

That thought came to him in the early predawn light. It was during such times Graham Michaels questioned whether he was running from something or actually seeking the elusive. Perhaps both.

He lived on the sea. Water surrounding him, his livelihood there, his existence, where he slept and planned and prepared for the next destination. The sea. Fluid movement. Unreliable. Unpredictable. Erratic and fickle. The place he was at home. Then something would catch up, uncover his hideaway. Sometimes it might simply be a line from a book, some random song on the radio, the scent of cold stone in winter that reminded him of the streets he once walked upon. Or someone coming to find him. His past was his shadow, ever present even if the glare off the ocean waves helped him forget.

This morning, he'd been found again.

It was a gray morning and Graham's eyes followed the wood grain of the main cabin's roof. He hadn't slept well and felt no desire to leave the warmth of bed. A car alarm from the harbor parking lot had awakened him in the night, wouldn't let him go back to sleep. Then the foghorn off the coastal barrier sounded louder and nagged, unlike the comfort its lonesome moan usually brought him. He'd drunk coffee before bed, perhaps that was the culprit. Even though it was cold and left over from the afternoon before—sometimes it tasted better that way, strangely reminding him of compromise. His entire life was a compromise, for both the good and the bad, and cold coffee in a busy day served as a simple reminder.

It was still dark with the predawn feeling in the chill of the hour. The sea slapped lightly against the hull of his boat. The fishing boats had already gone out for the morning, engines waking, creaks of footsteps and hulls knocking against docks. Their wakes rocked his sailboat as they turned their way from the harbor toward the currents of fishing fields out in the open sea. Next would come the newspaper boy zipping along the dock, tossing papers onto the remaining boat decks with a soft thud, occasionally a soft thud then a splash, then a profanity or two.

He listened to the day's approach as he stretched beneath the white down comforter. Graham had gone to bed with socks on last night, but now felt the remaining lumps invariably kicked to the bottom along with the top sheet crumpled in a ball. It seemed he was waiting for something, though he couldn't fathom what. Until the ringing of his cell phone. No one called this early.

Graham found the phone by the greenish light it produced, tucked in a corner cubby beside his clock. The caller ID told him who it was.

"Jasper, I thought retirement meant you'd sleep past the sun."

"Hey lad, how'd you know it was me?"

"I could feel it. I've told you that before."

"Don't know how you do that," Jasper said with a laugh, knowing a tease when he heard one. "Then guess you already know what I have to say too."

"Yes, I do. Breakfast at the Shack, you're buying—that's awfully nice of you."

"Oh, you," came the chuckled response, then Jasper turned serious. "Gotta tell you something Irene told me this morning. Guess a woman stayed over at the Sea Lion Inn and started asking about you. She, the woman that is, not Irene, asked directions to the harbor and whether your boat was in or not. Irene might have been too helpful."

"What does that mean?"

"You know Irene. That woman doesn't know how to give a simple answer. She could talk for hours to the cat. Don't know all she told the woman. She don't know that you like to lay low and all. Irene was pretty sorry when I told her. At least she didn't give out your cell phone number. But I 'spect you'll be having a visitor pretty quick. Thought I'd let you know aforehand."

"Thanks, Jasp. And tell Irene not to worry herself. I'm sure it's fine. Maybe that clearinghouse sweepstakes I sent in, or most likely someone wanting to book an outing on the boat." Graham was already tuned for the sound of footsteps on the dock.

"Well, sorry anyhow. If you'd like, I'll meet you at the Shack, though seems it was your turn to buy. Or you could come hide out at my place."

Graham laughed, wondering what exactly Jasper believed about his need for privacy. Did the old fisherman have ideas of prison breaks or bounty hunters chasing his tail? Maybe he looked through the post office wanted flyers expecting to see Graham's face one day. And still he remained loyal.

"I think I can handle this. And I'll take you to the Shack. I was waiting till half-price Tuesday."

"Oh, you." Jasper laughed again. They talked about the weather then, every fisherman and boatman's favorite subject, then said their good-byes.

Graham liked Newport, Oregon. Years earlier, he'd traded life in an apartment for a forty-one-foot Morgan sloop at a harbor dock. On the sea, Graham could forget. He could live in a small harbor town, head for open sea, or explore a chain of islands in a foreign landscape. There he'd forget the past, forget that people searched for him, forget he couldn't run far enough. He'd been here a year and planned to stay at least another winter. He hadn't even the inkling to go until Jasper's phone call. Then the usual escape routes advanced in quick succession. Where this time? Maybe some warmer climate; he hadn't been to South America yet.

Just as quickly, his plans halted. He'd taken a small loan for boat equipment, opened a checking account, signed a lease with the harbormaster: all commitments to keep him from another impulsive departure.

Graham rose from the fore cabin, leaving the blankets on his bed in perfect shambles. The scent of fresh-brewed coffee drew him to the galley. That scent was his alarm clock, preset on the coffeemaker the night before and welcoming him to another day. The wooden floor felt cold on his feet, and he wondered where he'd stuck his slippers. He walked bent down through the short passageway from the fore cabin, passed the head, and moved into the galley where he could again stand fully upright. He'd been teased about that before by the few visitors and the clients who came aboard. "You're too tall for a sailboat," he'd heard more than once. But something about the compact surroundings comforted him. Once he'd rented a spacious house and had hardly slept the entire three months he lived there. A boat was his secret hideout, insulated and confined, but ever ready to pull anchor and sail away.

Drawing the galley door inward, Graham hopped up the stairs to the deck. The morning mists lay heavy over the floorboards and his bare feet were cold and wet as he searched for the morning paper—it never was tossed in the same place twice. He raised his head, holding the boom, and looked toward the end of the line of boats where the parking lot would be found. No one yet.

Newport, Oregon, was the closest thing to a permanent residence he'd had in years. The waitresses knew him at the diner; the guys at the dock fought with him over whose turn it was to buy. The baristas at the Wired Whale Espresso Shop waited for him every morning. One regular had told him the women would announce, "Here he comes," and immediately start his cappuccino. He liked to joke with them a bit, get a smile and laugh, comment on how nice they looked. And they made a perfect cappuccino, comparable to the ones in Europe. He was no longer the newcomer, the foreigner, the curiosity. He attended church a few times, was a regular at the dock pub, played on the local softball team last year. The old fishermen called him "lad" after Graham humored them with his flawless Irish accent, an imitation mastered by having his father's Northern brogue in his ear and from his time in Ireland as a boy.

Yet he hadn't invested enough to really mourn a departure. If he had to, he could leave in a moment.

The paper now opened before him, Graham poured a second cup of coffee, then stopped to listen again. It was too early for a visitor, he reminded himself. The woman, whoever she was, would come later.

Who was she? What was it this time?

He'd been in small locales all over the world. And still someone would find him. Maybe he should try harder. He could change his pattern, move inland, maybe disappear into the wilds of Alaska. And yet, he couldn't imagine leaving the sea. He loved it like his mother once had. Was it because of her love of open water that he'd never left it? An honor of sorts to a life cut short?

Mother and the sea and the stars, he recalled. On a night in Ireland, when Graham was missing home during their six months away from the States, she'd taken him to the beach one night. His father worked late in the heart of Belfast, so this was an adventure for just the two of them. She brought a star chart with a wheel to show the constellations in each season. They'd lain on the sand, a wool blanket folded nearby for when the night turned cold.

"There, do you see Orion's belt and the Great Hunter?"

He'd tried to see the images in the stars and sometimes he'd say he did. Years later, he would know the stars like friends and wish to show her all he'd learned.

"It doesn't matter where you go, Graham, if you can reach the sea or see the stars, then you'll feel at home. It could be in the Pacific where I grew up, or this cold Irish Sea. You could travel to Kokomo, you know, like in the Beach Boys' song, or the Great Barrier Reef, and still the sea and sky will whisper the same words to you. It will remind you that I'm near, that God is even closer, and that you have a journey of worth ahead of you. Find the stars or the sea, and you'll be okay."

Graham would go to Kokomo and the Great Barrier Reef. He'd go inland and outland, but always he sought the water and the sky. He found his mother there and something akin to the God he'd once believed in with such innocent faith. When life became bleak, as it always eventually would, he'd find them. It wasn't some supreme comfort as perhaps his mother hoped to give him. The sea was infinite loneliness; it understood him.

From outside, Graham heard the soft patter and jump of cat's paws. At the meow at the door, he reached and flicked the hatch back open. "I think you're trying to move in, Captain Salt," he said to the white fluffy stray. "Have you seen any strangers wandering around out there?"

A meowed response and then Salt gazed at him in the usual feline disdain and walked to inspect his cat dish for approval or rebuke. Today, rebuke. Yesterday's remains of Fancy Feast chicken delight.

"Ordered around by a miniature dictator who doesn't even live here. You remember that. This is temporary, got it?" he said as he filled one dish with clean water and the other with a fresh can of cat food. Then he noticed that the cat's hair was more rumpled than usual. A tuft near his shoulder stood at an odd angle. "And off fighting again, eh?"

As he watched Salt from the table, Graham wondered at his thoughts of his parents. They hadn't been on his mind for some time, and yet, this was how they always came to him, in unexpected moments. The up-and-coming visitor, he told himself. That was why. The woman might be asking questions about Ireland again. Or it could be the cousins or Aunt Fiona, or his mother's family— someone might have died.

Just the thoughts of the various notions brought the past knocking. *You can run, but you can't hide.* Clichés were called clichés for a reason.

He sat on the edge of the built-in bench that wrapped around the table. Soon, this woman would come, and then he'd decide what to do. Where to run this time. Or what to face.

And so he waited. Graham realized he'd been waiting for years.

LAUREN RENDELL NEVER did things like this.

Now Carrie, this was something Carrie would do. And yet, it was for her best friend that Lauren was commencing a journey she never wanted to take. She'd never planned to do it alone. Most likely, the next days would take her around the world. She'd know for sure today.

The hotel room smelled slightly of smoke, though she'd

requested a nonsmoking room. Lauren smelled her pajamas as she folded them but couldn't detect any scent transferred into the linen material. As she placed them in her open suitcase, neatly packed and organized, she thought of how much she'd use that suitcase in the days ahead.

Yesterday Lauren had rented a car and driven north along the Pacific freeway from California to the rocky Oregon coast. Worries for her grandfather attempted to be an excuse to abandon the cause. Yet, he'd waved from his yard as she left, saying, "I'll be fine. You can do this, kiddo. And be sure to relax while you're over there! Savor life a little!"

She pictured Grandpa like a rebellious teen enjoying a reprieve from a watchful eye. And it wasn't as if she had a husband or children longing for her return, only an office staff who might appreciate her more by the next week, some houseplants, and her bulgy-eyed fish.

Of course, there was also Carrie.

This was for Carrie, she reminded herself even as her nerves fidgeted at the thought of a plane ticket dated the next day, destination Firenze, Italy, and Lauren still unsure whether she'd really find this person from the past. Without his confirmation, Lauren might as well be off to search an Italian village for that proverbial needle in the haystack.

She stared a moment at a nondescript watercolor in typical hotel décor, then returned to packing her suitcase on the bed. Lauren hated hotels, especially after watching a TV news special about the less-than-sanitary conditions of such places. Now she could nearly visualize the hundreds of people who'd been there before her, their germs in the air, underwear and socks on the floor, their bodies using the same bathroom. Disgusting. Many unfamiliar places awaited this week; she was leaving behind the comfort of her safe and scheduled life.

Carrie. If only they could be doing this together. Or at least taking the trip to Europe as they'd planned. And a return that wouldn't end in mayhem as the last trip had fourteen years earlier. But Carrie could not go. And this was the least Lauren could do, or the most perhaps.

She gazed at herself in the mirror. Dark hair in a disheveled mop and even darker circles beneath her eyes. If anyone believed there was "no place like home," it was Lauren. And just great—she'd forgotten her favorite shampoo and would be using the Sea Lion Inn special, surely the cheapest brand known to mankind.

What am I thinking? Carrie always gets me into trouble, but this time I'll be in trouble alone. She won't even know to help me out.

The compelling thought would not let her rest. She'd prayed again and again to get rid of it. Still it remained. This "quest" called to her as nothing ever had, except Carrie's adventures that brought her kicking and screaming behind. This one wasn't Carrie's doing, it was hers.

First, she must face him.

Lauren researched at home and then the night before in the hotel room. His name was in the local directory. Graham Michaels Charter Co. and *see advertisement*. His forty-one-foot sloop provided chartered excursions, sunset cruises, and day sails. A business on the sea. The woman at the hotel counter confirmed enough for Lauren to be certain it was the same Graham Michaels from Carrie's past.

"Oh, you can find him at the docks; most every morning he's there." The woman told his boat's name and the location of the harbor. It was almost too easy. And yet, there was nothing easy about facing an old enemy. Yes, Graham Michaels sounded like a favorite in town by the woman's description—if only she knew the Graham that Lauren had known. Lauren tried to imagine what he'd be like now, the teenager turned man. She knew some about his life from years earlier, a little about his childhood, but everything would be changed.

He wouldn't remember her, she expected. This was not the meeting of someone from her past. Well, not exactly, for they had spent a week together long ago. And yet in a sense this man had been present in her life. People do that, Lauren knew. They influence other lives without permission. She might pass someone a thousand times, drive by where they work every day, sit a row behind them on an airplane, eat at the same restaurant, then somehow they become important, essential even, life-changing perhaps.

It wasn't exactly like that for Lauren Rendell and Graham Michaels. Their association came through someone else. They had both loved Carrie. Lauren had loved her since childhood; she loved her still, or else she wouldn't be here. Graham might have loved her one summer fourteen years earlier. Beyond that she couldn't say.

A taut curiosity filled her. Curiosity and something akin to hatred. Who was this man who'd stolen something of her best friend so many years ago? Who was this man who'd nearly destroyed Carrie with his betrayal? Who was this man Carrie still thought of longingly, and why did she wish him to remember something beyond them all? Whoever he was, he didn't deserve it. And as she thought of it, replayed her part in the betrayal, Lauren knew she didn't deserve it either.

THE REMNANT OF dreams.

Of late, many nights were filled with subconscious journeys Carrie couldn't recall. Were they dreams, or were they nightmares? All that remained was a great need to know the narrative and the meaning.

It felt like near obsession, this desire to recall them. The study of the ceiling as she awoke gave no answers. The little notebook beside the bed yielded nothing. She read about people in the Bible who were visited in their sleep—was that it? And yet the message she was supposed to know was forgotten as the sun rose up another day.

After several nights of forgotten dreams, this early morning Carrie felt drawn toward the dusty steamer trunk stowed away in a back closet. Once long ago, she'd put a postcard in there, a dream-like picture from Salvador Dalí's mind. *Impressions of Africa* was the title, though Dali hadn't actually been to Africa when he painted it. Was that postcard what brought her toward the trunk and its treasures of the past? Would it offer some clue to her night-time haunting?

Carrie walked slowly as the now-constant ache crawled through her muscles. Passing the wall of family photographs, she continued down the hall, passing her son's bedroom until she reached the farthest guest room. She opened its back closet. Here the past was boxed and locked away, nearly forgotten beneath dust and darkness, yet never truly gone. For Carrie Timmons, the past was like the scar on her right hand—constantly lived with, yet so familiar as to be forgotten.

The opening of the trunk brought the reminder of letters.

I want to believe that I'm stronger now. I might be strong enough for both of us. At least, it feels that way today.

These words were written. And many more. They returned to her as she found, instead of the Dalí postcard, a stack of worn and faded envelopes buried deep inside the steamer trunk. Was this what she was meant to remember? Envelopes sealed and unsent. Pressed together, wrapped in twine and stored away.

Carrie didn't need to open them to know the writing inside. She was their author. She'd placed them inside their paper prison, licked the sickly sweet edge, locking them away from herself.

Not one had been mailed.

Within a single moment I loved you.

I've defined by when the moment began.

An opened trunk, her grandfather's but not unlike Pandora's perhaps, held the mementos of her earlier years. There was a buried life behind the trunk's latch, the buried life her own.

You may not believe me, but despite the mistakes, both yours and mine, you made me better in ways you cannot comprehend or imagine. I wish there'd been time to tell you.

The words were inside the letters, words she recalled without opening the seals.

Two lives. One viewed by the outside world. She was wife, mother, substitute puppeteer for children's church (even if she wasn't very good), and all those roles enjoyed that amplified her, where she smiled, made small talk as she held a shrimp on a cocktail napkin or sipped coffee and chatted with friends and acquaintances.

And then there was the buried life.

Was it our wish for more beauty? Or did we find in each other an escape from the sorrow we endured? How can pure motives turn so harshly against us?

In that world, she existed far from the people around her. Even with her faith in God, she sometimes felt a sense of herself as being meaningless in the agelessness of time. It could be blamed upon the past few years of illness, and yet, it had existed long before the diagnosed disease began eating away her organs. And perhaps the illness was a physical manifestation of the disease that had been killing her since that summer.

That summer.

The disease of a season gone by. A brief couple of months that haunted her these many years later. It existed as a shadow over her entire life, even back to the farthest memory. For now, childhood memories were clouded by what would come. Her days lying in her tree fort with a book, dreaming; she was always dreaming. The "what would come" marred those youthful moments of innocence like watching from afar as a predator made a stealthy approach toward that child.

I will say this again in two years, ten, seventeen, a hundred. You'll tell yourself it couldn't be true; you'll think time has taken it away or that we didn't share enough for its continuance. I know, it makes no sense to me either. It doesn't fit neatly in this world, and it was such a short time. But you are part of me, and always will be.

Far away came the sound of a foghorn. If she opened a window, Carrie could hear the waves against the rocks. Even as morning grew outside, darkness pervaded the room, pressing around where she sat on the floor. Carrie glanced up for a moment, finding it strange to be here as if between two worlds, two lives. How strange to know the words inside the envelopes. To have them suddenly return, and yet, had they ever truly left her? Were they not like every breath or the blood moving through veins—ever constant despite any consciousness of their existence?

One summer changed everything. And she had never quite recovered.

She'd learned to live with the shadowed presence. Sometimes she embraced it, believing it heightened who she was. Sometimes she attempted another round to kill it, to live without the longing and want. If only she had some answer. If only he'd said good-bye. If only she knew he was well and happy and that he remembered. If only . . .

I'm not asking for everything, just as I can't give everything to you. But I wish for even a small place within your heart. And hear me this time when I say—it would take eternity for me to forget you.

Find me someday. Please. I will need you. You might even need me.

But he had never come.

Carrie was curious to open the letters, to read each word and live inside them again. She shoved the envelope stack to the bottom drawer.

Instead of opening those age-old seals, she returned to the other mementos of the past, suddenly wishing for hot tea to warm the chill away. In one drawer, she found her old pink diary with its metal clasp, a baby blanket, first shoes, and her baby book with a lock of blond hair taped inside. School papers, crafts, and awards. Then a folder from her high school days with front covered in graffiti: *I love John Cusack. Depeche Mode rules! Carrie and Tom Cruise. U2 forever! R.E.M. is awesome!*

Carrie opened the folder to find various writings, sketches, and her list of life goals written at the ripe age of seventeen.

Travel in Europe; have own art gallery; go skydiving; see my favorite paintings with my own eyes; live a long and meaningful life; get arrested over some meaningful cause; kiss Bono . . .

She then noticed the section dedicated to her best friend and their conjoined life goals.

Get an apartment with Lauren; make Lauren go skydiving; take Lauren to Europe; have kids at the same time as Lauren; always be friends . . .

As she read the list, Carrie was surprised at how many goals she'd accomplished, and how many she didn't care to fulfill now. Except for one: live a long and meaningful life.

This was her most certain failure.

Carrie picked up a stack of miscellaneous photographs; it was like a slide show of the events of her life.

One photograph made her pause. Had she really been looking for it all along?

It was Italy on one of the last few days.

Sitting on a bench, legs crossed, she looked at Graham with a mischievous grin. She'd been so unaware of what would come. Was that really her? It didn't seem like the person she'd become, not with the mistakes and hurt she'd cause in the days following and in the years since. Carrie never got to keep one photograph of Graham; he'd always been behind the camera. She'd believed she had time, all the time in the world, never imagining that he'd disappear completely from her life.

You said, "This has never happened before, where the floodgates open in such a way. I feel a connection with you, I can be myself."

Such words shared, between two people, it's like an agreement, or a promise. Sure, it didn't always seem real, as if we existed outside or above all things mundane and existential. Yet, that does not erase what was spoken.

If only she could return to it, start again, take the steps over. Say something different, make him believe in her or at least make him understand. Not leave a perfect summer in Europe such a mess, with wreckage unresolved behind, and a scarred hand her only visible wound.

And then she knew.

Something of this photograph had been in her dream. Could it be the secrets left behind that day might still be reconciled? For fourteen years, she'd wondered, did Graham bury the box as they'd planned, as he'd promised? If so, it would be there, beneath that bench, at least that had always been her guess. She tried picturing it, the stone seat on the rocky cliffside on the coast of Italy.

But now, I simply love you. There's nothing expected; sure, there's much wanted, but I'll love you still.

The words of her final letter written six years after she'd last seen Graham. It was the day before she met Jason and journeyed down a new path.

Graham, where are you now?

15

A tiredness swept over her. It took enormous effort to return to her bed with the floor hard beneath her aching joints. *This must be part of those dreams,* she thought. *This is what I seek in the deep of sleep.*

The unresolved. The good-byes. The final search for meaning. Should she find the box that carried the secrets, or make sure they were never revealed?

She had to make a plan. She was running out of time.

HE'D NEARLY CONVINCED himself that either Jasper or Irene had been mistaken. He'd scheduled the week's cruises on his laptop, checked weather forecasts, played a game of online poker, worked on an advertising idea, and ordered a new winch for the boat. His shower was done, though he didn't shave, worried that someone would arrive while he was in there. The cabin and galley cleaned up, he'd packed dirty clothes for the Laundromat and replaced the cables to the engine battery. All the while he was also pausing to listen. When he went above deck to test the engine, he peered toward the parking lot for the umpteenth time.

Finally, he decided to get out of there. He'd done all his morning duties, and it was only 9:00 a.m. As he grabbed his keys, Graham heard footsteps. They were the halting pace of someone unfamiliar to the docks. The fishermen had hard, confident steps. These were softer on the wood, and hesitant, definitely hesitant, probably reading boat names as she went. Graham looked at Salt, who yawned lazily at him. "Hey, if I wanted a pet, a nice little dog could replace you." The steps grew louder. This would be the visitor looking for him. He considered locking the cabin door and peering from a porthole until whoever it was left. Oh well, why not see what this was about?

"Hello?" the woman called.

He picked up his laundry basket so he could give that "you interrupted me when I was leaving" look and bounded up to the main deck. There she was, about his age, no business clothing like someone handing out subpoenas or what a lawyer might wear. Jeans and a casual wool jacket. And not bad-looking either.

"Graham Michaels?" she said, lacking all warmth in her tone.

"That would be me. What can I do for you?"

"You don't remember me, then?"

He took a step forward, grabbing the boom and moving it back behind him while trying to recall her features. "Should I?"

"I didn't know you very long. It was in Europe. You were sort of dating my best friend."

"Carrie Myles," he heard himself say, though he couldn't recall this woman's name. He remembered her, but she looked different . . . an adult, that was it. A hundred thoughts flooded his memory at the mention of Carrie and that summer.

"Yes, Carrie Myles Timmons. I'm Lauren, Lauren Rendell."

"Oh, yes, Lauren, that's right." He stood there, wondering what he should say. *How are you? How is Carrie? Why are you here?* "Would you like to come aboard?" He motioned over his shoulder. "I have coffee."

"Well"—she glanced back toward the parking lot but didn't move—"I guess, sure. It's just . . . I'm here . . . there's a reason. You see, I need your help."

Lauren regretted it immediately. She didn't mean, "I need your help." Where did that come from? Where had all her practiced words gone? She'd planned resolve, strength, anger if necessary. Not need. Never need. Especially with him.

Here was the one person who nearly destroyed her best friend. Images came in quick succession: Carrie drenched in the rain, hand covered in blood, the months afterward when Lauren wondered if she would ever truly smile again. Here he was, rising from the mouth of his sailboat, laundry basket in hand, grinning that smile Carrie had written about before Lauren herself met him in Italy. She'd hoped back then that Graham Michaels was all Carrie believed him to be.

Now, with her slip of words, Lauren felt a nauseous churning in her stomach. Slightly tanned from the sea, brown wavy hair, blue eyes, a white T-shirt that didn't hide a fit body, he appeared happy, or at least healthy—unlike Carrie. This shouldn't surprise her, she knew this, had found him on the Internet and then learned more about him the night before. But seeing him was different. Somehow he'd become fiction, never truly real, not after so many years. Yet here he was . . . alive and well. Only hours away from Carrie. How long had he lived in this town so like their own? How easily it seemed he'd survived that summer, when Carrie barely had.

It's been fourteen years, she reminded herself.

Graham set the laundry on the deck and rubbed a hand over his chin.

"What do you mean, help?" he asked, stepping back as if to revoke the offer of coffee.

"I'm not asking for money or anything like that," Lauren said, then stopped talking. Everything was coming out wrong. She sighed, thinking how to rephrase it.

"How is Carrie?" he asked carefully.

How could he just ask that, such a simple, normal question? As if Carrie were an old friend from high school.

"You remember that summer," she said, then again felt dumb for saying the obvious. Her purse hung awkwardly from her shoulder as she felt a sway in the dock beneath her feet.

He sat on the edge of the fiberglass cabin, gazed back down the dock as if looking for a way of escape. Typical Graham, just as she'd expected. Carrie would defend that, would offer an excuse for his behavior as always.

"Of course I remember," he said so softly she barely heard. "That was a long time ago."

His sudden unease strengthened her. "All I need is information. I wouldn't be here if it wasn't essential. You left something back there, in Italy, remember?"

His dark brows furrowed for a moment in thought. "You mean . . . Carrie told you about that?"

"Yes. And I need to find it. You're the only one who knows where it is."

He stood in silence, staring at her for a long moment, his eyes haunted. Then, raking a hand through his hair, he said, "Come aboard. Did you want some coffee? How did you know about the box? Carrie and I promised never to tell anyone."

"A lot of promises were broken," Lauren said. She stepped onto the boat, grabbing a rail for support until she found her footing. "Carrie needs something from the box. It's important."

Now they faced each other on equal ground. He was taller than she realized, but her tenacity was gaining. She'd come here for two reasons—confirmation that he'd done what he promised, that he'd buried the box that summer in the place Carrie believed it to be, and to get that exact location.

"So she sent you to find out where it was?"

This caught her off guard; she quickly recovered. "No. She doesn't know I'm here."

He again rubbed the day's growth on his chin. She noticed a half circle on his chin that looked like the nick of a razor. Lauren knew from Carrie he'd had that since a young age, a scar from a tragedy that took his parents' lives.

"This doesn't make sense. Why now? And why is it important?"

"She's not expected to live through the winter. She's sick. Maybe she wants whatever is inside for her seven-year-old son." His composure dissolved and for a moment, he looked hurt, even as he processed the facts. He surely hadn't known that Carrie had a son. He wouldn't know she was sick. Lauren hoped it hurt. He'd hurt Carrie beyond what he could ever imagine.

This was nothing.

"I promised coffee," Graham said, disappearing down the steps into the galley. He was glad she didn't follow.

From above, Lauren called, "Tomorrow I'm going to Europe. That's why I'm here. I need to know if it's there."

Everything so fast, tumbling over and over, memories, Carrie, that summer, the last night, the buried box several days later—what else to do after everything fell apart but do at least one thing he'd promised. He'd thought of the box from time to time, wondered if it was still buried or lost or destroyed. And Carrie sick now, dying, and a son. She had a son. Seven years old. He remembered being that age. Knew tragedy at almost that same age. Taking a mug from the wall hook, he poured a cup of coffee and stared into the black liquid, suddenly not knowing what to do with it.

"So is it there, or did you destroy it?" She was peering inside.

He took a drink, then remembered he was getting it for her.

"It's there," he said, wondering why he didn't lie. This was something, if ever anything, to lie about. And he'd spoken enough lies in his lifetime.

She hesitated, seemed to want to ask more, then looked like she might leave.

He remembered the contents of the box. "But wait," he called and hurried up the stairs, hot coffee spilling from the cup and splattering across his chest. "You don't want to do this."

"Do what?" she said, staring at his shirt.

"It's better left buried."

"Yes, that would be your philosophy, wouldn't it?"

She had no idea. Carrie hadn't told her everything, this he knew. And Carrie didn't know his part either.

We'll both put something important inside. Something no one knows about . . .

"I'm warning you . . . ," Lauren said.

"Warning, or threatening?"

"Okay, giving advice, how's that?"

"If you find it . . . it will change things. It's not just a box that two kids buried. It holds secrets. Some things should stay buried. Forever."

"Now I'm intrigued."

"I'm serious about this," he said firmly. She knew nothing, not really. But something stirred inside Graham, an old need to set things right. If he could get the box's contents from her . . . "Listen, sit down and give me a second." This time he did bring her a steaming cup and found he had to know. "So she's . . . married?"

"Yes. Happily. Very happily. Their son is the best kid in the world. She couldn't be better, well, except . . ." The facade was crumbling.

"What's wrong with her?"

"A rare form of multiple sclerosis."

Graham knew nothing of the disease. "What's her son's name?"

"Eddie, Edward."

"Eddie . . . after her uncle, right?"

Lauren didn't like his question, or maybe she didn't like recalling the closeness between him and Carrie. She set the coffee mug down and pulled her purse over her shoulder. "Where is the location exactly? I don't want to be overturning rocks for days on end."

He didn't know if she should do this. The uncovering could set off cataclysmic events in other people's lives. It wasn't something to flippantly give in to.

"There are a few things I have to tell you first. And I need you to promise me something."

"Promises, eh? You're asking me to keep a promise to you?"

Her comment hurt and also brought further distrust. How *could* he trust her? Why should he? She'd shown herself un-trustworthy in the past. Carrie had trusted her, but then Carrie had trusted him too. *Because of Carrie, that's why.* He owed her at least that much.

LAUREN ACCELERATED ONTO Highway 101 north toward Portland. Tomorrow morning, she'd be on her way to Italy. Nothing to stop her now. Right? She tried in vain to find a good reason that would keep her from this insane adventure. Her usual excuse that her grandfather needed care was even relinquished with his new part-time home nurse and housekeeper.

Her main consolation was anticipating Carrie's reaction. Surprise. This was so unlike Lauren, Carrie would hardly believe. *Surprised* was too light a word, more like *stunned, floored, astounded, shocked.*

But there were rules attached, or promises rather. She thought for a moment of Carrie and Graham in that lifetime ago. How romantic and idealistic they were to bury a box and promise to open it together in a year. It was something from a book or a movie. Not reality. And yet, Lauren found herself wishing to have someone of her own to do something like that with.

Once she found it, she'd make one last contact with Graham. But surely what was inside couldn't be as bad as he'd insinuated.

Surely.

PAST THE LAST harbor buoy, Graham pulled the lines and let the sails whip into the wind. There was a moment, like a pause, after the engine was shut off and the boat dropped speed and the sails unfurled. That dramatic pause when the canvas caught, and the sails harnessed the wind, tempting and taming it at the same time.

The sea had power to quiet a soul. The rhythm of waves like eternal breaths brought perspective. Graham needed the melodic width around him to ease the day's events. Lauren Rendell. He should have never told her the location—why had he? If she didn't do as promised, everything could change—and not just for him, for many people.

There were dots of memory on the map of his life, pinpoints like cities that Graham could return to, but most of them were regrets. There were occasions of beauty, times of joy and peace, momentary though they'd be.

More evident were those places along the journey that changed him. One stood bright and clear—the day when he was seven years old that changed him, beyond repair, beyond healing, beyond redemption.

And from that date, there were other places he could stop and remember. One was a summer. One lone summer in the maze of his thirty-two. The summer he remembered and yet loathed to remember. Yet today it was brought back beyond ignoring.

He turned the wheel and pulled the rigging with a zing of line in the pulley. The boat shifted upon the waves toward the south, bouncing for a moment, then catching the wind again and surging forward.

He hadn't wanted to break his promises or betray Carrie. Surely it appeared to her that he was heartless. But he *had* his reasons, good reasons really. And he'd written her, called, shown up in various locales where he might find her. She didn't know how many conversations he'd shared with her. He'd come back, found her, been there right when she needed him most.

Only she knew nothing about it. The heroics he envisioned hadn't translated so well into real life.

For a time, he'd all but put her behind him. He'd met other women, fallen into infatuation or whatever it was he occasionally experienced, and fallen out again. There'd been a fiancée for a short time when he thought perhaps settling down might work for him. The fact that he was allergic to his engagement ring whenever he tried it on was the sure sign of failure. Erin was now married to a stockbroker and lived in New York. Graham had turned toward being successful for a while. It just didn't satisfy him—the games of golf as business meetings, the corporate lunches. That life that itched of facade to him. The sea called for his return.

But there were always the times Carrie came to him. Something would trigger the memory of that summer together. Perhaps a new novel he knew she'd enjoy, a mention of Europe or an Italian movie, or the way the raindrops hit the glass window and slid all the way down. And there she was. He could nearly reach out to touch her face, that line of her chin, the curve of her lips. His fingers would catch every tear, and she'd nestle herself so perfectly against him.

He'd imagined a thousand scenarios. Yet, this was for the best.

For him. And for her. Their future impossible. *Some things in this world don't make sense.*

Surely Carrie had moved on. Convincing himself of this helped. His own trumped-up arguments kept him from finding her again. He told himself every possible lie. *She manipulated you. She never loved you. She wanted to take you over, make you her own. That summer wasn't real life. And Carrie didn't know what you did— if she had, her allegiance would only be from sympathy. The poor victimized little boy. The childhood lost. The pity party with hats and horns. She'd say God forgave you, or that you hadn't done anything wrong.* And that would be the greatest lie. She, she, she. Any accusation became a mantra, repeated and reminded and believed.

In moments of honesty, he accepted his own manipulation. He knew he'd betrayed her. He could admit that he hoped she remembered him, and that he wanted her connected to him, even in a small way. He couldn't bear the regret truth brought, so instead Graham busied himself with a new voyage or an adventure of some kind.

Graham looked at the compass on the gear panel. He was going south. Suddenly he realized Harper's Bay was south. He'd come out for a short sail, a day on the water. But how easily he could keep going and be in the town where Carrie lived.

Carrie. Her name never fit her. It was common when she wasn't.

He had hated Carrie for a time, for as long as he could. It kept him away, and he *had* to stay away. "You can't make me hate you," she'd told him, one of the last things she said though she was crying at the time.

Someone once told Graham he could hate only what he once loved.

Carrie was dying.

He needed to see her one last time.

Three Months Earlier

Carrie had come to this appointment alone.

Jason wanted to be there, but she assured her husband it was another simple appointment, and after all, North Coast Bank did need its VP. The bank president had been patient the first year of her illness, the second a little less, so now, Jason didn't attend the routine doctor visits. He would wish he'd been here today. And yet, she was glad to hear the verdict alone, to attempt to process the words, the impact that they wrought, and to walk into the bright sunshine of an ordinary July day.

She felt more alone with people all around than sitting solitary beside the sea. Such news deserved an epic setting. Not a bland doctor's office with elevator music in the background instead of a dramatic Andrew Lloyd Webber composition. People drove in SUVs and minivans with errand lists, lunch hours, destinations. Carrie sat on a bench and watched them. A group of teenagers jogged across the street, trails of cigarette smoke drifting behind. Summer vacation, she thought, probably up to no good. And really, why did it matter? A century from now, they'd all be dead anyway. It wouldn't even be close to that long for her. It wouldn't even be a year.

Dr. Linn tried to make sure Carrie had a ride home. *You shouldn't be driving. You shouldn't be alone.* She assured him she was fine. It's not like this came completely out of the blue. For over two years, she'd faced such a possibility. And yet, this news arrived when they'd believed finally life could be normal again and health, like for everyone else, taken for granted. Movement unencumbered. A hospital no longer a second home. Their son would know kids in the park better than kids in the pediatrics ward down the hall. She and Jason might get a few romantic weekends together.

Another thought, how they popped at random through her mind. Plane tickets. Two sets waiting in their protective sleeves, dated several months from now, and yet they'd been so excited—both she and Lauren. How would Carrie tell Lauren that she couldn't go now? In three months, she might be too sick to leave home. They'd planned and waited; Carrie's improved health appeared a miraculous U-turn. They'd promised to return to Europe, a redeeming trip.

Maybe this was punishment for a past Carrie had yet to forget. It might be justice, this death by slow, destructive disease. Except then she thought of Jason, Lauren, and especially of Eddie. How was this justice to him? What in his seven and a half years could bring Eddie such a fate?

How could she tell him good-bye?

THE RECESS BELL sent Eddie's classmates hurrying toward their various favorite places on the playground. Four square, monkey bars, the catch-and-kiss tree. His favorite was usually tetherball. Eddie was nearly the best tetherball player in the second grade, if only he could beat Mia Chavez. But today, he didn't race to the tetherball line. Instead, he walked carefully with the wooden box tucked beneath his arm. He headed toward the picnic table he'd told Tanner to meet him at when they'd seen each other on the bus. Tanner wanted to know all about the games inside the box, but Eddie wouldn't risk the pieces being lost on the short ride to school.

"I'll beat you," he heard Tanner call from behind him. Eddie tried to walk as fast as a run, but Tanner went speeding past, bustling through a group of girls.

"No fair," he called after his best friend.

A sudden whistle brought them to a halt.

"Come try again, Tanner," the lady on yard duty said. "You know not to run until you reach the play yard."

Eddie couldn't help but grin as Tanner stomped back toward his classroom.

"I won," Eddie said in triumph when Tanner finally reached the picnic table.

"No fair," Tanner said but with a smile. "So, can we play now?"

"Sure. We can pick from five different games."

Eddie patted the smooth polished wood that rested on the table between them. He carefully opened the rectangular box with game pieces inside. It had been a gift from someone; he couldn't remember if it was Uncle Mike or someone else. He only recalled them sitting in the hospital waiting room and going through the different games it provided, all with small magnetic pieces.

"We could play chess," Eddie suggested.

"I don't know how to play that."

"How 'bout backgammon or checkers? Checkers is easy; I learned that when I was five."

"Okay, I've played checkers too. I learned when I was three."

"Yeah, right," Eddie said as he pulled out the metal plate with colored squares covering it. Then he slid it into the grooves on top of the box so it was ready for the magnetic pieces. He loved the little click when the magnetic pull snapped the piece and metal together.

"How come you can bring this, and I can't bring my GameBoy?" Tanner asked.

"I don't know, but I did ask Mrs. Smith before I brought it. Maybe we should ask."

Something familiar caused him to look past Tanner toward the street behind the tall school fence. It looked like his mom's silver car. It was his mom's car. There she was getting out and waving.

"Mom?" Eddie said, setting the game on the bench. They met at the tall chain-link fence that separated them.

"Hi, honey," she said, then over his shoulder, "Hi, Tanner."

"Hi, Eddie's mom." Tanner smiled and turned toward the game board.

"Are you helping in class today?" Eddie asked, wondering if it was Wednesday, then at the same moment remembering they'd already had library so it was Thursday.

"Oh, I was driving by and saw it was recess. I wanted to spy but you spotted me."

He laughed, imagining his mom in black clothes, running from tree to tree. "You needed my spy glasses."

"I know," she said with an exaggerated sigh. "If only I'd thought of that."

Her fingers gripped the metal fence again, her pinky waved at him. He smiled and looked behind him. Tanner had returned to the picnic table and was playing with two game pieces, putting the magnets toward each other until the forces pushed them away. Eddie reached up and curled pinky fingers with hers.

"How's your day so far?"

"Pretty good. Nicki's mom is bringing dirt cupcakes 'cause it's her birthday."

"Dirt cupcakes?"

"The kind with gummy worms and broken cookies on top so it looks like dirt. We ate them last year at the harvest festival, remember?" Then he remembered she hadn't been there; that had been Grandma Stella with him. He felt bad for saying it, for bringing back that day. He'd heard her crying because she was too sick to come. It wasn't even her usual disease that time, but some sickness in her lungs because she'd been in bed so much. So Mom missed another fun thing. Her blue wig was on the bathroom counter—she

29

had planned on being a rock star—and she hurt badly. She started coughing so hard there was blood on the tissues and on the counter. He'd thought of it all night at the Halloween party, whenever he'd seen a vampire or scary person with fake blood on their face. He told Tayler H. that his mom had real blood on her face; Grandma told him to not talk like that. He decided it was good to not think about it either. Thinking made him sad.

"Wanna have lunch with me?" Eddie asked. "It's pizza day."

"Would love to, but I have some errands. We'll get ice cream after school."

"At Frosty Cone or Espresso Joe's?"

"You pick."

"Hmm, I'll think about it."

"Okie dokie . . ."

"Artichokie. In a while . . ."

"Crocodile." Mom glanced over her shoulder, then blew him a quick kiss. Eddie jumped back as if it smacked him on the cheek, which made her laugh. He liked it best when he could make her laugh. It was pretty easy, even when she was really sick. He stayed at the fence while she got back in the car.

"Next time, I'll bring the spy glasses and you'll never see me."

Eddie was about to respond when Tanner called behind him.

"One of the magnets fell out!" He had crawled under the picnic table and was searching the concrete with his hands. "Gross, there's a bunch of gum under here."

Eddie ran back; he had to find that magnet. He'd stay there all night if he had to. He'd get one of those machines that his grandpa had, the one that found gold and money. They'd used it once on the beach and found an earring and eight dollars in coins. What if they still couldn't find it? But before he reached the table, Tanner held up the magnet in triumph. "Found it! Oops, there it goes again!"

Turning back toward the road, he saw his mom already leaving. He waved even though he knew she couldn't see his good-bye.

SHE'D HAD NO intention of stopping by the school after her doctor's appointment. In fact, Carrie had planned to stop by the bank to see Jason. She didn't want to interrupt him at his office, but she longed for the strength his presence immediately afforded. But the compelling to see Eddie was gravitational. The quick touch of fingers more than enough to renew her.

Now Carrie drove from the school, pausing at the stop sign to look back toward Eddie and Tanner as they crawled under the table. They were probably imagining it was a fort or something. There seemed no limit to the imaginations of those two.

Strange to watch him from a distance and see Eddie without him seeing her. As if she were already gone and viewing him from afar.

How could she leave him behind?

Logically, of course, Carrie knew it wasn't her fault. Her mind reminded, reprimanded, defended. And yet, it was the betrayal of her own body that took her away. Her organs had given up, they'd put up the white flag of surrender, and soon they'd be defeated, a saluted departure as they sank into the depths.

Another car braked at the four-way stop to her left, and the driver peered at her expectantly. Carrie accelerated through, glancing once more at the playground receding behind. She wouldn't see him in third grade. Who would know which teacher to request? She'd have to make a note of it—there'd be lists of things that needed instructions like that. She imagined the class parties of next fall, the ones she wouldn't volunteer in or bring goodies that received excited welcomes. Her son wouldn't hear classmates announce, "Eddie, look, your mom's here."

God, I can't do this. You can't let this happen to us. At least, let it be longer, give me more time.

And with that plea she realized it was one she'd prayed three years earlier, and here she'd been given all those days and holidays and moments. Still, she couldn't keep from asking. If the answer was no, what then? What could she leave behind? What did it matter that she'd ever been here? Her husband could someday remarry, hopefully to someone who loved him as Jason deserved. That man was a rarity in this world. Eddie would adapt somehow. Vague memories of her might return, but would he become more bitter about what he'd lost than thankful for the time they'd shared? Perhaps she'd leave one of those videotaped messages, maybe several, to be watched at different stages of his life. Graduations, wedding, the birth of his first child. But then, in a way it might be a little creepy to have continuing messages from the dead over the course of someone's life.

How she wished to give that little boy on the playground something more than illness and death. How could she bottle up a mother's love to last an entire lifetime?

THEY WERE MEETING and both with news. Café Francais was their favorite lunch spot—a newer restaurant offering a hint of European flair and a healthy menu to satisfy two small-town women who considered themselves somewhat cultured.

Lauren had one hour for lunch from her job as a supervisor at Harper's Insurance Company. She'd advanced up the corporate ladder at the north coast branch since starting as a receptionist her senior year of high school.

"How's the career?" Carrie asked with a smile. Often she inquired about the ins and outs of Lauren's life as a working woman. Some-

times Carrie considered going back to work or school, but something always kept her from getting there—her years of illness especially. "Did Mr. Barney call this week?"

"Of course. He asked what dosage I thought his wife should be
taking for this new disease she had."

"And you told him you're in insurance, not pharmaceuticals?"

"I've tried, but he is lonely and cares for his wife all alone. He
just needs someone to talk to . . ." Her voice trailed off as the waitress set down her coffee and Carrie's mango green tea. Carrie's gaze
seemed distant, and Lauren wondered if she was feeling down again.
She knew her news would cheer Carrie up. "Okay," she said once
the waitress was gone. "I'm going first—I found the perfect little
place for us in Paris. Already booked it and everything."

The long pause from Carrie surprised her. "Lauren. I can't go."

Lauren waited a second for the joke that didn't come. "What do
you mean? Why not?"

"I saw Dr. Linn yesterday."

A dark foreboding washed over her. She'd known about the
appointment and hadn't even thought to ask. It was one of so many
appointments, and they were past the devastating declarations by
now. "And . . . what did he say?"

Carrie stared into her tea. "It's so strange to say. So strange to be
sitting here with you and be saying this . . ."

"What?"

Carrie looked up then, and Lauren knew. If ever she'd been
stunned to silence, this was the moment when she knew with
absolute clarity what those words meant.

"It's back," Lauren said. "What kind of treatment?"

"None that will do much good this time."

Lauren could hear the attempted lightness in Carrie's tone.
Lauren's mind did a slide show of the last few years, from Eddie's

birth to the first diagnosis. It had even sounded hopeful, no big deal really. Then all those years of illness, trying this and trying that. Then at last something worked. Carrie was back. A future—a healthy one even—awaited after all. Life would return. It would be one of those stories other women told of sickness and recovery.

"How long?" Lauren heard herself say.

CARRIE HAD SPENT the day before rehearsing. She couldn't spend every moment thinking about it, going through the prognosis would lead to fear if she considered things like pain and suffering and slow agony. Instead, she focused on the immediate. How would she tell her loved ones that she was going to die? She wanted to be brave, yet she also knew they'd want to be brave for her.

What words to say? They would be as individual as the person she spoke to. The rehearsal began. She tested and tried different versions.

So, I went to the doctor today and he didn't have good news.

Well, I guess I'm not going to be around for long.

I'm going to go to heaven before you. Maybe I can help Jesus prepare a place for you.

It looks like this will be my last summer. We may need to have an early Christmas.

Jason had been first. He simply reached out and held her tightly as she cried. His own tears fell in silence down his face and into her hair. But Jason was also the fixer. Already he'd begun Internet research and was talking to experts and making appointments for second opinions. She wanted to hope as he did. Hope was good, of course it was. But so was reality.

He'd said with confidence, "You and Lauren need that trip. All the planning and excitement. You couldn't wait to see your favorite painting at the Uffizi and go to that town on the Italian Riviera. You should go."

"I don't want to be gone from Eddie. Or from you."

"You could do a quick trip to Paris."

"Too far away. What if I hit some bad spell, or some terrorist attack kept me over there?"

"So, you mean it, you don't want to go back?"

She knew what he was saying. This could be her last chance. Maybe she should think about it. But Carrie didn't need to consider. "I asked, and the doc thinks I won't be up for travel."

That stopped him. His hopeful expression dissipated. His shoulders fell. It was only a few months until the trip. How could she deteriorate so quickly? She knew Jason was thinking, *How can she be leaving me so soon?*

She knew Jason would continue his research, continue seeking alternative methods of healing.

Eddie should have been next. She wanted to tell him. It was going to be the toughest. He'd already been through more than a seven-year-old should experience with all her stays at hospitals. But Carrie didn't want to live with the shadow of death continually hanging over, and Jason was convinced there'd be some new procedure or some miracle from God. So they decided to wait before telling. Eddie could enjoy the next months without worrying over his mother's condition. More time of normalcy sounded good. Maybe she'd even get a few short day trips. There were three paintings she had wished to see. Only one was within a day's drive now. The Bouguereau in San Francisco, but no chance for the Dalí in Belgium or Lippi in Florence. The Bouguereau would have to do.

Now the words were spoken to Lauren. How strange to see her friend across from her, sitting at their favorite café, quiche and hot drinks before them. How strange to know this wouldn't be forever. Oh, the many things she'd taken for granted.

Lauren seemed speechless.

Carrie spoke instead, knowing visions of their trip together struggled to die inside Lauren's mind just as they did in her own. "I feel terrible about Europe. There was so much we wanted to see again, and the new things we'd planned. Seeing those paintings too, just one more time. And everybody raves about Prague."

"Heard the food is cheap in Prague," Lauren said. Her voice was small, distant.

"Oh, the *apfelstrudel* in Vienna."

"*Gelato* in Italia."

"Café mocha and crème brûlée in Paris," Carrie whispered as if they were holy.

"Do you notice it always comes back to food?"

"I guess so," Carrie said with a smile. Then a sudden seriousness came over her. There was something else, other than food, that she'd especially hoped for. "There had been something else . . . ," she began. "I'd thought of seeing if Graham really buried that box as he promised."

Lauren didn't respond, but she didn't appear surprised.

"Of course, he probably didn't bury it anyway. So that mystery will always be . . . well, a mystery."

Still Lauren didn't respond. Any mention of Graham over the years always brought cold contemplation on Lauren's part.

"Is there anything I can do?" Lauren asked.

"Are you sure you mean *anything*?"

The pause. Lauren was famous for her pauses, but she always took the bait. Carrie's best friend, who had risen up the professional chain of command, had a difficult time with decisive confidence outside the office doors.

"Yes, I think," she said with reluctance and a slight smile, "I need to get out of here."

"Huh?"

"Just for a few days. I want to see something. It'll be my last time. Jason wants me to go to some specialist in San Francisco anyway. So, I thought since Europe can't happen for us, why not at least a little trip to the city? It won't be the Uffizi Gallery in Florence, but I'm dying to see the Impressionists at the Legion."

Lauren smiled, a sad and weary one but a smile nonetheless. "That'd be good. Yes. We'll go to San Francisco."

"We'll get to see our favorite Bouguereau. One of my favorite three. Remember when we first saw it?"

"Sophomore-year French club field trip. What's the name of the painting?"

"*The Broken Pitcher,*" Carrie said. "And the others too, Renoir, Degas, and wasn't there a Seurat?"

"I think so. And of course, the Monets. It'll be good to see them again. When do we go?"

"Soon. We need to go soon."

EDDIE KICKED THE wooden box, sending the small magnetic pieces scattering across his carpet floor. Mom was gone for the weekend. Dad said it would be fun for them to spend time alone together. But he wasn't being very fun. Something was wrong again. Dad pretended to smile and be cheerful. He was calling Grandma and Grandpa a lot, even Eddie's weird aunt Mags. And he kept saying things like, "We'll do something extra special," a sure sign of bad. He was on the Internet right now and seemed nervous when Eddie asked what he was doing.

Mom . . . she was sick again, Eddie just knew it.

Walking through the quiet house, Eddie went outside and sat on the back patio. He watched a few leaves make a dancing descent toward the swimming pool. Soon they'd cover it for the winter. The gate that separated the pool from the deck was locked. He loved the short months of warm weather and wished he could live in a place like Palm Springs where they'd once visited his aunt. They could swim all year there.

There was a noise at the corner of the patio. From behind a potted plant, Eddie saw Pepper raise her little head, all sleepy with blinking eyes. Then she stretched her chubby legs, yawned, and wiggled over, excited for some company.

"Go away," Eddie said. The little black Lab wagged her tail all the more. She jumped up and her front paws scratched mud onto Eddie's jeans. "Don't! Go away, stupid dog."

He pushed her back and hopped from the lounge chair. At the gate to the pool, he stared into the still blue waters. Paws again landed on his back, and Eddie shoved Pepper off him.

"Quit following me." Why didn't Pepper just go away? She was so annoying. Whining all the time, waking him in the night.

Having a puppy wasn't what he'd envisioned. Well, maybe a little. He'd wanted a dog for so long, had dreamed of his very own puppy. Every movie seemed to have a dog in it. Some cute tiny thing with floppy ears and big brown eyes. He came up with various names: Bandit, Chompers, T-Rex, Henry.

Actually getting a dog seemed to take forever. His dad kept making promises. "When your mom gets well. It'd be too hard to have a puppy with us at the hospital so often."

Eddie would argue back, "I'll take care of it. Mom would love a little dog, like another son."

"We'd come home to dog doo and chewed-up shoes."

"I'll train him."

"When Mom gets well."

And then finally, after an eternity, he got to choose a black puppy from a litter of five. Pepper, already named, was the first dog to spot him. As Eddie knelt before the wiggling mass of black, she came toward him and licked his hand. Eddie was sold.

The first problem, his puppy was a she. This was easily overcome with the idea of the future babies she'd have. Next problem, dog doo and chewed-up shoes. Pepper did eat everything in sight. And she jumped up on him, knocking him off balance sometimes. She didn't listen to him. Everyone said it took lots of time to train a dog. He'd tried to teach her to fetch for two whole days in a row, and still Pepper simply stared at him or jumped away to play chase. Eddie didn't mind so much—those occasions when Pepper slept in his bed made up for everything. He loved her sighs and the way she'd flop her head down beside him, then the little tail would wag before she hopped up to lick him.

But today, he didn't want Pepper bugging him. She seemed to have gotten the hint. He turned to see where she was and noticed Pepper chewing on something.

"What are you doing?"

Her head shot up, tail wagging slightly, then went back to chewing. Eddie recognized the red something being gnawed on. That was his mom's slipper.

He ran toward her. "Pepper! Bad dog, give me that!"

Pepper picked up the red slipper and ran. She sure was faster than when they'd first brought her home. She stopped on the lawn, the red slipper between her teeth

"This isn't funny! Give me Mom's slipper!" Eddie was almost to her when she sped off. She dropped the slipper in her haste, and turned back to snatch it up right before Eddie grabbed it.

"Bad dog, bad!" He chased Pepper around the yard. That was his mom's birthday present. She loved those slippers, probably wanted them when she went back to the hospital. And now they'd have dog slobber all over them.

Finally Pepper dropped the slipper. Her tail wagged, she barked, made a false jump toward him, then sped off. "I'm not chasing you. This isn't funny. I hate you. I wish I never had a dog! Stupid, stupid dog!"

Tears rolled from Eddie's eyes as he held the wet, mangled slipper.

He thought of his dad's words: "When Mom gets well, we'll get a dog."

They'd gotten the dog. Now Mom was sick again.

AFTER A QUICK game of rock-paper-scissors, Lauren settled into the driver's seat.

Lauren didn't particularly like driving in San Francisco as it was, and Carrie's overconfidence made her nervous.

"I'm not afraid to drive, but you are, so let me," Carrie said as Lauren navigated the congested streets. Joggers populated a sidewalk along the marina district, their bobbing heads moving at various tempos. The choppy blue waters of the Bay were dotted with sails, cargo ships, and ferryboats. It was one of those perfect San Francisco days—sunny and brilliant, as if the usual fog were really a cleaning instrument, scrubbing the air and brightening the lawns and houses and bridges. One of U2's newer CDs played on the car stereo, though Lauren had turned it down while she drove.

"You lost, fair and square." Lauren didn't want to debate right now—there were cars to avoid and lanes to pay attention to—otherwise, she'd be headed off in some wrong direction. This was why she lived in a small town.

"Oh, you aren't fair, but you are square. I know these streets better; now I have to give instructions. Does my driving really make you that nervous?"

"Uh, that would be a yes. You zip around like Mario Andretti."

"Get in the next lane or we'll be crossing the Golden Gate out of town . . . hurry!"

"I'm trying!" Lauren's stomach twisted, but she moved over just in time with only a single honk from behind. "A little notice would be nice."

They drove through the city, weaving around the Presidio, trying to find their way with Carrie's memory as their map. Lauren wondered if they'd find the museum before closing time.

"Doesn't this look familiar?" Carrie asked. "I think this looks familiar."

"You think? Great. Remember, it's been a while since I've been down here."

"Just think, we would've been leaving in a few months for Europe."

"Can we not talk about the canceled trip again?" Lauren said with the aggravated whine that always made Carrie laugh. And she did.

"I can't believe I forgot my map."

"Me neither. You'd go to your grave . . ." Lauren stopped and darted a look at Carrie.

"Funny how you don't realize all the little lines that have to do with death and dying and such."

"Yeah, so very funny."

"Okay, this really does look familiar. Turn at the next, hmm, how about right?"

"'How about right?' That's comforting."

"Remember the time we parked behind the golf course and had

41

to walk all the way around 'cause you wouldn't run across the green?"

"We might have been hit by a golf ball. Or gotten in trouble."

"And I listened, walked an extra mile—see, you always say I get you in trouble, but that's not true."

"You do get me in trouble."

Lauren glanced over to see Carrie kneading her own neck.

"You hurting?" she asked.

Carrie merely nodded. Lauren knew she hated talking about it. Already, Carrie seemed to be losing strength. Her eyes showed the weariness—it was almost always there, and so quickly it had come back.

"I do think this is familiar," Carrie said, pointing forward up a sloped street. "It's at the top of a hill, and it's close to the Golden Gate Bridge—remember those pictures we took with the bridge in the background?"

"Yeah, I thought that guy was going to steal our camera."

"I need to find those photos. Hey, look, I know I remember this. Turn there; look, there's a sign."

"Unbelievable." But there it was, as they drove by the golf course on the right, the Legion of Honor museum emerged above them. With its columns of white, the museum was an austere prince atop a grassy clifftop hill in San Francisco's Lincoln Park. Lauren drove around the upper parking lot, found no open spots, and turned past the museum, where she finally saw a parking space. Views abounded through the trees: the reddish orange Golden Gate and the vibrant bay waters had white party hats atop each rippled wave. "It's a Beautiful Day" should've been playing at that moment from the U2 album.

They walked beneath the first columns into the open courtyard, then stopped before the large sculpture that rested in the center.

"*The Thinker* comes to San Francisco," Lauren said, looking at the black sculpture resting his chin on one hand. He seemed smaller than she remembered—but it had been years since she'd seen it. The museum, with its Impressionist collection, had been one stop in the cultural experience of Miss Davis's high school French class. Since then, Carrie and Lauren had visited several times, but Carrie had come most often.

"What do you think he's thinking?" Carrie said, and Lauren smiled. Carrie always asked that when they stood before him.

"'Why do Americans stare so?'" Lauren said in a deep voice.

"'How come I can't be the original and stay in Paris?'"

"He's plotting how to get his clothes back on without the crowds watching."

"Maybe Rodin had a naked-in-public dream and decided to sculpt this guy as a way to release it."

After paying and picking up several brochures about the current exhibits, Lauren wondered if they'd go straight down the corridor toward the more modern artists of the nineteenth and twentieth centuries or turn toward the left and into the Renaissance wing as they usually did, savoring each painting until reaching their favorites.

"I can't wait," Carrie said. "Let's go straight to our old friends."

Sometimes they stood like art critics, staring with heads tilted in the same accord, index fingers to lips, brows furrowed as if they could decipher exactly what the artist was intending.

Today there'd be no "funning around" as Jason called their antics. Carrie seemed to be on a mission. They zipped through the first room, barely taking time to gaze at the paintings along the way. Lauren would often peruse at her own pace, but she followed Carrie, mindful that this was probably their last time here together.

"There it is," Carrie said in a hushed voice. She stopped in front of the large painting.

EDWARD-ADOLPHE BOUGUEREAU
The Broken Pitcher

The young girl, a peasant, stood at a well above a village in some old-world country, probably Italy, considering the French artist spent much of his time painting there. The girl's eyes caught Lauren's immediately, just as they always had from the first time she'd seen her as a girl herself. It took a moment to understand the title of the painting. At her bare feet rested a large water jug with a cracked and broken bottom. The background colors of the country-side were softly muted, while the girl's clothing and the blue pitcher were brought forth vividly.

But it was her eyes that brought Lauren back. As she stood shoulder to shoulder with Carrie, the girl seemed to gaze so deeply into her, those dark brown eyes leaping from oil paint and pene-trating the core of her. They were like Carrie's eyes—seeing so much with so little effort.

"She never disappoints me," Carrie said softly.

"I know."

"Do you know, it was like this the first time I saw Graham."

Lauren was surprised to hear her talk of Graham again. For so long, Carrie hadn't spoken of him, perhaps in years. Then in the last week, she'd brought him up several times. "It was like what?"

"One of those moments that kind of stops you."

Lauren wasn't completely sure what Carrie meant, and though she'd heard quite a few Graham stories, she was sure there were many more she didn't know. Mr. and Mrs. Bender were the chaperones on the European adventure. But Lauren's practicality kept her from going for the whole summer. The opportunity couldn't be passed up at the insurance company where six months earlier Lauren had taken a part-time job while finishing their final year of high school. Lauren had come late, promising to catch up with Carrie and the Benders once they reached Italy. Oh, how Lauren later regretted that when she had to travel alone to meet them. The flight had been terrifying even with Mr. Bender picking her up at the airport. And then when she arrived, tired and grouchy and wishing for familiar things, Carrie greeted her with a stranger in tow. Graham. Carrie had already written about Graham, yet seeing them together, Lauren realized how deep the feelings were between them.

"Did you first meet him on the beach?" Lauren asked. Her gaze roamed the painting, the backdrop of Italian countryside. How poignant that Italy met them here on canvas and in memory.

"Yeah. The Benders went to Milan for a few days to shop. I hadn't been feeling too well so I stayed behind. Figured I'd catch up on writing to you and try to get you to hurry up and meet us. I went down to the water, thinking a swim would feel good. These little kids were playing a game . . ." Her voice drifted off for a moment as if she'd journeyed into this painting, traveling around Italy until she arrived at that Italian seashore. "Their ball kept rolling over to me, so I grabbed it and joined in."

Lauren smiled. She pictured Carrie laughing with those Italian children whenever Carrie told this story.

"Along comes this guy that I noticed a long way off, before he noticed me. But I kept playing, ignoring that this good-looking guy was approaching. He stopped and started taking pictures of us playing. His poor Italian quickly revealed he was American, and he assumed I lived in the village. He asked us to pose for a picture. It was so strange, when he raised the camera up it seemed as if I was the only one he could see through the lens, and he knew I was looking right at him, right through the camera. We connected there somehow. Of course, I didn't think it was real. The photo was taken, I said something in English; I can't remember what. And that was that, the moment over."

"But it still isn't over," Lauren said, turning toward Carrie.

Carrie looked at her. "No, I guess some things you never get over. Or some people. His eyes were blue, did you know that?"

"Yes. I remember."

"It's strange; somehow he doesn't seem real anymore. And yet, in another way, he's more real than anything. I wonder if God works all these things out, you know, in the other life. Or if it's all just over."

Lauren touched her arm, struggling to express something she'd read several times in the last week. "Would you like to hear a quote?"

"Ah, a Lauren quote? I'd guess you have the perfect one."

"Of course. C. S. Lewis even. He wrote books for me to memorize since I have no life of my own. Here we go: 'But for them it was only the beginning of the real story. All their life in this world and all their adventures in Narnia had only been the cover and the title page: now at last they were beginning Chapter One of the Great Story which no one on earth has read: which goes on forever: in which every chapter is better than the one before.'"

Carrie bit the side of her lip and a lone tear streaked down her cheek. She nodded and turned back to the girl lost inside the painted world. "Maybe that's what I'll tell Eddie. That I'm starting Chapter One of the Great Story."

"I can't imagine telling him."

"I don't know what to say. And Jason believes there'll be a miracle, so he doesn't think we should say anything yet."

"We do believe in miracles. So why not for you?"

"I don't know. I can't explain it. But I just know this time. Sure, I'll doubt myself, I'll go back and forth, but at night, when I'm praying, and there aren't other voices in my head, then I feel at peace. I've been having strange dreams too that I don't really remember in the morning. I can't tell Jason to give up looking for a cure. And maybe I am wrong. But I don't think so."

Lauren didn't know what to say. How could Carrie just give up like that? And how could she ever let her go?

"Someday, will you show this to Eddie for me?" Carrie said. "Will you take him on this art journey and show him the paintings his mother loved? Will you, please?"

Lauren nodded.

"I should have brought him. There are so many things I wish I'd done with him. Maybe there will be time still. But if there isn't, show him this, and tell him that quote, again and again if need be."

"I will."

THAT NIGHT, CARRIE fell asleep before Lauren. They were both usually night owls, and here Carrie was exhausted and sleeping at 9:00 p.m. Curled on her side, the pillow bunched up and her hands holding the edge of the blanket, Carrie looked so much as she did as a little girl. They'd been friends so long that Lauren could barely remember life without her.

Lauren adjusted the pillow beneath her and glanced at the book she'd brought. There never was time to read it seemed. And this was the book Carrie said had changed so much of life for her. Somehow Lauren fought against reading those life-changing books—she didn't really want a changed life. And yet, change was coming, the greatest, most horrible change she could imagine. Without Carrie,

Lauren had no one. No one who knew her, no one who loved her. Not like Carrie did.

A loneliness swept over her, one she'd never experienced. Deep and penetrating, like osmosis it spread through her entire being. There was only once that she'd been this alone. It was that summer.

After that final night in Italy, Lauren was the escort home. Carrie had a bandaged hand and cuts on her face that would heal and disappear, unlike the scars on her heart. The journey from the Italian coast to Harper's Bay was a twenty-four-hour eternity. Carrie barely spoke, barely seemed to know where they were going. She functioned, could smile and communicate with basic human responses. But Lauren knew something foundational had shifted. She feared another crack could occur at any moment, a fracture that would unleash the flood, crumbling the barely shimmed exterior. Then what would Lauren do to help her?

Lauren's grandpa picked them up at San Francisco International Airport. Carrie had spoken to him, accepted a hug, told a few things about Europe, then the silence grew as they journeyed into the familiar landscape. Lauren said they were exhausted, an excuse for Grandpa to turn on his oldies station on the radio of his Cadillac.

Carrie didn't close her eyes, just stared out the window as the '50s classics played through the speakers. They both spotted the sign:

WELCOME & STAY
HARPER'S BAY

Then Lauren saw long, silent tears streaming down Carrie's cheeks, falling unchecked from her chin. When she reached for Carrie's hand, it was cold, clammy—like somebody dead. She grasped tighter, willing her own lifeblood to flow into her friend.

"We're here," Grandpa said as they pulled into Carrie's drive-way. "Welcome home, girls."

The car stopped. Carrie didn't move. She stared out the opposite window, her body rigid except for the flowing of tears.

"We'll be right there, Grandpa," Lauren said when he peered through the window, a worried expression on his face. He shuffled off, no doubt confused by the emotions of the female gender.

The tears turned to sobs, and the rain outside began as if to cry with her. While Grandpa opened the creaking trunk for luggage, Lauren took Carrie into the house.

No one was home. Carrie's parents were on some business trip, or so Lauren thought. Later she'd learn it was the first rehab attempt for Carrie's mother, and Carrie's father's first meeting with the one who'd become "the other woman."

As Carrie crossed the threshold of the front door, the sobs pushed out like crushing blows. Lauren stayed that night and came every day after. Carrie wanted nothing to do with life. Her body had become merely a shell. Sunlight unwanted. Food a burden. Water her only sustenance. Lauren became frantic. Should she call mental services? Call their pastor? Who?

The pastor in the end. Prayer and counsel didn't seem to help much, not at first. Lauren was sure her best friend was gone. Graham, that fool they'd left in Europe, he'd destroyed her. And Lauren had helped him. If only she'd known beforehand how Carrie would respond, she never would've been part of it.

Days came, passed, began again. Carrie stayed the same. Dull, quiet, harmless, emotionless—everything about her appeared diminished. She was nearly gone.

Then, like a shift of wind, something felt different in the dark, musty bedroom. Carrie's ascent began like a glimmer of light on a darkened sea. She nearly didn't believe she'd glimpsed it. Was it true?

Had she really seen it? A spark in Carrie's eyes, a hint of strength. Lauren found Carrie painting one day in the near darkness by the light of a lone pale bulb in her bedroom lamp. She used one color only—gray.

Thus began "the gray period" as Carrie would later call it. "Many artists like Picasso had blue periods; mine was definitely gray." Though after her gray period, Carrie would put away her paints and canvases for good, except to sketch something for Eddie years later.

But for a time, canvas after canvas, papers, watercolors, oils, charcoal. One entire wall of her bedroom. Gray. First, flat and indistinguishable. Then a touch of black on an edge, or a shading of darker to lighter gray. A drop of red, or white, once yellow—which brought Lauren to finally believe that Carrie really would recover. Lauren would find her friend again. The snap was repairable if not slow in healing.

With painting, Carrie added writing. Lauren didn't need to wonder what Carrie wrote or to whom she wrote the sealed letters. And yet, none were mailed. One day they disappeared from view.

"It's my only way to say what I didn't get to say," she said once, when Lauren had sat for a full fifteen minutes wondering if Carrie even knew she was in the room.

On this day Lauren said, "Carrie, the leaves are changing."

They both loved autumn best.

"I had wanted to see autumn in Austria," Carrie said and continued writing. They'd originally planned to stay in Europe until November, watching the colors change in the Swiss and Austrian Alps.

The next day, Lauren tried again. "You're missing a grand one. I'm getting all the best leaves."

Carrie lifted her paintbrush from the canvas. They'd collected leaves since childhood, seeing who could find the most vibrant or intriguing mix of colors.

Carrie's eyes gazed deeply into Lauren's for the first time. "There better really be leaves out there."

Carrie had stayed indoors for six weeks. Her sweats and T-shirt hung from her, and flip-flop sandals revealed toenail polish chipped and faded, a lasting testimony of the summer. She stood for a few moments at the open sliding-glass door. September was gone, and October was dressed in full-colored regalia. The coastal forest was an infusion of evergreen pines and ferns and deciduous trees covered in oranges, reds, and gold. An ocean breeze carried the scent of pine, sea, and autumn, brushing back Carrie's hair from her face. Her step outside was like some great moment; there seemed a pause, and Carrie said, "We need a dramatic sound track right now."

They laughed and Lauren said, "How about *Dirty Dancing*?" as they walked onto the back porch. "You could jump into my arms, though I might drop you."

Carrie smiled and took long breaths of autumn air. "It's like breathing for the first time."

"Well, it's so musty in that house. It smells like you've been living in a moldy sock."

They walked around the backyard, picking up leaves as they had so many different times over the years, comparing colors and designs.

When Carrie's hands were full of gold and red leaves, she stopped. "And so on October . . . what's the date?"

"The seventeenth."

"And so on October 17, I begin life again." Her smile appeared weak, her face pale. She looked small and fragile. "We can begin it together."

Lauren felt a burden lift, not entirely, but enough for now, enough to believe in a renewed life. "October 17. Together."

Years later, here they were.

But their renewed life had stalled out again.

Eight Years Earlier

They met in the Safeway supermarket parking lot, looking from opposite ends of a car's smashed-out windows. Carrie's car windows.

Carrie had received a call at work to pick up her mother from the Rusty Iris Bar. Again.

"I only had a couple of drinks," her mother slurred as they rode in the car.

"Mom, it's three in the afternoon. How do you get this bad by three in the afternoon?"

"This bad? This bad? Don't talk like that to your mother. If your father heard you speak to me that way . . ."

Carrie was tempted to say that her father divorced her mother for this very reason. Instead, she said, "Mom, I just have to stop by the store. I'm making dinner for Lauren and some friends from work tonight. Then I'll take you home. Don't go anywhere."

The crash made everyone inside the store jump; one woman screamed; a clerk dropped a gallon of milk, bursting its lid and splattering white liquid across the floor. Carrie knew, just knew it was her mother again. She ran outside, leaving the groceries on the counter. The front of Carrie's car was smashed into a light pole. Her mother was behind the wheel, and a guy in a suit and tie was pulling the mangled door open.

Carrie ran to the passenger side where she'd left her mother. "I was going to fill up the tank, that's all. It was on empty," Mother was saying; her forehead was cut and bleeding. Carrie caught the man's expression from the other side. He reassured in a glance, "It's okay, I'm here." Later Carrie would say the look said, "Here I am to save the day!" Everyone would laugh at the idea, Jason in a Superman suit, but in effect Jason did save that day and many days to come.

Jason Timmons was an executive at the local bank. He owned his home, ironed his own shirts every morning, had a respectable retirement fund by the age of thirty, and was involved in leadership in his church. He was stocky, slightly overweight with thinning dark hair. His boyish smile reminded Carrie of one of those adorable little boys with pinchable cheeks. He stayed with Carrie through the police report and as they watched her mother's protesting departure in the ambulance. Later, he drove her to the hospital. He made the call to Lauren on Carrie's behalf, and he stayed with them late into the night, carrying bad coffee in Styrofoam cups from the cafeteria's vending machine.

Carrie stared at him as he slept with his head against a wall in the waiting room.

"He's a great guy," Lauren said from beside her.

"He seems like the kind of responsible person you'd like," Carrie said.

"He didn't look at me the way he was looking at you."

She couldn't deny the safety his presence offered. A safety Carrie hadn't known existed, especially since the weight of her mother's drinking had rested so long on her shoulders.

Jason was gently persistent. He asked her out the next week while also helping with her mother's legal problems. When he didn't call—his attempt to not be overly persistent—Carrie found herself missing their talks. He'd lived a disciplined life, rising at 6:00 a.m. and going to bed at 9:00. As dependable as a well-crafted clock, he said. Now he was staying up late to talk to her on the phone. He said she brought more life to his world than he'd ever known. Her teasing, spontaneity, love of life, and humor he didn't always get— she was water to a desert land, or so he said. Carrie replied that a desert did just fine without water.

Jason had no dreams to leave the north coast. Carrie couldn't conceive of another person besides Lauren and old folks who didn't want to see the world or at least something outside the small-town life.

"This is home to me," he said when she asked. "My parents moved around a lot when I was a kid; maybe that's why they divorced. This feels right; I might live here the rest of my life. It's where I want to be."

They'd come to the beach for a picnic Jason had prepared. Carrie tried to argue, give the reasons why the world was just waiting to be explored. "But I like it here. I like the sunsets over the Pacific. Every night is a different one, as different as the many places you think are waiting to be discovered," he replied. "For me, every day is a new discovery, right here. Especially now that I've met you."

Carrie wasn't sure how to respond. A distant foghorn called its mournful song, and a seagull cried in duet. The waves made their steady slides across the pale sand. She thought of the many places she'd been and all the places she wanted to discover. He seemed to read her thoughts.

"Beauty can be found in most every place. And in most every person."

"Yes, but . . ." She couldn't think of an argument. It was the first time she'd questioned the wanderlust that moved through her.

It had been nearly six years since that summer in Europe. Carrie was twenty-four and still wandering in many ways. After returning home and the recovery afterward, Carrie's parents arrived back from their "trip" and announced their separation. Carrie stayed awhile in Harper's Bay, then moved with her father to Portland, starting community college—her fresh start, she hoped. Her mother's drinking progressed and soon included prescription drugs—she needed Carrie. And Carrie had missed Lauren terribly, though they talked daily, and she'd nearly convinced Lauren to move north.

Back in Harper's Bay, Carrie took a job working at a book and music store and quickly fell into mothering her own mother. Lauren offered Carrie a guest bedroom in the small house she already carried a mortgage on. Carrie traded time between her mother's house and Lauren's. Full-time at either place brought the walls closing in. Lauren had been her best friend since childhood, but they didn't particularly make the best roommates. Neat, organized, deliberate Lauren. Carrie wished for life to be full and vibrant—who cared if she left for the day with dishes in the sink? Lauren, of course.

The house she'd grown up in was sold now, divided like everything else in her parents' divorce. Her mother's new house hadn't been finished or fully moved into. There was a lone couch, no pictures on the walls, baseboards missing down the hall, cabinet doors unfinished, one bathroom without fixtures. It smelled of cheap paint and cigarettes. Carrie took on the Lauren-role at her mother's house—the responsible one; the one scrubbing, vacuuming, doing laundry, paying bills, stressing over the future. Her only hope was that she'd be leaving soon, very soon. Surely she could convince her mom to get into another rehab; surely her mom would stop drinking and seek a new life. Then Carrie could escape. The weariness lasted for years.

Then the car crash at Safeway.

Soon after, Jason and Carrie started dating, if Carrie could even call it that. She enjoyed his company even if there wasn't that passion she'd felt for Graham.

As they sat on the beach and the sun fell into a pink horizon, he said, "I fell in love with you at the hospital. That first night, I just knew."

He kissed her then, and Carrie's cares dissipated beneath the warmth and security found in him. Two weeks later, he surprised her again.

"Marry me," he said after they attended a local theater production together. It slid from his lips so quickly, even he looked surprised. And yet, it seemed to give him courage also. "We could ask Pastor Nickels, or drive to Vegas; maybe Tahoe would be nicer. But marry me. Will you?"

"But . . . ," was her response.

"I know," he said. "You were hoping for something you might watch in a movie. But what we have is so amazing—can't you see that?"

Carrie didn't know what to say. "Yes," she began. "I mean, I don't know! I'm afraid I'd be cheating you of something greater; you deserve more than me."

"Being with you, every day, for the rest of my life would never be cheating me. I don't want to push you into anything. But I believe in you, in us. I feel this love so strongly, unlike anything I've ever known. We can have a really great life. I'll always love you. I can take care of you, and I'll always be here. Carrie, I believe God brought us together. I've never believed something like that before."

Something in Carrie yearned for such words, though she'd never realized it before. "Jason, you don't know everything. There's really little you do know about me, about the past," she said in protest.

"But I *do* know you. I know you're a kind, good-hearted, loving person. You love God more than anything. You're beautiful and creative, and I know I don't deserve someone like you. I know you might later find me dull and boring, but I promise to do all I can to love you the right way. I promise to try to be worthy of having—"

"Jason, stop. Don't talk like that. I don't deserve you. My past is a burden. You don't need that."

"Even if you were an ex-con—"

"Who told you?" she said, then laughed at his stunned hesitation. He realized the joke and laughed too.

"Just think about it," he said. "I'm not going anywhere."

Carrie worried and wrestled over the thought. She knew Jason would be faithful, trustworthy, financially stable, and he'd be a good father someday. He wouldn't betray her, or leave her crying in the rain as that other someone had. He wouldn't cause such pain as she'd experienced. He wouldn't drive her to near madness, madness that caused her the greatest regrets of her life. Jason loved her. She wished to love him as much as he loved her, wished to feel what she'd had with Graham. But it wasn't there, and those memories in Europe would not depart from her life, no matter how much she told them to leave.

The next day, her mother called from jail. Another DUI.

Jason went with her, filled out the papers, talked to an attorney. The weariness crept over and deep inside. She was tired of being strong—years tired. Jason held her while she unraveled, and somehow his presence sewed her back up.

"You don't have to do this alone. I'm here for you. No matter what happens between us in the future, whether we stay friends or if it becomes more, just know I'm here. I love you."

From within his arms, those safe arms, she said, "Tahoe sounds good to me. Do you ski?"

Jason pulled away. "Tahoe, you mean, you will, really?"

"I will."

"I'll take a skiing lesson."

Carrie would marry Jason because he loved her. And he knew enough about her past, knew that though she cared deeply for him, she'd never quite recovered from someone else. He loved her still. And she loved him for it.

It would be more than enough.

JUST OVER A month after meeting Jason, here they were in Tahoe, supposedly dressing for a wedding.

Lauren could only shake her head at the whirlwind she was once again sucked into. One downfall of her friendship with Carrie was times like this—when things sped so fast she could barely keep up. And yet, wasn't that also one of the good things about their friendship?

Carrie was getting married.

But instead of pulling the gown over her head with that bridal glow, Carrie sat in the empty bathtub in her pajamas, her hair in rollers and fingers and toes freshly painted, cotton balls stuck between her toes. And she was crying.

Lauren stood at the window. The town was still snow-covered on this early spring day. Sunshine sparkled over the fresh crystals. Carrie's cream-colored dress hung on a hanger beside her, ready for the small, casual wedding scheduled to begin in one hour. She sighed. Carrie was getting married though she wasn't fully in love. And yet Carrie believed and hoped this was the right path. What could Lauren say to that? But Lauren had seen Carrie in love, and it nearly destroyed her. So why not take this safer path? The fairy tale wasn't what it seemed to be. Happily ever after wasn't really for this life.

"Are you okay?" Lauren said, walking to the open bathroom door.

"It's the life I never wanted," Carrie said.

Lauren had a sudden desire to shake her; and the anger surprised her. "I can't believe you're acting this way! He's an amazing person. He wants children and a home. He has an income that won't require you to work unless you want to. What's wrong with such a life? Can't you see the blessing in it? It's more than most people get. I know I'd be happy with it."

"I'm sorry, Lauren," Carrie said, rising clumsily from the tub. "I don't want to be ungrateful. Jason is a gift; I know that. What's wrong with me? Why can't I be more content?"

Lauren stood at the window, staring toward the white peaks that surrounded the lakeshore town. "Sometimes I think you weren't meant for this world," she whispered. "You don't know how to live here. Everything normal people want holds little value to you. I don't know how to change you, or if you should be changed."

Carrie stepped carefully beside her, trying not to damage her fresh toenail polish. They stood there a long while, looking at the mountains and chalets. A gondola rose along its wires toward a mountain peak. Carrie took her hand. Lauren knew they were both thinking of Europe and that last day on the Italian coast. Though they had not spoken of "him" or of "that summer" for many months, Lauren knew he was as ever present as the scar on Carrie's hand.

"I wonder what happened to him," Carrie said. "I hope he's happy."

"You hope for more than I do."

"You don't want him to be happy?"

"If I wasn't a Christian . . ."

"Uh, but you are."

"And being a follower of Christ, I know I should hope for his happiness too. But I'd rather just not hope for anything for him."

"Remember when we were kids, and we'd sleep outside and talk about our future husbands? We were full of wishes and dreams."

Lauren smiled at the image—two young faces staring toward the heavens. "And here we are—me husbandless and you unsure with only hours until your wedding. Maybe we should've wished a little harder, or prayed instead of wishing."

"How could we wish or pray more than we did? When I met Graham, I thought he was that answered wish. I believed so surely, I never once doubted it until that last day. Maybe God wants to be the thing we wished so hard for back then. And maybe He gave us long ago what we wanted so badly—true friendship with each other."

"Yeah, I think you're right." Lauren squeezed Carrie's hand.

"You've been an amazing friend, the best person one could dream of. I can't imagine surviving the things I've survived without you."

"Well, you've done all right; just don't think marriage means leaving me behind," Lauren said.

"Let's get me married before you start worrying about that."

THREE MONTHS AFTER the wedding, Carrie's mother died from a mixed dose of alcohol and Valium.

"Mom." Carrie stared at her mother in the coffin, wanting to shake her arm—sometimes it took a while to wake her mother up. This woman was a stranger. The mom Carrie had known in childhood had died somewhere along the way, without her ever knowing when, or why. Carrie could look back and see the wrong turns, but as a child, she'd missed it. Lost in a protective bubble. The mother of her adult years had various personalities, wanting to be Carrie's best friend, needing Carrie to be her caretaker, and despising Carrie for any minor infraction of her imaginary rules.

The many arrangements and complex details of putting a life beneath the ground and then sorting out what remained took weeks. Jason and Lauren, the church, old friends—people swirled around Carrie, all helpful and lending a shoulder. The burden of her mother's life was gone, replaced quite firmly by the burden of guilt. Worry turned to mourning. All her surefire plans to help her mom were too late. The ring of the telephone didn't make her jump; it only brought an empty and bitter sorrow.

As the patterns of life calmed into a rhythm again, a fleeting thought overwhelmed her. She could leave now, envisioning some Pacific island or maybe South America where she could escape and grow strong beneath a tropical sun. Her small inheritance would allow for no worries, no responsibilities, no burdens for a time.

But . . .

She was married. Jason had put an offer on a new house in an upscale subdivision. There was even a chance she was pregnant. She'd made a commitment. And she'd never leave Jason; he'd done too much for her; he cared too deeply. How could she hurt him?

The commitment was made—she had to accept it.

This was her life now.

Italy, Fourteen Years Earlier

Graham watched her from the shadows.

She stood at the window; her finger touched a raindrop that had splattered against the glass outside. From his view, the raindrops fell all over her. From the top of her head, like fingers that trailed from her head to her feet. He wished those raindrops were his hands. He wished to encase her within his arms, pull her close and closer until she disappeared inside him. In some ways, he realized this was what he was doing. He was taking her inside, and she would never fully leave him despite how she would move on.

And Carrie would move on, he told himself. And it surely wouldn't take long. Someday she'd be thankful that he did this. She'd be better off for what he was about to do. It wouldn't be fair to give her the same sentence he endured.

Today would be good-bye. Today would be the last time he saw her. Today would be remembered and relived. He'd wish he'd said more or maybe less or had done something impulsively romantic that would cement him forever into her mind. Because he wanted that. He wanted her to never forget him. He wanted her to never get over him. It was selfish and ridiculous, he knew. Yet he couldn't deny the truth of it within him. And he'd never quite get over her. Ever. He knew this in the moment of watching the rain fall over her without one drop getting her wet.

"It feels as if we were made for each other," she said as she turned around. The gray shadowed light filtered in, the room growing darker around them, yet she was softly illuminated by the last of daylight outside.

Carrie inspired him, but he would no longer believe in the innocence of love. He'd seen too much in his life to continue fooling himself as he'd done these past weeks. There were rules, barriers, the past that taught him early lessons she had yet to know. There was life beyond the days they'd spent together.

He was older really, even though her birthday was seven months before his. An old man at eighteen.

"Carrie." He wanted to make her understand, but he didn't understand himself, only felt the weight of them upon him. He wanted to keep her close, to protect her from the pain he would soon deliver.

"Why are you looking at me like that?" she asked.

"Do you know that you're beautiful to me?"

"Oh, stop," she said, embarrassed yet pleased. How was he going to walk away from her? "You're beautiful to me too," she said then, serious.

He tried to laugh. "Beautiful, eh? Not quite the compliment I was going for."

"You are. Inside and out. I don't know very much about you. Sometimes you seem so guarded, but I want to know you. This has all been so strange and out of the real world. But what I've seen . . . I know it's real. And you're beautiful."

He sat slowly in the chair, his hands moving over his face. Words came to him and he spoke the words that didn't want to leave his throat: "I'll never be what I want to be."

"What do you want to be?"

"I don't even know."

"Someday, Graham, you'll be happy. Someday, you'll just . . . this sounds strange, but the only word I can think of is *shine*."

He lifted his head, amazed, hurt, sick. His mother had used the same exact word when he was a child. *My Graham, you shine like the stars. You're the shiniest boy I've ever seen.*

"I need to get out of here," he said, his breath constricted in his throat.

"Where are you going?"

"I'll talk to you later. Tonight. I gotta go."

He walked outside, stunned by the slap of cold and rain on the late summer day. His legs moved faster until he was running. He didn't think he'd ever stop.

Maybe he never would.

Twenty-four Years Earlier

A chain-link fence surrounded the well-tended lawn. White rocks along the borders. Plastic flowers stuck from metal vases inside the rocks, creating the illusion of a garden when viewed from the road, though it reminded Carrie of the cemetery. Lauren's grandma and grandpa were inside the double-wide trailer; Grandpa was watching the evening news and Grandma had started dinner. Soon, Lauren's thirty minutes of piano practice would be finished, and they'd be free until dinner was ready.

Carrie sighed as she waited on the porch, listening to the same piano concerto for the umpteenth time. At times like this, she wished Lauren had younger parents rather than grandparents who liked things "proper." Lauren had been adopted as a baby; then her parents died in an auto accident, and she moved in with her grandparents. Poor Lauren. Her birth mom didn't even live in this country.

"I'm done!" Lauren said, bursting from the screen door.

"Yippee!" Carrie cried. Off they went.

They climbed the tree they weren't supposed to climb, though Lauren wouldn't go to the fun top branches that swayed like a rocking chair. Next they played Star Wars, both pretending to be Princess Leia. After barely escaping Storm Troopers, they made the dramatic exhausted fall backward.

"I'm tired," Carrie said. "What next?" Thick grass blades pressed into their shoulders and against tank tops and shorts.

"That looks like a giant caterpillar," Lauren said, staring upward. The clouds were a dancing circus across the sky.

"Fire-breathing dragon," Carrie said, pointing at an especially large puffy cloud.

"Where? You think so?"

"Yeah, see the fire coming from his mouth?"

"Maybe. Hey, that sort of looks like a kitten asleep on a blanket."

Carrie didn't see anything that looked like a kitten but pointed in another direction. "Luke Skywalker and, hey, over there Jabba the Hut."

"He's creepy." Lauren shivered, which made Carrie chuckle.

"Hey, Winnie-the-Pooh."

"Where?" Lauren said, rising up on her elbows.

"I was kidding. How boring."

"Winnie-the-Pooh is not boring. He's adorable."

"I like Tigger. He's hyper and never wears out."

"He's annoying. Christopher Robin is my favorite."

"Yeah, you'd like to marry Christopher Robin." Carrie liked to say that Lauren wanted to marry everyone just so she'd get a sock in the arm and hear her say *gross*.

Lauren socked her arm. "Gross."

Carrie doubled over in laughter, then considered, "My favorites are Piglet and Eeyore; even if Eeyore is kind of whiny, he cracks me up. And Piglet's just his own person."

"You're weird." Lauren lay back down beside her.

Carrie closed her eyes for a minute. The sun had come from behind a cloud and now warmed her face. When she opened them, she sought the clouds and decided to make up some imaginary formations that she didn't actually find. "Hey, one of the flying monkeys from the *Wizard of Oz*." Carrie knew Lauren hated those monkeys.

"Why do you make everything scary?"

"To scare you," she said, giggling. Carrie wondered how high exactly those clouds were. Her uncle flew all around the world for his business, and he said from an airplane the clouds were below you. She wondered how that would look. But she didn't want to see them from an airplane. Carrie wanted to be like Superman or Mighty Mouse or Peter Pan and zip right through them like a knife cutting butter. She envisioned each one of those characters and the way they'd each fly, choosing Peter Pan gliding through the sky as her favorite.

"If you could be anyone, who would you be?" she asked Lauren, who was weaving two blades of grass together.

"Anyone, hmm. Maybe the president of the United States."

"Too much work."

"But then you could have all the power in the world. Or at least a lot of power."

"I don't want power," Carrie said, thinking of all the people wanting her to do things for them if she was the president, all those hands to shake and babies to kiss.

"You could help the poor people."

"That's true. But you sit in an oval office all day and have to sign papers. Who else would you be?"

"I don't know. I like being myself."

"Do you want to know who your first parents are—the ones who had you?"

"No. I told you a thousand times. They're probably some homeless family or something I don't want to know about."

"But it could be exciting. They could be rich, or maybe you were separated from them, and all these years they've been looking for you. Or maybe they are Gypsies and they travel around Europe and have wild Gypsy parties. Or they're exiled royalty . . ."

"Or maybe they just didn't want me, or they'll want to be my parents now and I won't like them. Maybe they're really mean, and they'd make me live with them. See, there's more than good make-believe; sometimes it's bad real-life stuff. Stop talking about this. What about you? Who would you be if you could be anyone?"

Carrie knew not to ask anymore. Once Lauren's grandma had talked to her about it, telling her not to mention Lauren's birth parents anymore. Just sometimes it was hard not to; she was so curious. How could Lauren not want to know? "Okay, okay. I'd be Peter Pan," she said, her voice turning dreamy, and she could envision it perfectly. There she went, flying through the clouds, fighting pirates, listening to stories from outside the children's window.

"Why wouldn't you be Wendy?"

"'Cause Wendy goes back and leaves Never Never Land. She grows up. I don't want to grow up."

"Everyone has to grow up. I want to grow up; then I'll have a job and my own apartment, and—hey, there's a covered wagon," Lauren said, pointing toward a cloud formation that had just driven from behind a tree. Carrie nodded her head. She was still flying through clouds, cutting straight through that covered wagon. Next she'd zipped high above the tallest sequoia redwood trees and all the way along the coastal sands, in and out of the crevasses of the rocky islands. Then she pictured Lauren flying beside her with hair whipped back, smile wide across her face.

"Lauren, the Bible is always right, right?" Carrie asked, thinking of the Sunday school class that Lauren's grandparents took them to each week.

"Of course."

"And doesn't the Bible say if we believe and have faith, then we can do anything?"

"I think so."

"Anything? We can do anything?"

"Uh-oh." Lauren rolled onto her side and stared at Carrie.

"What *uh-oh*?"

"What is it this time?"

"Nothing bad. It's just, well . . ." Carrie sat up then, wondering if she should tell Lauren. "Like Peter when he walked on water, if we believe, if we really believe . . . I know we can fly."

"Okay, yeah, whatever."

"No, really. Come on. Up, get up." Carrie was already on her feet, pulling Lauren from the lawn.

"Oh, itchy back," Lauren said, scratching her bare shoulders.

"We have to concentrate. We have to believe."

"Sure."

I can fly. I can fly. I can fly. Carrie repeated it in her head again and again as she ran around the lawn taking leaps of practice flights. Didn't they say at church that all things were possible with God? Lauren was doing ballet leaps, then cartwheels. She obviously didn't believe.

Carrie kept trying to believe, kept repeating, concentrating, praying, knowing, and then she did believe. Suddenly, in dual moments, Carrie felt herself stay in the air longer than she should have; and a voice interrupted from the front porch.

"Girls, come in for supper."

She collapsed onto the lawn. Then up she jumped, realizing that she had flown. "Did you see that? Did you see?"

"What?" Lauren said, already starting for the porch. Her grandmother had closed the screen and returned inside.

"I started to fly," Carrie said, the moment now memory. But she was sure, sure that if her concentration had remained, she'd be in the air still, right now flying around.

"Yeah, right."

"No, really."

But Lauren's face reflected supreme doubt. Her legs skipped toward the porch and up the steps. "Come on, I'm thirsty. Let's play with our paper dolls after supper."

Carrie wished to protest, to convince her best friend. But it would never happen. She thought of trying to fly again. If she could do it once . . . and practice did make perfect. For now though, Carrie followed slowly toward the porch, passing plastic flowers and a pink flamingo. She'd try again. Later with a sheet off the roof of her house on such a windy day that she'd been sure the homemade parachute would hold her up. The broken arm was proof it didn't. And much later, it would be in an airplane going to a foreign land, and a day of skydiving with Lauren dragged along. Every swim afterward would feel like that flight, only in water. None of it would be quite the same as that moment, but Carrie wouldn't forget.

For a moment, frozen in time, she had flown. It seemed she'd spend the rest of her life trying to recapture that one instance of flight.

THEY WERE MEETING his father in Belfast that afternoon. Eight-year-old Graham was excited about a weekend in the city; they hadn't seen Dad all that week.

He took the fat black marker and made a straight line across the calendar week. Only three more rows and they'd be leaving Ireland for home. He couldn't wait to pet his dog again. How he hoped she hadn't grown to like their neighbor better than him. Would she remember him? It had been nearly six months.

While there, he was being schooled by his mother in the small

Irish village. He watched from the window as the other children carried their lunch pails to school, laughing and playing games as they passed by. Sometimes he'd rush to the door and wave; they'd make plans to meet when school was finished. Except not tonight; he'd be seeing his dad tonight.

Graham had another journal entry to write, as he did at the start of every school day. His mother grew tired of his usual essays about how much he missed home—surfing, baseball, Frisbee on the beach, food on a stick, or the roller coaster at the boardwalk in Santa Cruz.

"You'll someday be glad we came to Ireland. It's a cultural experience," she'd say. "It'll seem such a short time once we get home."

But to an eight-year-old boy, six months was an eternity.

"Today write about some of the things you've learned in Ireland," Mom instructed while packing his small suitcase for the overnight trip to the city. Dad didn't like them staying in town—it was sometimes dangerous, so they'd spent these months in the country village. But Dad worked long hours, leaving them alone more than Graham liked. And Dad wouldn't hear of them living close to his Irish family.

"I haven't learned anything here," Graham said with a frown.

"Write about your cousins."

His frown deepened at that. Graham knew not to write about them; Mom would know the truth then. She had no idea how crazy and wild his Irish cousins really were. They were unlike any kids he knew, not even his craziest friends who could go to the boardwalk at night and race their bikes over the train trestles. Manny, Malachy, and Murphy were crazier than that. They raced through ruined buildings and had their clubhouse in the basement of a demolished theater. And on his last visit to their house on the outskirts of Belfast, Graham had seen something that was worse than anything they'd seen in the past. He still wanted to tell his parents, or someone, but his cousins swore him to secrecy. There was no breaking such a vow even when death was involved.

Perhaps his parents had sensed the trouble though, because Graham's father put an end to their playing when his parents picked him up and saw how dirty he was. It became a big family argument between his father and Uncle Fergus, like none he'd ever heard. His cousins didn't seem the least affected. "'Tis how our dad always be. He yells as often as we laugh."

Graham was terrified of Uncle Fergus, terrified and fascinated in the same breath. Uncle Fergus was raging fun and raging terror. He drank his pints like a true and honorable Irishman, at least that's what he told Graham, especially when Graham's father wasn't around.

"You don't let that America take away yer Irish blood. Yer Irish first and foremost, ne'er forget that, eh, lad?"

"I won't forget," Graham would say, unable to break from those piercing blue eyes. He wondered how many men had cowered beneath that stare as Graham wished to do.

"We needs our family, we do. When yer father takes you back to America, you don' forget 'bout us here, now. You come back to yer land. She needs ya, she does."

Graham promised, though he didn't want to move to Ireland someday. His vow of silence might keep him from telling his parents about what he'd seen in the backstreets of Ireland, but the memory stayed close, especially at night. It filled his dreams and caused him to wake sweating and breathing heavily.

He was still picturing his uncle when his mom said, "Let's forget today's assignments and get ourselves to Belfast. Maybe I'll get a new dress for our dinner with Dad."

Graham cheered, happy to not have schoolwork, but he also

found it funny how his mom's stomach looked exactly like a small basketball beneath her shirt. She needed a new dress 'cause none of her old ones fit anymore. After they packed everything up and his mom went to the loo (she said the baby must be sitting on her bladder—whatever that meant), Graham carried everything to the small car in the driveway before she came out. She loved it when he surprised her with stuff like that.

Green hills and blue sea—that was Ireland. The radio played, and they sang along as they drove the coastal highway. Funny how it didn't seem weird anymore, driving on the left side of the road. Returning to the right would be strange when they got home.

"So we aren't staying with Aunt Fiona and the cousins?" Graham asked, thinking mainly of Uncle Fergus.

"Dad said we can stay at the hotel. There's a swimming pool."

"Great," Graham said.

By that evening, Graham had forgotten all about his cousins and Uncle Fergus. Dad had the afternoon off from his job—some big business that had to do with oil or something. Graham listened to Dad tell Mom that everything looked good for the transfer back to California. They both rubbed Mom's stomach, and Dad finally got to feel the baby kick for the very first time—the baby always seemed asleep when Dad was around. For some reason, Graham and Mom thought it was a baby girl in there.

That afternoon they swam at the indoor swimming pool at the hotel and visited the Botanic Gardens, then changed for dinner.

"Tomorrow, we'll go to a fancier place," Dad said in the hotel room. "Tonight you can see where I eat when I'm alone and missing you and Mom."

Dad's favorite dinner place reminded Graham of any other he'd been to since arriving in Ireland. McFallon's Pub brimmed full of people, some sitting at tables, others surrounding the bar. Graham's stomach rumbled at the smell of roasted meat, cabbage, and Irish stew. They found a table in a back corner, or maybe Dad had specially reserved it, Graham wasn't sure. The hard wooden chair was fun to tip back in, and he looked at the flags and decorations covering the wall while Mom and Dad talked about work. He wondered if he would miss all this when they went home. *Maybe*, he thought. *Probably not.*

"Mom, I need to use the loo," he said.

"Just a minute and I'll take you."

"The boy can make it to the loo by himself," Dad said. "He's eight years old, ya know."

"But . . . ," she said.

"He's a big lad now, aren't you, Graham?"

"Yes, Dad, I be a big lad now," Graham said, using his Irish accent that made them laugh.

"Be careful, and don't talk to anyone," Mom said, a worried frown on her face; then she winked and smiled.

Graham wove through the crowd, looking back to see his mother watching nervously. He waved and she smiled in return. The loo was crowded, and he waited his turn, then went to wash his hands. He knew Mom would ask if he washed.

On his way back, someone familiar caught his eye. Graham wasn't sure until Uncle Fergus turned his head to the side as he worked his way toward the door.

His uncle turned, and then, when their eyes met, a sudden terror-stricken expression came over his uncle's face. Graham stopped, afraid to go toward him. Uncle Fergus hurried back.

"Graham, boy! What you doing here? Where are your mam and dad?" he asked, his eyes scanning the restaurant for them. "Where are they?" he asked again.

"In back," Graham sputtered.

Uncle Fergus took a step as if to run where Graham motioned, then he stopped as quickly, grabbed Graham at the elbow, and pulled him toward the front door. "Come now! You come with me."

"Don't!" Graham struggled to get away as Uncle Fergus pulled his arm hard. "I have to go right back."

"My God, my God!" Uncle Fergus was saying as they reached the doorway.

Graham felt tears on his cheeks both from the pain and the fear. The laughter and chatter around him hummed in his ears.

"Hurry! Oh God, oh God," Uncle Fergus cried, now at a run, practically dragging Graham, who gasped at the taut grip around his arm.

The blast was almost soundless.

A sudden gasp and pause, then the exhale of destruction.

Graham found himself on the ground, pushing away debris, seeing blood and charred bits of things. A loud ringing filled his ears. Turning his head, he saw flames and the sign to the pub falling to the ground. People were running or staggering away—one man was naked and he didn't seem to understand why until he looked down and saw that his body was burned; a woman was screaming with a child in her arms; an old man knelt on the ground just feet from Graham, coughing and choking until blood spurted from his mouth. Graham couldn't remember where he was, what was happening, who he was. Then he remembered and jumped up to find his parents. He saw Uncle Fergus then, off to the side, holding his ears. Their eyes met, and then his uncle turned and ran away.

Later at the hospital, a policeman in a white shirt and black pants explained that his parents were dead. Graham remembered staring at his badge with the words "Police Service Northern Ireland." There had been a bomb in the pub, the man said. Someone had left it, and all those people died.

The ringing in Graham's ears hadn't subsided, though it had diminished. Bandages covered his forehead and his arm, but nothing really hurt; he couldn't feel much of anything. The police asked what he'd seen, why he'd been outside during the blast, but Graham couldn't answer. When the policeman came back, Graham had already had a visit from a different uncle, Dad's eldest brother, Terrance, whom he'd met only once. Uncle Terrance said to tell the police nothing. But that didn't seem right. All Graham could think of was his mom's smile as he left them at the table, and how happy he'd been to see his dad and swim at the pool. And his baby sister . . . Graham realized he didn't have a baby sister now.

Graham told the police he didn't remember anything from that day. He remembered that his mom wanted to buy a new dress and they'd gone swimming; after that he could only remember being in the hospital.

And so Graham stayed silent, protecting the man who murdered his mother and father and the baby he thought was a girl. Uncle Fergus.

Graham would return to America to live with family friends, but he couldn't have a dog there. He never saw his dog again.

But before leaving Ireland, Graham would get the evidence to send Uncle Fergus to prison. That evidence stayed with him as he considered what to do. He would bury it in a box on a rainy day years and years later, knowing he wouldn't retrieve it in a year; he might never retrieve it again.

He was always burying the past. It just seemed easier that way.

RETURN

Now: with things as they are.

2

Lauren heard her flight called as she stood in the midst of travel commmotion at the Portland International Airport. Simply hearing her flight number sent visions of a TV reporter announcing, "Flight 33 went down over the North Atlantic, killing all aboard."

She was hours from Harper's Bay and going three thousand miles farther on this quest. How such a thin-threaded compelling kept her from hurrying home, she couldn't figure out. But somehow she kept taking the next step, and here she was about to catch a flight. She wiped her sweaty palms on her jeans.

Lauren tapped another round of numbers into the pay phone. She'd already called her grandfather's daytime nurse, her neighbor to feed her fish, and the office to check messages and confirm that she really was taking this vacation instead of popping back to work early like usual. Her supervisor had said, "It's about time you took a vacation—you make the rest of us look bad. Get some rest over there." Lauren had time for one last call.

"Hey," she said when Carrie answered, unable to hold back a smile.

"Lauren? Hey? What do you mean, hey? Where have you been? It's been two days, and I've been worried sick. I've called your cell phone a dozen times. Is everything okay? Are you home?"

"My battery was dead on my cell phone until I finally bought a new car adapter last night."

"Where are you?"

"I'm at the Portland airport." She could barely believe it herself as she said it. Lauren's smile widened at the silence over the phone. "Hello, did you hear me?"

"Portland, Oregon—and I'll follow that with a big *why?*"

"Well, I had our tickets, nonrefundable, though I did have to change departure cities. And I found my passport, so I'm going to Europe." Lauren waited for the coming shock, reveled a moment in it. How many times had she been on the other side—the recipient of stunning news? She never astounded Carrie.

"Lauren, what are you doing?"

"Florence, Italy, is the first destination of course, after the eleven-hour flight to Paris and the layover and next flight. But there's a painting I need to see, then on to the Italian Riviera, where there's a box to recover."

Silence. Stunned, lovely, flabbergasted, trying-to-believe-her-ears silence.

"Where are you really? This isn't funny."

"I promise, I'm at the airport. Already checked my luggage in, made it through security—even had to take my shoes off. Here I am at Gate 34."

"You can't go alone. You don't like business trips back east by yourself, and this is to Europe. And . . . the box? You don't even know where the box is. *I* don't even know."

"I found him."

No response again, but this time, Lauren didn't revel in it. Sure, she said it easily enough, but this was the part she wished not to mention.

"Him?"

"I found Graham. He lives on the Oregon coast. He told me where it is." Just then Lauren heard her flight called again and noticed the line of people waiting to board. "Carrie, it's my flight. I gotta go."

"Oh no, you can't leave it at that."

"I'll call as soon as I get to Florence, or Paris during my layover."

"Wait."

Lauren didn't want to wait. She didn't want the questions that were about to assault. Another announcement over the speaker saved her. "They just called my row. Don't worry, and just know that the box is finally going to be recovered. You'll finally get back whatever it is that's bothered you all these years."

"But Lauren . . ."

"I'll call, I promise."

"Okay, okay . . . I just can't believe this, that this is you. Off to Europe, alone?"

"Crazy, isn't it? I love you," Lauren said, drawing it out so Carrie would hear the meaning behind the words, trying to be brave and trying not to worry.

"I love you too. But wait, I can't believe this, and—"

"Talk to you tomorrow, or whatever day it'll be when I arrive." Lauren hung up after Carrie's hesitant good-bye.

It was now or never.

CARRIE SAT ON her back patio as a light rain fell more as a mist, bringing an illusory quality to the deepening night. She was chilled through and knew she needed to go inside. This was foolish, childish, stupid. Her body ached as it so often did now, even more with the brittleness of cold. And yet, she couldn't move.

Lauren was going to Europe. Unbelievable. Carrie kept waiting for the call saying it was simply a joke. But Lauren wouldn't joke about seeing Graham. She really had seen him. Talked to him. He lived on the Oregon coast, along the same seaboard where she lived. A rush of melancholy swept over her—the feelings, the wonder, the regret rose again as if to pull her down to the shallow grave they'd come from.

Lauren had seen him, but for Carrie all the details were missing. He was alive, breathing, thinking, and dreaming—at this moment, right now. Of course she knew this; it was ridiculous to be stunned by the reality. And yet, she'd tried to appropriate that part of her life to something akin to a dream, or at least a secured memory. Now it was present, once again part of the immediate now.

An envy came, strange in its way, of the eyes that saw him every day, of the ears that heard him speak. Why couldn't she see him? Why were her ears sequestered away? That summer they'd laughed so easily together—who laughed with him now? Did he have a wife? Children? Why couldn't they at least be friends? She'd take that; she'd take any little bit of him.

And with that, guilt swept in, deep and consuming. Eddie slept inside with stuffed animals surrounding him. Jason had been reading *Time* magazine; there'd been some article about medical miracles. He was probably asleep too, with the magazine pressed against his face, lamp still on beside his recliner, mouth open with an occasional snort. How could she let herself think such things? How could they arrive unbidden after so many years? After all the wonderful things she'd been given with Jason and Eddie.

All those years of wondering if he'd really buried the box. Now Carrie knew that he had, and Lauren knew the exact location. Had he done it the night she left? Or later, years later? What did it all mean? Why hadn't he ever found her? Why hadn't she been enough for him to want to find?

And why did it matter now?

"Tomorrow we'll bury it. I have the perfect place," he'd said with that smile, that ever irresistible smile. But there had been no tomorrow, at least not for them. It flooded over her, those days together, the sunlight and rain.

It shouldn't be Lauren. Carrie should be doing this instead. The recovery had the potential for devastation, Lauren's own in particular.

"Stupid, hateful body, how could you fail me in so many ways?" Carrie wrapped the lap blanket tighter around her legs. She pictured Lauren somewhere in the clouds, trying to be brave but not doing the best job. Lauren had opened the past—for all of them. She thought this was all about helping her best friend. But there was something in that box Lauren should not see, perhaps ever.

EDDIE HELD THE flashlight under the covers of his bed. He illuminated the stars and moons on his sheets. Then he pulled the light away and shone it on the stars and moon on his ceiling. Then, flipping the flashlight off, his sheets and ceiling glowed. The places where he'd shone the light the longest glowed the brightest in the dark.

Everyone was sleeping, but he couldn't. His pajamas felt scratchy and his eyes wouldn't stay shut, no matter how many times he counted sheep. So he played this game of light and dark and glow-in-the-dark as Tiger, Snakey, Bandit Bear, and his other stuffed animals watched, lined up against the wall. Maybe he should find his shirt with glow-in-the-dark animal footprints. Or he could get some glow paint and decorate the walls; then it would be seen only in the dark. He'd ask his mom about that.

Slipping out of the bed, he decided to write himself a note.

That's how his parents remembered things. His dad kept a list on his PDA. Mom wrote on Post-it notes. Eddie was hoping to get both for his birthday—a kid's PDA and a big stack of sticky notes. The house was quiet, but the living room light was on. He turned into the library where the computer's screen saver shone in the dark room. Eddie climbed up the chair to grab a Post-it; Mom didn't mind if he took some once in a while, but she'd said no more crafts with them after he used a whole pad to decorate his desk. Jumping back down, his elbow hit the computer mouse, flipping off the screen saver.

Eddie stopped at the words he saw there. Mom said Dad drove the doctors crazy with his research. He was always reading up on things. Eddie noticed other papers on the desk that had been printed. Portions were traced over with a yellow highlighter pen. Why was Dad looking up information like this again? Maybe his mom was sicker than he thought.

The highlighter reminded him of the glow-in-the-dark color. That's why he'd come in here, to write a note. He picked up the pen and wrote:

Bye Glow Painte!!!!!!!!

He wondered if he'd spelled it right, thinking then of the upcoming spelling quiz in Mrs. Smith's class. With a smile, he realized he couldn't see the words very well because of the yellow ink on the white paper. It could be a mystery for his mom in the morning. Eddie carried it down the hall toward her bedroom and peeked inside. The bed was still made. Maybe it wasn't as late as he thought, except he remembered his digital clock said 10:17 p.m. just a few minutes ago. Dad, at least, was always in bed by 10:00 p.m., and usually earlier. Sudden worry swept through him.

Hurrying toward the living room, Eddie found his dad asleep

in his chair with the lamp on beside him, a magazine on his lap and more printed papers beside him. Mom wasn't in the kitchen or back in her bathroom. Then Eddie remembered her other favorite place to sit and think, out by the swimming pool on the back porch. He opened the French door. He could barely see her in the dark, a blanket draped over her, looking small with her legs curled up.

"Eddie, you're still awake?"

"I couldn't sleep. Why are you outside? What's wrong?" It was raining, but the spot where she sat was under cover.

"Nothing's wrong. I was just enjoying the night. It's okay, honey. Go back to bed."

He came toward her anyway. She slid her arm around his waist and gave him a little squeeze. She was cold, like an icicle.

"Brr."

"Yeah, let's go inside. It is pretty nippy. I'm nearly too cold to move, so you saved me from frostbite."

He smiled at that. They liked the frostbite game. "Then you couldn't make coffee without fingers."

"Or smell flowers without my nose."

"You'd have to get one of those big horn things to listen through, 'cause frostbit ears just snap right off."

"And so do the toes."

They laughed. Dad thought they were weird, and sometimes Mom embarrassed him in front of his friends when she tried their games in front of them. But she didn't care, and he didn't really mind either.

"Let's get ourselves inside. And you get to bed, little mister."

Back in the house, Eddie paused as she walked with the blanket draped over her shoulders.

"Will you tuck me in?" he asked.

"Sure thing. Just let me get your dad off to bed."

"We could tickle his nose with a feather," Eddie said; they'd done this before, and it was so funny to see him twitch and itch before finally waking up. Mom didn't seem to hear him, seemed like she was thinking too loud to hear him.

"Mom . . ."

"Eddie, go on to bed. I'll come kiss you in a minute."

He didn't want to do what she told him. Why was everybody acting so strangely and up so late at night too? Slowly, he trudged down the hall, glancing back to see her shaking Dad's arm to wake him up.

Back in bed, he slid the flashlight under the covers, remembering why he'd gotten up in the first place. He lay still, staring up toward stars and planets that had lost all their glow and were only visible from the hallway lights. Finally, Mom came in.

"Snakey, are you keeping Eddie up again?" The blanket was still around her shoulders, and her hands were cold on his forehead.

"No, Eddie's keeping us up," Eddie said in a slithery voice. Putting his arms straight up, Mom covered his whole body with his sheet and comforter, then took his hands, pulling them downward with the blankets that were perfectly tucked under his arms.

"There you go. Now you can sleep snug as a little bug."

Eddie smiled. Grown-ups were just weird sometimes. With her kiss on his forehead and the fuzzy warmth of bed, he began feeling sleepy.

Everything was fine. At least, he sure hoped so.

3

A ll the way to the deep blue horizon, the sea was moonstruck.
It surprised Graham how alive he became upon the sea. After
too many days close to shore, it was easy to forget. A journey, however short, provided a different sense of being.

The portable stereo caught some coastal station playing classic
rock from the '50s to the '80s; funny, how the '80s were sometimes
now called *classic*. Weren't they just yesterday? The CB burst into
activity from time to time—Coast Guard instructions or a freighter
calling a harbor. Graham's boat lights were on, and he figured he
could sail all night at this rate, or if not, pull into some bay for a few
hours of sleep. The invigoration of a salted wind made him feel he
should turn west and sail straight on to the South Seas. A part of
him wished to, and he could at least sail a day or two, then turn
back. Perhaps he'd slip into Harper's Bay; it wasn't too far, really. Not
that he'd actually go find Carrie. But what if he did? She'd said once
that if something unforeseeable tore them apart, she'd always welcome his return into her life. But that was years ago, did *always*
really mean *always*? She couldn't mean it after their bitter farewell.

The change in breeze snapped through the sails, and Graham
wondered if that was his answer—was it a *yes* or a *no*?

Water and moonlight. The sea captured light in every turn of
wave. How it reminded him of that first night in Italy.

He'd only been eighteen. That seemed so young now. Traveling as the personal assistant, or "personal servant" would more aptly describe it, of a woman who could've been his grandmother. How glad Graham was that she wasn't a relative except for the inheritance Mrs. Preston would leave an heir, had an heir ever been. The most aggravating person he'd ever met—that Mrs. Preston. He carried packages while shopping the cities of Europe, lugged luggage to and from her rented villas, a companion for the social functions she attended—whatever suited Mrs. Preston at the time. That was his position. Do whatever he was told. Part of him hated it.

But at eighteen, it mattered little with the offer of travel, granting an escape from his position at the country club as a golf instructor to the rich and nonathletic—Mrs. Preston one such client.

The job was secured for a minimum of six months. They'd arrive at a city such as London, Berlin, Rome, or Vienna. Mrs. Preston would demand a car—right now. Instructions were made on how to stack the luggage in the trunk even after Graham had been doing it in a dozen cities. The driver would be told how she liked to be driven—no potholes, no sharp turns or quick stops— and the gratuity would reflect how well her instructions were carried out.

A request, or rather dictum, from Mrs. Preston sent Graham back to Italy from the French villa where they'd recently arrived. Mrs. Preston wanted her favorite dried pasta. "No one makes it like Martina." It would take him two days to travel by train; she wouldn't let him take the rental car.

Grateful for the escape, Graham packed his camera. By the next afternoon, he was in the small village of Monterosso al Mare off the Ligurian Sea. Graham easily found Martina and picked up the order, then strolled the rocky beach where he watched a young woman playing with some children. He lifted the camera and took several shots before they noticed him.

"*Per favore*," he said, giving a smile as he lifted the camera. The children made funny faces, showing off tanned cheeks and missing teeth. The young woman, pretty with dark eyes and wheat-colored hair, appeared shy at first, uncomfortable before the camera. But in one photo, she looked directly at him, right through the lens as if she could see him completely. It surprised him.

She blushed and asked in perfect English, "What part of the States are you from?"

"You're American?" he said.

She nodded and her eyes met his again, this time with no camera to shield him.

"I'm from California. What about you?" he said.

"California."

They left the children to their game; she didn't even know them, which he found intriguing. Carrie Myles was staying in the coastal village while the family she traveled with went to Milan, shopping. Her laugh came easily, at everything. They talked about being Americans in Europe, about the differences in cultures, about what they missed back home. For some reason, Graham would remember that she missed Dairy Queen Dilly Bars the most, even though she loved Italian gelato.

Together they strolled the village shops, watched part of a boccie game, and drank cappuccinos at an outdoor café. A breeze off the blue Mediterranean cooled the summer air. Carrie and the Benders were staying another month in the village. Strangely enough, two days later Mrs. Preston would insist on returning to the Italian seaside after becoming angry at her French proprietor—it meant he'd have the month with Carrie in Italy. She said it was divine planning. He was just grateful for the time.

But that first evening, Graham missed his train back. Another would come in the night, so they ate dinner, platefuls of pasta, and spent the eventide on the water's edge where they'd met that afternoon—it seemed they'd known each other for years.

When the moon came up and the breeze died down, the air grew stiflingly warm again. Carrie couldn't resist the allure of water any longer. Graham stood on the shore as she swam. The water caught the moonlight, surrounding her with a diamond dress. Finally, he tore off his shoes and dived in.

An altogether perfect moment.

One of few times of perfection that stood out so starkly in Graham's lineage of existence. Every moment of it remembered with precise clarity. The sound of crickets, the lap of waves against the rocks, the lights of the village rising up the steep mountains, and stars dangling from above. The word *dreamlike* came to mind as he recalled it. They swam, talking and laughing, until their fingers pruned, the air turned cold, and the moon faded over the horizon.

Though colder here in the Northwest, still this was a night not unlike that one, Graham thought, feeling alone. He leaned over the railing of his boat, staring across the light caught upon the waves, willing the memory to return to life. He wished to see her swimming out there, waving, calling him to join her.

But she's in a house, or a hospital. Sick, dying. She isn't that Carrie anymore.

A horrid image arose in colors of gray and black. Carrie in an open coffin. Carrie hooked to a thousand tubes and IVs. Carrie's face sinking into the waters below him, eyes frozen open, mouth gaping wide. Or Carrie swimming away, not calling to him, not saying good-bye.

He shut his eyes, a sudden shiver running through him. *I wish*

I could go back and make everything right, he thought. Didn't he believe as a child that prayer was more than a wish to the heavens? He wanted to believe again, in something, wanted to know there was more to life than regret.

A slight gust of wind keeled the boat toward starboard. From the galley, Salt's meow tinged with a growling sound. He'd already fed her; maybe she didn't have sea legs after all.

Graham tried to force his mind from the past. His instincts were alert, checking for other vessels on the water, watching for a change in current or anything unexpected. This was real. In many ways, that time with Carrie had never been real. Everything from that summer seemed an alternate dimension. It had captured them both, torn away reason, and granted something beyond complacent existence.

No doubt she'd take that last night's memory and carry it with her to the grave. Unless he saw her one more time. Unless he asked her forgiveness, or at least let her know that she'd meant something to him, more than something. Some final words might free them both, resolving the past before it was too late. Before she was gone.

CARRIE BOLTED AWAKE. A nightmare, it was only a nightmare. Sweat drenched her back and neck beneath her hair.

"Are you okay?" Jason asked, half-asleep and rolling toward her.

"Just a dream. I'm fine."

"A bad one?"

"I don't remember now," she said. The moonlight through the window outlined his face, and she saw Jason's eyes blinking.

"Okay, good, good, get some rest then. Love you." He was already sliding back into sleep. In a moment, his breathing grew deep. How easily he said he loved her without need of reciprocation.

Graham, yes, the dream had been about Graham. Graham, who never said he loved her, who perhaps could not love, or so he'd once confessed. She hadn't believed him at the time. Now Graham returned to her in the lateness of night.

Rising from bed, she walked step after aching step toward the bathroom to wash her face and change her damp shirt. The tile floor felt cold on her toes, and the mixture of cold and dampness made her feel feverish . . . or maybe she already was. The dream had dissipated, but not the feeling it had left. It settled on her heavy and dark. There'd been some kind of drama, running, crying, shouting. But nothing distinct. Probably for the best. Dreams had a power, even when forgotten, to settle over and drag down. As Carrie returned to the edge of the bed, she wondered where Graham was at that moment. A sudden prayer came to her. *God, be with him. Guide his way. Let him know Your eternal love. Take him on a journey toward You.*

It was all she had to give him. It was all he would accept from her. He couldn't give that back. He couldn't turn away. He couldn't run from it.

Carrie again wondered what he looked like now. What had Lauren's eyes seen? No description could fully create the picture. If it was possible to see him, would she want to? Graham represented her most vulnerable moments. That summer had incited both the best and the worst of who she could be. Carrie had never known she could love so deeply in such a short time. As much as she'd moved on, he came to her often, especially when she prayed. The habit of praying for him had been all she had for so long, now it was part of her routine, even after all these years. And just as Graham Michaels uncovered a love she'd never experienced, he also revealed a selfishness, a depth of greed Carrie hadn't known she possessed.

Wouldn't she have given her future to him? And yet, he wanted nothing of her in the end. Her want was so great, the loss so deep, she'd have done most anything to have him stay.

The mere reminder sent a fresh shiver through her. The faces of the Benders, who had taken her all over Europe, as they stared at her as she bled, hysterical and soaked from the rain.

How could there ever be reconciliation? How had she ever gotten herself back when she had lost so much of who she'd been before?

Jason.

He had come into her life and loved her even when she struggled to believe she could ever love again.

"Are you okay?" Jason asked. She hadn't seen that he was awake when she'd sat on the bed.

"I think so," Carrie said, wishing to be okay. What was wrong with her that she had not fully escaped that summer?

He sat up and took her hand carefully. "You're burning up," he said, touching her forehead.

"I am?" she said. "I feel cold."

"Honey, I'm really sorry you couldn't go to Europe. Are you thinking of Lauren, or are you thinking of him?"

She was surprised at this. Jason rarely asked about that time in Italy, knowing it brought painful memories. He loved her, was her support, the rare spiritually seeking man who truly wanted God's will. She believed Jason deserved much more than her—the flawed Carrie, the least of Christian wifely examples.

"You don't have to answer that," he said. He rubbed his balding head and pulled back the covers for her to climb under. "But you do need your sleep. I don't want you worrying about all this."

"Me worry?" she said with a laugh.

He chuckled. "I love you," he said with a secure firmness.

She smiled. How did she deserve this? "And I love you. You do know that, right?"

"Yes. I knew it before you did," he said with a tease. His worried expression quickly replaced the smile. "Now, get beneath these covers. I'll get some water and some Tylenol for that fever."

Watching him leave the room, Carrie shook her head. *God, thank You for that man. I'm sorry I waited so long to see him.*

4

The plane was flying over Greenland when Lauren again questioned, *What in the world am I doing?*

Sure, there were better times for such a question than while making a path over the glacier-covered island, but why not then? For a moment Lauren pictured the Boeing 777 plunging down into those icy waters. The only reference to Greenland she could recall was from the movie *The Princess Bride*, and her life was anything but a fairy tale.

"You'll end up back where I found you. Alone, hungry, unemployed in Greenland," the Sicilian said to Fessick in the movie. She smiled, her forehead against the glass of the airplane window. Carrie was always asking for references.

"What's the line, that one from *Princess Bride*? Not 'Inconceivable!' but the other one."

"'You killed my father, prepare to die?' Or 'no more rhyming and I mean it. Anybody want a peanut?' Or there's always, 'Boo boo bow to the queen of filth. Bow to the queen of slime—'"

"Boo boo, to you. I wish I had your memory. It's so aggravating. They're right here." Carrie would tap her head at that. "Stuck, and I can't get them out."

"Kind of like the jokes you can never remember?"

"Yes, those too. Maybe I have ADD, or I was dropped on my

head as a child. Maybe I have a brain tumor. I'd drop lines like they were going out of style. A quote for every moment."

"It would become a pride in your life."

Carrie laughed. "You could be right. But really, there has to be some calling for people who remember movie lines and good quotes. Until the day I die, I'll be trying to get you to use your talents more."

And wasn't that the truth? Lauren thought now. Here she was, on a plane to Europe all alone, and wasn't that really because of Carrie? Sure, it was her choice. But so often it began with her friend.

Just then, the elderly man at Lauren's right let out a snort, his head drooping precariously close to her shoulder. She leaned against the window, staring down onto the world of ice and water. Memories raced through her mind as if this speeding plane would take her away from her life forever.

Her newfound spontaneity had fed her until a few hours into the flight. Then the realization . . . she was really going. She had really done it. Or at least taken the first step. There was an entire week of being brave ahead of her. Places to go, people to see, a treasure to recover.

Have I lost my mind?

Lauren hadn't particularly wanted to go on their first trip to Europe. That was Carrie again, the dreamer, the adventurer. Just like when Carrie decided they needed to try skydiving. Lauren had clung embarrassingly tight to the man she'd been strapped to while Carrie encouraged with that exhilarated smile.

"Just jump!"

If her health hadn't deteriorated so quickly, Carrie would be on this plane herself. But it seemed so quickly after the diagnosis that her body began to succumb. Lauren hated to be away from her best friend for even a week. But to give her this, it would mean so much.

That's why I'm doing it. I'm giving my best friend a gift. One she can't get on her own. Maybe the last I'll ever give.

5

Graham had spent the day farther out to sea, far enough that the California coast was a thin wisp along the horizon. He'd had consistent inklings to keep sailing west. He could wire money back for the loan; call Jasper to take care of things. Sure, his supplies and gear weren't in the best order for a long journey, but they'd suffice. And yet, throughout the day, that stretch of land kept calling him back. There were plenty of things he'd left unresolved. Why now this sudden desire for finality?

Because there won't be another chance for resolution. Carrie will be gone, and it'll be too late.

But she's married. She's a mother. She won't want to see me. Her husband certainly won't roll out the red carpet.

Graham stopped cold a moment. In his shock of seeing Lauren and her news, he hadn't considered as he should have one important element. He'd entrusted too much to a stranger. A stranger he once knew, who disliked him.

Her friend will retrieve what was left in Italy. I need to get it before it causes a real problem. Sure, Lauren said she'd give me what's mine, but that was no guarantee. This has the potential for real disaster. Why hadn't I thought more of that? he chided himself, though the shock over Carrie's illness kept him from thinking clearly.

His inner conflict flowed like the to-and-fro of waves. Graham looked at the cat that had seemed a little under-the-weather since setting sail. Salt returned a wary stare.

"After all I've done for you, do this for me. Meow once if we throw caution to the wind and head toward the Cook Islands. I have enough cat food for you, though you might have to share with me. Or, meow twice if we go to California."

Salt gave a dismissive look. "Humans," she seemed to say, and then resumed licking the one matted area on her otherwise perfect white hair.

"Exactly why pets are worthless."

A while later, Graham heard Salt meow. He looked up from the map he'd unrolled, hoping it was his sign to go. She meowed immediately again—twice. What did a cat know anyway?

And so by evening, the land loomed close again. If he didn't turn back, by tomorrow evening he'd see the lighthouse on Orion Point beckoning off Harper's Bay. Tonight he'd find a cove to drop anchor. In the morning he'd have to decide.

Years earlier, Graham had passed by Harper's Bay while driving up the California coast to consider a boat for sale. He'd known it was the town where Carrie had grown up, but he didn't know if she'd returned after their summer in Europe. On that trip, he'd driven to the next town of Crescent City. That night, after several hours at a local pub, he'd looked for her name in the phone book. She wasn't there, though of course she'd have a different last name if she'd married. Or maybe she had never returned as she'd promised herself. There was another Myles in the book, her parents perhaps? He nearly called to find out. After so many years, it was strange being close to where she'd lived and might still live. He'd walked back to the dilapidated motel that greeted him with further emptiness.

Now Graham knew she had been there. So close. When he

calculated the dates, he realized she hadn't even been married yet. If he had called, would it be different now? Lauren said Carrie returned after that summer, their summer, and despite several short times away, Carrie had become entrenched in the small-town life. Was that somehow his fault, just as so many other things were?

As the day fell silently into the western horizon, Graham spotted the first star of the night. His mother once said not to miss a night without spotting the first star—no matter what the hour. He wondered where she was now. He wished for something of certainty. Something beyond this world and the lasting thought of his parents' burned bodies amid corpses and terrorized screams.

On his bookshelf in the galley, Graham kept a scrapbook with the newspaper accounts. It rested beside the ship-in-a-bottle that his father had given him. The bombing received international press for a few days, just another example of tensions between the Catholics and the Protestants in Ireland. The bomb killed twelve people. Four members of a soccer team, a couple recently engaged, three pub employees, a respected Irish philosopher, and Graham's parents. The baby inside his mother wasn't counted. Only Graham knew they thought it was a girl.

The weekend before that last dinner in Belfast, Graham stayed at his cousin's house. His parents were going down to county Cork, where his mother's grandmother had emigrated from. Some distant cousins or something were there too, but they didn't interest him. Graham's mind was already plotting the excitement and raw survival of a weekend with his cousins, without Mom and Dad around.

His parents wouldn't allow him to play in the Pit—the district next to his cousin's house that was nearly reduced to rubble. The ruined graffiti-covered buildings and dingy streets were dangerous.

"I won't go there," he promised with a twinge of guilt, but not enough to stop the mental plotting. It was what boys did; Mom couldn't understand such a thing. Dad had spent his youth in similar settings, even if he seemed to have forgotten.

Graham's cousins were rare and untamed animals, Irish versions of Huck Finn, or the Lost Boys from Never Never Land. Wild and irreverent. Demeaning, insulting, dirty, scurrilous, and the best fun he'd ever had, even if Graham had to muster courage and strength to run with them. Every game ended in someone injured or near tears. Every adventure balanced the line into danger. Every child became a warrior, at least for a few hours. It was pure exhilaration.

Graham waved good-bye after a kiss from Mom and ruffled hair by Dad. Mom made him promise not to leave sight of the house; he crossed his fingers behind his back. She also received the promise from Aunt Fiona to keep Graham safe. Aunt Fiona tried to hold true to her word, admonishing them again and again, "Stay inside or in the front yard, I promised yer mam."

Aunt Fiona handed baby Polly from her hip to Aideen, her fifteen-year-old daughter, as they cared for a house full of men talking and drinking and arguing. Her patience for wild boys was minimal. At last, she shooed Graham and his cousins from the attic where their game of hide-and-seek sent flakes of downstairs ceiling dropping into the men's pints below. "Stay close," she said. "I promised yer mam."

And they were free on the streets.

Only several blocks away and a scramble through a broken section of concrete wall, they entered the Pit. It looked like a war zone. Burned-out cars, crumbling walls, rats and stray dogs. An occasional human moved by, and they moved clear of a gang of guys who lingered on a street corner, talking and listening to a boom box. The boys ran through the Pit like spies on a secret mission. Creeping through the alleys and between cars and doorways wasn't play anymore. They could get in real trouble. This was danger, and it pumped like electricity through his veins.

Soon, they were sufficiently dirty, had staked out several areas, and Graham had a cut under his eye from some metal on an old car he'd shimmied past. Manny led them through a building, climbing stairs that were missing steps until they reached the third floor. As they investigated an abandoned apartment, Graham heard voices from outside.

"Hey, somebody's out there," he said, crawling toward the broken window where an old couch rested. He peered over and saw a group of men walking down the alley below. "It's a bunch of men and yer dad."

Malachy jumped up to see. "Dad, out here?"

Manny quickly pulled him down, knocking his head as he did. "You shush now, hear? We better go."

"I wanna see what Dad is doing."

"He'd kill ya if he knew."

"You've seen this 'fore?"

Graham then noticed that this room had empty Coke bottles, empty potato chip bags, and cigarette butts littering the floor beside the couch—Malachy's favorite snacks.

"Don't you never tell Dad. You either, none of ya," Manny said with a fear unlike any Graham had seen in his cousins, especially the bold Manny. That fear was electric, shooting straight into Graham. Manny motioned that they could look over the window ledge, whispering, "People hardly never look up."

Peering over the edge, Graham saw four men surrounding another man. The one in the center stood proudly, his left eye so swollen and bloody that it made Graham cringe. But the man stood

with jaw clenched and bloody fists squeezed tight. The four men—
Uncle Fergus included—didn't speak, but kept expressionless faces
firmly on the man within their circle.

"That's Johnjack Kerry," Manny said, his voice sounding
surprised.

"Nay, not Johnjack Kerry?" Murphy said in his young voice.

The other boys seemed to understand what was happening, but
Graham didn't want to sound stupid not knowing, so he kept silent
and watched. He wondered why the hurt man wasn't taken to the
hospital. He appeared to need stitches by his eye. Blood ran down
his face. Something in Graham made him not want to understand
the scene before him.

Then one man talked in a low tone to Johnjack, strode forward and pushed him. Johnjack barely moved, but his head hung.

Manny suddenly jumped up. "Let's go, we gotta go, really."

Graham hurried after him, though Murphy lingered until his
brother called again from the door. They were only halfway down
the stairwell when a gunshot rang out, causing them all to drop
down. Graham and Manny held each other's gaze.

"It be done, then," Manny whispered from the stair step below
them.

Murphy smiled wryly. "Bloody traitor, deserves his share."

The hard expression on Murphy's face stunned him. Graham
had to fight the panicked impulse to run, run anywhere. But where
was he safe in the Pit? So instead he followed, moving closer to
Manny as they walked.

They stayed out past dark, wandering the streets and trying to
reclaim some of the earlier sense of exploration. Graham kept
thinking some shadow was following them. While Murphy kept
trying to conjure up fun, Manny's dark mood prevailed. When
they finally turned back toward the house, Graham wanted to slink

inside and call his parents to pick him up. He sure didn't want to see Uncle.

Manny grabbed his elbow before they walked inside. "We be taught, most important, be loyal to the family. 'Tis not ours to question, and we never speak of such things as these."

Somehow Manny's words brought a darker dread. Graham chose to trust Manny and let the words settle inside him.

Aunt Fiona appeared surprised to see them when they returned, as if she'd forgotten all about them. There were dark circles under her eyes, and she had been crying, or maybe Graham was simply looking for signs to believe what had happened in the Pit was more than a bad dream. Or maybe it wasn't anything abnormal. Killing a man they knew might be as normal as taking out the wash to these people.

"Supper's cold, boys. Go wash up and come eat. Oh, and, Graham, you wash your face too; got dirt all over it."

She never asked where they'd been but stood at the kitchen window with her hands wringing a dish towel. The men weren't back yet. Even among the brothers, there was a subdued air within the house.

Graham didn't think he'd sleep that night. The terror of the day kept washing over him. Uncle Fergus, his father's brother, was a murderer. This wasn't the Wild West or a Celtic battlefield. He could go to prison. Graham wondered about the family. What would happen to Murphy, Manny, and Malachy then? The cousins had talked about Johnjack on the way home. He had a daughter in Manny's class; Murphy whispered that Manny was in love with her. Johnjack had been at their house; he'd known Uncle Fergus since childhood. Even as these thoughts roamed through his mind, he couldn't stop seeing that man's face, and picturing him dead with a bullet through him. He pictured the blood on the street and wondered if the body had been left to the rats.

That night, the room was hot, and his breathing came in tight gasps for quite some time. Murphy shared his bed, and Graham was pressed against the wall. Everything became unfamiliar, stifling, and lonely. He wanted his parents. Wanted their house by the sea in California. If his cousins caught him crying, they'd pummel him. He turned with his face an inch from the wall and blinked his eyes.

A wave of nausea hit as images assaulted him. Johnjack's bloody knuckles that would now be cold and stiff. Just when he could no longer breathe or stay in this house another second, he remembered his mother's secret weapon.

"Our Father who art in heaven . . ." He whispered the prayer his mother taught him, and added the simple words, "Help. I'm all alone."

And then, even with the smothering heat, a calming force settled over him. Like a gentle rain. A deep sense of rest, or peace perhaps. He yawned and closed his eyes.

Late that night, Graham awoke to deep baritones in song. Men, several, singing an Irish folk tune mixed with shouting, cheering, crying. Graham realized Murphy wasn't beside him. Malachy was gone too. Only Manny remained, stretched across his bed, covers kicked off, taking long drags from a cigarette. He didn't turn Graham's way when Graham called to him. Instead, he waved a hand toward the door and stared at the ceiling.

Creeping forward toward the darkened hallway, Graham spotted the younger brothers lying at the top of the stairs, peering downward. He slid beside Murphy, who gestured to his lips, then across his neck: "Quiet or die!"

Uncle Fergus stood with a hand against the mantel, a pint in his other hand. There were three other men Graham recognized. The men from the Pit, except no Johnjack Kerry. Seeing his uncle sent a cold shiver through him.

Aunt Fiona's living room was littered with empty beer mugs, cigarette butts, and the tangle of men swaying and singing. Holding up his pint, Uncle Fergus would join in the drunken singing, then cover his face with the back of his hand.

And when sergeant Death's cold arms shall embrace me
Oh lull me to sleep with sweet Erin go Bragh
By the side of my Kathleen, my own love then place me . . .

Graham noticed the tears streaming down his uncle's cheeks.

The boys seemed enamored, and Graham caught a glimpse of his cousins' future. This would be their life too. Someday their children would peer from above where "people hardly never look up" and watch his cousins, drunk, singing with tears for the man they'd killed that day. This was life for his family, though surely it couldn't be life for everyone in Ireland. This would have been his own life if his father hadn't left.

Just as he thought of telling his parents, he remembered Manny's saying, "'Tis not ours to question, and we never speak of such things as these."

Panic to leave this house, leave this country, filled him. Get his parents safely away. His father and Uncle Fergus didn't get along. Graham knew now what that could mean. Only one month before they would leave. It couldn't come soon enough.

Graham had discovered something. He'd felt it when he'd prayed. God was with him. He believed it as he never had before.

PAIN CREPT INTO the edges of her day.

At first Carrie wondered if it was real or imagined. Was she waiting for every ache to be a sign that heightened it all the more?

This morning, Carrie realized the impact of pain, how it slowed her and took her breath away.

Sure, Carrie knew it wasn't a mystery that time was running out. Yet knowing it was different from feeling it crawling over her, pulling her down toward the grave. Fear popped up and brought panic. She'd want to cry out for help, but her heart would constrict and her muscles freeze up. She was going to die. She really was. It would be painful; this pain would only get worse. And what had she done with her life? What, if anything, important had she done? The thoughts and fears and panic wrestled behind her closed eyelids. They danced around the room and mocked from every corner.

Carrie barely made it out of bed when it was time for Eddie and Jason to leave that morning. Now she cleaned house at a snail's pace, but any distraction was a respite from picturing Lauren's journey to Europe. It was driving her crazy, imagining and wanting answers to her many questions. It made her restless, though the energy wasn't there to actually allow her more than mental agony. If only she had the strength to hop a plane and intercept Lauren from retrieving what was better left buried. Pain, instead, had become her closest companion. Like tiny shards of glass pricking her skin, but from the inside out. It reminded her with every step of what was coming, more of this, more *than* this.

As Carrie dusted through the house at her hindered pace, objects kept jumping from their places and into her consciousness: figurines, photographs, cherished doodads, earrings, favorite nail polish, a roll of undeveloped film, trinkets Eddie had made, an old watch with a dead battery, favorite CDs.

Strange how little things were seen so differently and how really their worth belonged to her and her alone.

After her mother had died, the question of what to do with everything was raised after the funeral and initial arrangements.

Carrie wanted to keep it all in its place and to never sell the house. Of course, this was impossible, Carrie knew. But the sudden disposal of everything "Mom" felt like another burial.

Her father came down to help with the arrangements. "Pick out a few mementos you'd like to keep, Carrie. We'll take what's left to the Salvation Army."

Carrie knew of the Scripture about not storing up treasures on earth, but it didn't fully register until they were hauling off the possessions of her mother's life.

Now what to do with her own things? Already in the past years, she'd begun organizing closets, putting photos into scrapbooks, writing in her journal, filling up Eddie's baby book. Just in case. But now that she knew, they knew, what effect would it have on Jason and Eddie to see her preparing to leave them? And how would it affect her?

At first, she wanted to box everything up for Eddie for some future date, to open and explore who his mother had been beyond what seven-year-old eyes could see. But she couldn't give him everything. It just wasn't practical.

In the living room, she sat on the soft leather couch and stared at the DVD collection of kid's movies, Jason's nature and action flicks, and her section of favorite foreign and independent films. On another wall, her bookshelf: books of magic tricks, travel guides, famous artists, and favorite novels, and those she'd planned to someday read. Figurines and souvenirs from around the world were displayed. All around—pieces of her. Her paintings and sketches from her younger days found in various places. In a basket, a strand of taupe-colored yarn from her short-lived and unsuccessful attempt at knitting after a teacher friend gave her a beautiful cream-colored scarf, saying she'd picked up on knitting quite easily.

Who to give it all to? Who would want it? Who wanted the pieces of her?

A month earlier, Carrie had gone on a frenzy, writing letters to people she loved, especially Eddie, to open during major events of his life. But letter writing took up her time and thought. She would crinkle them up if the handwriting wasn't good enough, or a word didn't sound right. It reminded her of that other stack of letters stuffed away in the steamer trunk. She envisioned Eddie through the stages of life, getting a message from her: graduations—eighth grade, high school, college. His wedding. A letter to his future wife. Letter at the birth of his first child, a letter to the grandchildren she'd never know. The stack of neat white envelopes grew. Then one morning, after Jason had taken Eddie to school, she picked up Eddie's letters and buried them in her steamer trunk where they might never be found. *He needs to live without his mother's death in everything he does. How to find the balance? How can I say good-bye in the way he'll understand all that he means to me?*

Carrie still hadn't told Eddie the doctor's diagnosis, even though it had been several months now. *He knows something.* Their old habits of illness were returning that he would recognize from the past years—Jason's worry and insistence that Eddie not "bug her," as if he could, especially when every day was now cherished. The video camera stayed on the charger in the kitchen and was often in use. Jason's medical research. Her slowed pace. The doctor visits. She needed to tell him. But the months of seeming health had been such a quenching respite. Yet the time bomb was ticking, faster than they hoped, Dr. Linn had said at her last appointment.

Carrie practiced what to say to Eddie. Maybe, "It's like I have an airplane ticket, though I'm not exactly sure of the day of my flight. It's coming pretty soon, but we can't just go sit at the airport and wait and wait. So we'll do all the things we can do until my trip arrives. Someday you'll get your own plane ticket, then you'll fly above the clouds and far away from here, and you'll find me. I'll be waiting at the airport, so excited to finally see you. And once we're together, it won't seem like it's been all that long. You can send me letters while we're apart and you'll get notes from me, in some pretty surprising ways, sometimes by a memory or maybe a song or a part in a movie, but not often 'cause you'll have things to do in this life that are important, and you'll need to focus on them."

Carrie imagined Eddie asking, "Like what important things?"

"That'll be part of your discovery. Maybe you'll be a scientist who will discover something to help people. Or you'll create beautiful paintings that will make people see differently. Or hopefully, you'll be a daddy someday, and you can raise your little son to be a good and kind person like you."

Such were the conversations she wanted to have with Eddie. But how to start them? How to say those things without falling apart and begging God to keep her. If only she could be the parent that she imagined or wished to be.

As Carrie walked toward the kitchen for her medication, a sharp pain in her hip caused her to reach for a side table for support. A framed picture slid off the edge and glass shattered across the tile floor, barely missing her bare feet. She wished for her slippers but hadn't seen them in a while. Carrie stared at the fragmented glass of their family photo. Eddie's birthday was the next week. They needed to tell him before then. Too many people knew now. She'd hoped to wait, but it would be worse for him find out another way.

His birthday. She had so much to do for it.

What can I leave him?

An idea began to formulate.

Something unique for all the uniqueness of that child's life.

Carrie thought of how differently Eddie viewed the world—how having a sick mother had shaped him. Doctors, nurses, and hospital patients had entertained him for years. He knew the difference between the good and the bad hospitals and waiting rooms. Death had been a shroud over his life for so long; in some ways it wasn't foreign to him at all. He loved humor and stories and imagination and . . . treasure hunts.

She sat in a chair, the glass shards littering the floor, and let the idea form. Instead of the pile of letters or hours of video, she'd put something away—yes, a treasure hunt for some year in the future. He'd love it. It would remind him of her in ways a bundle of letters couldn't. Someday when Eddie was grown, he would find it.

The thought became visual. Eddie as a young man going to Italy, finding the box, discovering a bit of his mother inside, a reminder that she loved him still.

"I've got to get over there." She'd join Lauren in Italy for only a few days, back in time for the birthday bash. Lauren would be thrilled—someday Eddie would be too. The idea became the sudden and singular thought. But even as she said it, the heavy weariness descended, pulling her down and down. Carrie made it to her bedroom and fell into bed. Eyes closed, curled on her side, her head tucked down, knees curled up, comforter pulled over her head. Her mind cried and cried, knowing the strength was gone.

A journey was as impossible as walking upside down on the ceiling. And yet, the future she wished to leave her son hinged on that very thing.

6

Carrie was going to worry.

So far, there had been no time to call.

Lauren hadn't planned for the details of arriving in a foreign country. She'd forgotten to exchange her money in the States; now here she was in late evening without a dime, or rather a euro. Lauren also vaguely recalled Carrie saying when they first planned this trip that they'd buy international calling cards while still at home—it was a cheap way to call. Oops.

On the connecting flights from Portland to Paris to Milan to Pisa, Lauren was reminded that some airlines weren't as advanced as others. The final plane appeared older, the seats worn, flight attendants dressed in uniforms reminiscent of the '70s or '80s. The in-flight snack consisted of a wrapped piece of soft cheese, a packet of crackers, and a small sandwich on a hard but tasty roll with cream cheese, another cheese, and cucumbers. She was in Europe, Lauren reminded herself again and again and again.

By the time she arrived, it was night in Italy—the flights had taken her through one day and into the next. Customs made her nervous, officers with their foreign flags and guns on their belts. Soldiers carrying semiautomatic rifles walked the busy hallways of the airport and no one seemed to mind. People smoked, chattered in their individual languages. The smells were different and not altogether pleasant.

Lauren retrieved her luggage from the baggage carousel, then headed toward the exit area and spotted an ATM. That was another travel tip Carrie had told Lauren about; ATMs were the best way to get money now. Lauren was nervous, especially when the strange currency appeared and the receipt was impossible to decipher.

From the terminal, she wrestled her luggage to the train station. Florence's closest airport was an hour outside the city in Pisa, which, of course, brought to mind its Leaning Tower. Tickets to purchase, signs to decipher—everyone else made it look easy. Some American tourists helped her find the train bound for Firenze, or Florence, Italy, renowned as a Renaissance marvel. Lauren wished for sleep but worried her luggage might be stolen.

She arrived in Florence and found a line of taxis waiting outside the station. After the train station challenge, she decided to pay for a cab to the hotel. How did the euro compare to the dollar? This was why spontaneity was surely a sin.

"No English," the taxi driver said when Lauren attempted to communicate. Instead, she pointed to the computer printout of her hotel reservation. The driver studied it, then nodded and opened her door. Yeah, this would probably be an hour's drive for a hotel around the block, she thought. She'd been told by a couple at church that she had to be travel-smart in Italy. Well, *smart* was a relative term.

As the taxi sped away from the airport, Lauren had a fleeting thought that she quickly banished, then it returned against her will. Her birth parents were from a village on the Italian-Slovenian border. That summer years ago, they didn't venture toward northeastern Italy, though Carrie had asked her to. Carrie believed they could find the village and track down the past if they put their energy into it. That was exactly what Lauren feared.

"Why wouldn't you want to know who your birth parents are?" Carrie had asked, just as she had a hundred times over the years. Even after the trip, Carrie would occasionally inquire if Lauren was ready. Lauren knew her parents were poor and from a village in northern Italy. They'd given Lauren to a missionary couple, Grandpa and Grandma's son and daughter-in-law, who were killed in a car accident on furlough in the States. Lauren didn't want to know more. "'Ignorance is bliss,'" she'd tell Carrie and quickly change the subject.

Lauren stared out the window as the driver zipped through traffic. Her stomach churned even more now than on the entire flight. Firenze, the golden city, was hidden by the night, though the streets and mass of scooters on the roads and the billboards in Italian all exposed its foreignness. Lauren pulled her jacket tighter around her. She wondered if the driver wouldn't mind just driving around forever; did she really need to get out and face more uncertainty? She could drive straight to the Cinque Terre on the sea, have him wait while she rushed out and retrieved the box, and then he could drive her right back to the airport. The quest fulfilled, and in such a timely manner.

The driver pulled in front of a small entrance to the hotel.

"*Excusi . . .*" He tapped the digital box, showing her the price for her delivery, then he bounced out quickly to open her door and retrieve her luggage from the trunk.

As she climbed out of the car, she was relieved to see a familiar Best Western sign.

"Thank you," Lauren said, handing the money to the driver. Lauren felt she was paying with Monopoly money. He looked it over, reached into his pocket for change, but Lauren shook her head and waved him to go on. That brought the first smile from him.

"*Grazie, grazie!*" the man said, and Lauren wondered exactly how much she'd given him.

At the front desk, Lauren tried to appear composed, as if she traveled the world constantly.

"Passport please?" the woman asked without even attempting Italian. Was she that obviously an American? Her genes were pure Italian, just like this woman's. Lauren remembered that the hotels often kept passports—a way to keep track of foreigners in other countries.

Soon, Lauren had her room key. A valet took her luggage up, giving her another wide smile after she tipped him—she really needed to figure out the money thing. The hotel along with the city teemed with the feeling of fifteenth-century Renaissance. Lauren imagined women in flowing gowns dressing in a room such as hers. The door closed, she was finally alone and fell into the bed in relief. The ceiling was decorated with a painting of a woman sitting beside a pool of water. From outside came the sounds of a city and a throbbing siren that reminded her she was in modern Europe. Sitting up, she stared at her suitcases and around the room. Alone in a foreign country.

She couldn't think of it all too much or panic would return, so Lauren found her travel bag and took out the itinerary she'd carefully planned with Carrie six months earlier. They'd bought travel guides and looked over maps. Jason shook his head with a contented smile—Lauren knew how relieved he was that Carrie was well again, that a sense of normalcy had come to their lives. They'd detailed the trip then printed it out on Lauren's computer. Their original itinerary consisted of two hurried weeks of travel.

Florence, the Cinque Terre, Nice, Marseille, Paris, Zurich, Salzburg, Vienna, Venice, back to Milan for the flight out.

But Lauren was veering from the itinerary and flying home as soon as she had recovered the contents of the box and gotten a post-card of one of Carrie's *three*—the favorite paintings she loved best. The revised itinerary:

Florence, the Cinque Terre, Home.

Florence brought her to the first major city where the painting by Lippi was found. She'd go to the Uffizi Gallery, buy some postcards and souvenirs, and then get to the seaside village.

Lauren crawled back onto the bed, then thought again and pulled the bedspread off—all those hotel horror stories of unwashed bedcovers flashed through her mind. Now she fell onto the sheets and thought again how very far from everyone she was. A prayer came nearly as a plea: *Well, here I am, God. And it's Your fault. I hope at least it was You prodding me toward this, not letting this crazy idea die. So, help me, and all of us. Guide us. Show us what You want done. Resolve what needs resolving. Give us strength to face what is ahead . . .*

Now that she was here, Lauren couldn't wait to get home. And yet, sometimes she realized, her very own prayers took her places she didn't necessarily want or like.

THE CLIFFS WERE turning dark along the deep crevasses while the lighthouse itself and outward-facing rocks were exposed by pink highlights where they gazed toward the sun setting in the west.

Orion Point Lighthouse.

It marked the southern end of the half-circle of Harper's Bay. Graham sailed onward, watching carefully for fishing boats and other vessels making their way into the harbor. The two greatest dangers on the water were overconfidence and complacency, or so he'd been told. Once a sailor relaxed on those waves, he became his own greatest enemy. And Graham knew its truth; he'd never traveled a decent journey without moments of fear. Such was life on the sea. Landlubbers often envisioned sailing as a relaxing hobby. Few understood the temperament of the ocean or that no seaman dared be arrogant in conquering it.

As he watched the flash of light from the tower, Graham knew it was time to turn back. He'd never planned to go this far, the outer shore of Carrie's hometown. Yet sailing north up the Pacific coast would be a rigorous undertaking. North was tedious, often requiring the engine to motor up—a slow, arduous task. Not a sailor's delight. But tacking out to sea brought the wind, then he could turn and come back toward land. He'd need four to five days to get back to Newport, double the time it took going south.

The cold seeped up from the ocean now, though thankfully the weather had been unseasonably warm. With October turning toward November, it wouldn't last long.

How strange, he thought, staring toward Harper's Bay. Carrie was in that town at that very moment. What was she doing right now? Did her illness make it hard to live happily? He imagined such a person filled with life wouldn't let her coming death destroy the remaining days. But what did he know of her now?

One downfall of the sea was its ability to make Graham think too much, despite his desire to escape. He lived with the memories, mistakes, and failures. Out on the water, he could look at them and feel their ache and wish for change. He could stare toward a small harbor town and know he'd hurt someone he might have loved, if love were possible for him.

Graham fixed a course toward the occasional flash from the Orion Lighthouse. There was a cove just beyond the lighthouse where he'd stay the night, decidedly avoiding a more relaxing night in the marina. He needed supplies, but this town could not be his stopping point. No way. He could not interject himself into her life; distance was a good thing.

Down below, Graham grabbed a chart and checked his position on the GPS. His cell phone caught his eye. The bars showed full reception. How easy it would be to dial information and see if they had her number. Then Graham realized he didn't know Carrie's married last name. That was good. He couldn't call.

Back on deck, the boat heeled to port. Graham flipped off autopilot, keeping his feet apart in a firm balance against the rocking and sudden jarring of the boat. He dropped the chart, GPS, and cell phone onto the bench seat as a gust of wind pushed hard and whipped through the sails.

From the helm, he again glanced toward the town. He could see a beach, the marina, and the town rising up the hillside. From the southern edge of town, dense forest and rocky shoreline covered the coastline all the way to Orion Point. Graham's chart showed a shipwreck on the inner side of the bay. He remembered watching a program about it the year before on his tiny nine-inch television—some schooner wrecked in a storm in the early 1900s. That it was off Harper's Bay had interested him. He'd watched closely, staring at any shots of the townspeople in hopes of seeing her. Why did he do things like that? He'd made the choice. This was the best life for him. And for her.

Lauren said Carrie didn't know she'd come searching for him. Did Carrie know now? What would she think of Lauren digging up the past? But what had Carrie buried that day—he'd never looked inside the envelope of secrets. That was one saving grace; he hadn't broken that promise. He'd broken only the most important one. If Lauren found the box and recovered the tape he'd put inside, Graham would have a decision to make.

Every few years, he received a letter or visitor asking about the bombing in Ireland. A lawyer, family member, or reporter—it was guessed he could identify the terrorist from that day. They wanted his help. Once a young woman and older man found him while he stayed in England, the closest he'd come to returning to Ireland. He assumed they'd tracked him down through customs, which irritated him. They gave a long plea to bring the killer to justice. The woman's brother, one of the soccer players, had been killed that day. She brought photos and told how her brother dreamed of a pro soccer career. It took several days of pleading before they left him alone. But that wasn't the last he heard from them. Every year on the boy's birthday, the woman sent him a letter, asking again for help.

But help meant facing the very past Graham kept trying to overcome or at least outrun. If he did turn back, he'd also destroy his family's lives, including the lives of the innocent ones like Aunt Fiona and the cousins. There was no good outcome, and the dead could not be resurrected. Still, death followed him wherever he went. Ireland was never fully gone.

He wondered how they were—his Irish family. Ten years had passed since the last time he'd talked to Aunt Fiona, though she annually sent a Christmas card with family updates to his mail service. He had no idea if the number was current or not. Sure, he could do an Internet search; he'd been saying he'd do that for several years and hadn't. On impulse, Graham jumped down and grabbed his tattered address book. He picked up the global cell phone and dialed the country code and phone number, all the while wondering why he was doing it. And yet knowing. Somewhere across the world a secret was being recovered. He had no clue what to do once it came back into his life.

As he so often did, Graham rode the impulse. Wasn't that how he'd arrived at the rim of Harper's Bay? He waited for the phone to connect. If he didn't try now, he'd put it off another ten years. He needed to know where they stood, what the climate was of his family in Ireland. Maybe it was the wrong number, but at least he'd have tried.

She answered on the third ring, the connection surprisingly clear.

"Hello."

"Aunt Fiona?" Graham couldn't hide his surprise at hearing her soft Irish accent.

"Well, I'll be. It must be my dear Graham to be calling me *Aunt*. That you, lad?"

"'Tis," he said, accidentally sliding into the brogue.

"Can't believe you called. It's been an age. Where are you, lad? Are you here, coming to visit? The boys be glad to see you. The boys excepting, as you know I'm sure, about Manny."

"I do. I sent a card and flowers; did you get them?"

"Yes, that be right. It was not a good time, it wasn't. Let's not be talking of that, unless . . ." She paused. "Unless, that is why you called?"

"No, I called to . . . say hello to my Irish family," he said. "How are my cousins?"

Aunt Fiona went through the list of the boys, telling about their jobs and marriages and divorces and the eight grandchildren, all provided by Aideen and her husband. "None of them lads are fathers yet."

Murphy worked for Uncle Fergus as pier supervisor just as Graham always expected him to do. Baby Polly was getting married the next summer, which made Graham feel older than he liked.

"And Uncle Fergus?" Graham asked, feeling a streak of anger and shame at that name upon his lips. "How is Uncle Fergus?"

"He's never home, always works, though I don't rightly mind

anymore. He's paying for a new house, 'tis nearly finished, and he bought me a nice new car—so can't be complaining now, can I? Not that I ever needed much in way of luxury."

The image of his uncle flourishing financially and Aunt Fiona's continued naïveté simply sickened Graham. He wondered how many families had been destroyed over the many years because of Uncle Fergus and the group of mobsters he belonged to. Graham had the sudden urge to yell the truth into the phone and throw it into the ocean.

"I was sorry about Manny," he said instead.

Their one chance for family redemption had died with his cousin. Manny might have done great things with his pursuit of an education and his interest in politics. His willful strength and sense of justice might have guided them all on the right path.

The tone in her voice changed. "Manny. He be one of those rare ones, he be. A shame, 'tis."

They talked a minute longer, then Graham promised to call at Christmas and said farewell. After hitting the Off button, Graham tossed the phone down. He never should have called. A never-ending string of mistakes. It could be worse, he knew. At least he was free of them, in most ways free. What if he'd stayed in Ireland? They had tried to keep him.

After the bombing, Graham's future rested in adult decisions. Aunt Fiona didn't know that Uncle Fergus was his parents' killer. At least, Graham didn't think she knew. She knew someone from among them was responsible, and that alone devastated her. Graham remembered Aunt Fiona and his mother laughing together, sharing recipes and secrets. She'd been the closest friend his mother had had in Ireland.

Once released from the hospital, Graham stayed at his uncle and aunt's house. Both his mother's brother and his parents' best

CINDY MARTINUSEN

friends in the States wanted him to come home, but it took a few
weeks to get the paperwork resolved. His cousins' house seemed
eerily quiet when he arrived. That night, he overheard his aunt sob-
bing. The cousins were moving statues around him. Their eyes
stared, but words fell silently to the floor. And there were enough
discussions and arguments among the adults that Graham faded in
as if he were a piece of old furniture carefully avoided.

Graham hid behind the leather chair, tucked between the stone
fireplace and the corner wall. It was a warm space that cocooned
him, made him feel safe from the enemies surrounding him. He
could draw in there or play with his plastic army men while over-
hearing the grown-ups' discussions. There was an argument over
where the bodies would be returned to the earth. Graham's mother
was American and his father an Irishman. Graham's maternal grandparents wanted their daughter's body brought home to U.S. soil. Yet,
it was argued that they should be buried together.

Graham shared space in Murphy's bed. Yet this time, Graham's
parents weren't coming to pick him up. He wondered where they
were. Where exactly on a map or chart was heaven? He only knew
that their remains were argued over, and what remained of him
and his future rested in the hands of those grown-ups—one of
whom was responsible for his parents' deaths. As much as he hated
and feared Uncle Fergus, Graham was reluctant to leave the only
familiar place he knew. Uncle Fergus was rarely home, and Aunt
Fiona and the cousins offered a measure of comfort and security.
California seemed far from where he'd last seen Mom and Dad alive.

The police called him to the station for more questions. Aunt
Fiona drove him down but wasn't allowed inside the dingy room
that smelled of cigarette smoke. Again, Graham denied knowing
anything. He said he'd gone to the bathroom and while walking
back, the explosion occurred.

"The record says you don't remember going to the bathroom, but now you do? Eh, lad?" the man asked from across a table. As the policeman leaned close, a sickening fear made Graham nearly wet his pants.

Graham gazed at the floor, certain his look betrayed that he did know something.

"Why do you protect the murderers of your mam and dad?"

"I'm not!" he cried, and tears stung the cut on his chin. He could picture their faces, but also the faces of his Irish family. It all clouded his head with what was right and what was wrong.

"Did you see something in the bathroom? Come now, lad. Everything on that side of the building was gone, all charred and embers, all the way to the back."

He shrugged, hoping they believed in miraculous escapes.

"You're a coward, that it, lad? You'd let the murderer go free 'cause yer a coward."

Graham left the station holding Aunt Fiona's hand. She wiped her eyes and said, "'Tis too much for such a young lad. Too much, I say." Graham wished and wished only to be with his parents. To play Frisbee on the beach with his father, to watch stars with his mother—he'd take the most meaningless moment with them; he'd do an essay every day for the rest of his life. If only they'd be back. If only they weren't gone.

That night, as he lay awake, he smelled Manny smoking in bed again. Turning over, he could see the red cherry light of the cigarette in the darkness.

"Do you know?" Graham asked.

"Yes."

The darkness gave Graham a sense of courage to ask what he wished to ask someone, anyone. "What would you do?"

The pause was so long, Graham would've believed Manny had

fallen asleep except for the movement of the cigarette in the darkness. Manny was staring at the ceiling now. Finally, "I would do what I had to do."

Graham understood what that meant to an Irishman. The vision of the Pit came to mind. And yet, Graham's parents did not believe in revenge even if his uncle did.

The next evening, his aunt, some other family, and the priest made arrangements for his father's wake to be held at the house. Graham retreated to his hideout until heavy footsteps sounded on the wooden floor, drawing Graham's attention from the line of soldiers he'd assembled on the floor. As Uncle Fergus and Uncle Terrance came into the room, he crawled close to the chair where his Uncle Terrance sat. Graham hadn't seen Uncle Fergus in the last few days, for which he was grateful.

"Our mam don't want to see you," Uncle Terrance said, his tone low. "She don't want you here for the wake neither."

"I got every right to be here. Silas was my brother. She don't want to see me, well, nothing changed from that. She always favored Silas. All we hears about is Silas in America. It always was of Silas. But he ran to America. He got important and forgot about our fight here—he forgot all it be to be Irish. Silas became a traitor when he became an American." Uncle Fergus's voice rose with every sentence.

"Fergus, don't talk of the dead like that. Silas was our brother. Don't you do it."

"What was he doing there that day?" Uncle Fergus's anger turned to something else. The image of him singing and crying over Johnjack Kerry came to Graham's memory. "Why did he go to that pub? Why would he do that to me?"

Graham wanted to leap from his hiding place and scream, "You killed them. You're the murderer. You killed your own brother!" His hands shook and tears rolled from his eyes. He thought of Manny's words. He would do what he had to do. How he wished to do something the Irish way.

Instead, he tried to believe that good would triumph. His mom sometimes read him stories like that, from fairy tales to Bible stories. He formulated a plan. It would take bravery and stealth. It was David against Goliath and all the other heroes against unbeatable odds. He would do this for his dad, his mom, and his baby sister. He would make them proud. There wasn't a cousin he could completely trust. Even though Manny knew, might even help him, Uncle Fergus was his father. And Graham would destroy the life they knew by telling the truth.

Without intending to, Graham caught himself staring at his uncle. Those eyes stared right back.

Go ahead, I dare you to tell, his uncle's eyes seemed to say.

At breakfast on the second week, Graham put his plan into action.

"Aunt Fiona, could I get a cassette recorder to listen to music on?"

They had little money—his father said Uncle Fergus drank their savings at the pubs every weekend. But Graham knew money from his parents' fund was contributed until he left Ireland. Aunt Fiona had bought him new clothes and asked him often if he wanted toys or anything special.

"Of course. I go to market tomorrow." She seemed pleased at his request.

All night, Graham couldn't sleep. His mind was plotting, and the wall was his mental planning board as he went through the various scenarios. He heard a noise from Manny's bed, turning to see his face flash with the flick of a lighter as he lit his cigarette. Manny stared his way. Graham stared back but didn't say a word.

Often, he'd felt a wildness at heart. A need for adventure, even a little danger. But this time, it wasn't a game. If someone found out what he was doing, they'd probably kill him. Traitor to the cause. Traitor to family. Traitor to country, and to the people. Deserving of death. He was a kid, wouldn't that factor in? Or would he too take a walk to the Pit?

When Aunt Fiona proudly brought home the black cassette recorder, Graham had a twinge of guilt. She included a David Bowie cassette that she'd heard was popular, a set of batteries, and a package of four blank cassettes.

Hurrying off behind the house and inside the cousins' fort, Graham put everything together and tested it: *one, two, three.* Retested it: *hello, hello, hello.*

"What are you doing?" he heard a voice, making him jump.

"Your mom bought this for me, that's all." Manny stood outside, then scrunched down to watch him. Graham worried his plan would be figured out, hadn't wanted anyone to know about the recorder. He quickly unwrapped the plastic around the rock-and-roll cassette to play it.

"I'd help you, ya know."

"What do you mean?"

"Johnjack was my girl's dad. She hates me now. I hate my dad for what he done, to Johnjack, and to Uncle. Your mam and dad were good people. Family. I'd help you, you know. Whatever you do. No matter what."

Graham nodded. He pulled out the cassette and replaced it with a blank tape. "This is what I'm going to do," he said, and they began to make trial tests together.

As usual for a Friday night, Uncle Fergus was drunk. The men met at the pub after work, staying until late or sometimes early morning. Graham and Manny waited for the telltale steps up to the door, the blundering movements of his entry. Manny crouched in the hiding spot, the cassette recorder ready. Graham waited on the couch to confront his giant. His heart pounded so hard it took his breath away. *Our Father, who art in heaven . . .* he began reciting to calm himself.

When Uncle Fergus spotted him, he growled, "Why you still up? Get yourself to bed."

"No sir," he said, shaking both from fear and anger. He let the image of his parents dead and in pieces rise to his mind. He'd envisioned it a hundred times, wondering how they looked; were they holding each other, was there anything left or did they look like charred monsters?

Uncle Fergus's demeanor changed, the drunken scowl turned boyish and pathetic. "My nephew, my poor nephew. You look like your dad as a boy, you know that?" Uncle Fergus sat on the chair, behind which Manny had hopefully started the tape. Uncle Fergus covered his face and tears fell from between his fingers. "How could this be? I didn't know they were there."

"You killed them," Graham said, standing before Uncle Fergus.

"What you talking of, boy?" he said, wiping his face with those large hands.

"You put the bomb there. It was you. I saw you, and I'm telling the police." Red anger flushed Uncle Fergus's face, but Graham was overcome with his own anger. "You're going to die in prison!"

"You fool lad! I fight for Ireland. That bomb shows our fight to the whole world. I put the bomb there for Ireland. Your father forgot his homeland; he be better dead for that."

"You're a murderer!"

The slap knocked Graham to the ground before he realized he'd been hit. He looked up at Uncle Fergus staring down at him.

"Don't you never speak to me again. You be dead too now. You go back to America where you belong, you traitor like your dad. I'm glad he's dead. I'm glad I killed him."

That night, Manny brought the cassette tape to him, handing it over with such a ceremonial pause that Graham knew it contained everything he needed—Uncle Fergus's confession. A sharp fear lodged in his throat as he accepted the tape. He thought of Johnjack Kerry and of the screams and images from the day of the bombing. Such memories brought conflicting terror and determination. But Graham would go to the police the following day.

The next morning, however, Graham awoke to the scent of breakfast. Aunt Fiona had risen early to make bacon, sausage, eggs, brown bread, black pudding, and potato cakes. As he sat at the table, eating with his cousins all around, he wondered what would happen to them with Uncle Fergus in prison. Aunt Fiona chuckled when he asked if she had ever worked outside the house.

"Oh, my, no, lad. I married yer uncle at the sweet age of seventeen."

Graham looked around at his cousins' faces. Baby Polly gave him a wide smile and with a giggle tossed a sausage on the floor.

Graham held firm to his resolution until after breakfast when baby Polly fell down the stairs and was rushed to the emergency room. That night, an exhausted Aunt Fiona and Uncle Fergus returned with the child asleep in their arms—bandages on her head.

His determination unraveled with Aunt Fiona's sobs of relief in the kitchen. Then Uncle Fergus burst in with a sledgehammer and unleashed a torrent of anger upon the stairs, cracking the wood as Graham and his cousins scrambled back to their room or outside into the dark for cover.

And though he knew what justice was, everything confused him in this place.

Graham decided he'd go the next day, but that day became the next, and the next. On the day of his departure, Graham walked down those still-broken stairs and faced his shame. He didn't have any courage after all.

His father was buried in Ireland. Graham and his mother's ashes were returned to California. Annually throughout his childhood, he'd returned to the cemetery with red tulips, his grandmother at his side. As the years passed, he'd travel the world over. But Ireland never drew him back. He'd never seen his father's grave. Even the Irish accent that reminded him of a lyrical song would become a mixture of longing and hatred. Once he'd dated an Irish woman, mainly to hear her speak, much to his self-disgust when he realized his motive. For a while, her voice brought back melancholy for his family and the good days in Ireland. But the end of his stay there would never leave him alone.

On his twenty-fifth birthday, while in Malaysia, Graham's mail caught up with him. A letter from Aunt Fiona, months after she'd sent it, but it wasn't a birthday note as usual. The letter was simple. Manny had turned up dead. In the Pit. The killers were never found.

With the memory of Johnjack Kerry's death, Graham knew what Aunt Fiona meant. That night, Graham drank several pints in an Irish pub he found on a crowded street in Kuala Lumpur. He wondered what made his cousin stand against his father's ways. Had it been Johnjack's murder? Or his parents' deaths? Did Manny always feel disgust for Graham's being so weak that he'd never turned Uncle Fergus in to the police? How did he feel when he realized his own father was taking him on the trail of death?

The last time Graham had seen Manny alive was the winter after that summer in Italy. His cousin tracked him down and followed Graham on the drinking binge he'd begun not long after leaving Carrie in the rain. Days of drinking and laughter all brought Graham's vague recollections of political plotting and Uncle Fergus.

The hatred Manny felt for his father was clear, but all discussions were spoken as frivolous, not with any serious conclusions. Their last night, Manny and Graham provoked a barroom fight with the owner, who called the police. They ran into the night and soon after said their good-byes—Graham off to the country and Manny back to Ireland.

For a moment, the sense of loss and injustice stirred righteous indignation inside him. When would his uncle be stopped? Graham could do it. He could bring justice down like a sledgehammer on a concrete slab. Uncle Fergus would break then, his pride, his position, and his career of killing. To the tune of "Johnny Boy," the only Irish folk song he remembered, Graham swayed and sang with a few other misplaced wanderers in the Malaysian Irish pub.

"To Manny!" he'd cried, with the others cheering what they did not know, and what did not matter. "I'll avenge you, Manny!"

Even in the thickness of his stupor, he imagined a box, buried far away on an Italian sea cliff. Inside would be all he'd need. Along with his testimony, Uncle Fergus would face justice at last.

But when he awoke the next morning, his head pounding and his stomach nauseous, Graham gave in to apathy again. This wasn't his fight now, he'd argued. It wasn't his country. His parents and Manny were dead, and nothing could change that. He was alone in the world. And alone meant doing what was best for him, and him only. The dead would exact their own judgment when time presented Uncle Fergus to them.

So, he sailed on.

Now the possibility weighed heavier again. This Lauren person would be pulling out the past with her quest to help Carrie. She'd promised to bring him the cassette tape he'd placed inside the box. It was probably ruined from the years beneath the ground. Or more likely, the box was long gone. If he didn't hear from Lauren, he'd simply forget the encounter. Carrie was better off with him far away, her last days on earth free from the pain he'd caused.

Hadn't he decided this before? Wasn't such logic what kept him constantly running?

Graham went below to where a map of the California coast was unrolled on the galley table.

"Ah, there's the stowaway," he said upon seeing Salt. "We need to find you a new home. This boat ain't big enough for the two of us."

A part of him wondered at that. He realized he liked the bit of companionship offered by this feline stray. And to think he'd always disliked pets, and cats in particular. Or rather, he disliked pets because he really disliked need. Graham knew this about himself; it was just who he was. A loner. Nothing wrong with that.

"Come here, you grouchy little beast."

She wasn't sleeping, but Salt wasn't moving either. Usually any opportunity for Salt to rub against him while he mapped a course was fully taken advantage of. Instead, she let out a hoarse meow, then rested her head down again.

"Are you seasick, a landlubber cat?" Graham went to her, unsure if he should pick her up or not. His fingers gently moved over her fur, then he saw some dirty spots of brown. Dried blood.

Worry came first, then annoyance. This was exactly why he didn't have a dog, or a cat, or any pet, for that matter. They got hurt, they died, or something took them away just when he really liked them.

Salt lifted her head slightly, catching his eye with her green ones.

"Okay, we'll get you some help," he said, gently smoothing the hair down her side. He moved up the ladder; the boat had floundered and turned, the current bouncing them toward the harbor. The lighthouse off Orion Point flashed around just then. Harper's Bay would have a veterinarian.

Guess he might go that way after all.

7

"Honey, do you want to wake up?" Jason's voice, Carrie recognized, but how she wished to keep all noise and movement outside of this darkened place. "Eddie's awake."

Sleep wouldn't let go. A corner of her mind nagged, *Go help with breakfast and lunches; be the cheerful homemaker other women are so great at being. Plan the best birthday party ever for your son.* Even before the illness, Carrie had never measured up to those other women in her Bible study. She disliked making lunches, though there was nothing of logic to explain why. Most of her attempts at crafts and gourmet cooking failed or appeared amateurish. While the other women cheered for kids and husbands doing their sports, she grew restless to be out there playing. But during the illness, she wished as never before to be even an inkling of that type of mom and wife who'd fit inside Norman Rockwell's painted scenes. The months of her second chance, Carrie tried harder, perfected some new recipes and baked cookies in the afternoon. Jason and Eddie seemed to enjoy the family meals at 6:00 p.m., the laundry without mounds in the washroom, and the evenings watching TV or playing board games with classical music playing in the background. It lasted a few weeks. Then Jason confronted her.

"This is nice—I can't deny it. But it'll give you ulcers, and don't forget, we love the unconventional Carrie." They'd laughed about it and found more balance. Jason and Carrie decided to take an art history class together and join a fitness club. They made plans for future family vacations they'd stopped taking for quite some time.

It was life as most had and took for granted. They had it for less than a year before disease crept back into their lives.

Wake up! How many mornings did they have left? But muscles reverberated with pain, and sleep became her only restless escape. Far away, she heard the sounds of Jason and Eddie getting ready for school and work. Her eyelids were enormously heavy. Eddie stood at the door, watching her. She could feel his gaze.

"Hey you," she said, forcing her eyes open and trying to sound cheerful. "It seems like someone has a birthday coming up."

He didn't move.

"Come here and give me a magic kiss, will ya? That'll wake up your lazy mom."

"No it won't," Eddie said and disappeared.

Carrie wanted to rush after him. Every muscle complained as she sat up. Head fuzzy, the room whirled, then slowed to a stop.

"Carrie?" Jason again. He was sitting on the bed beside her; she must have fallen asleep. Her head was back on the pillow.

"Where's Eddie?"

"Just caught the bus."

"But I didn't kiss him good-bye." A panic welled in her chest. They'd made a deal he'd never leave without kissing her good-bye.

"Sorry, Care. I told him not to bug you."

A tear fell from her eye, and then a whole trail of tears. It was happening; it was coming. The inside destruction she'd carried for so long was showing itself to the outside world. Taking over, taking her down, stealing away life in little nibbles until soon, soon, she'd be gone.

"Carrie. Carrie, I'm staying home, okay?" Jason's fingers wiped away her tears.

"No, it's okay. I'll be fine."

"You aren't fine. I already called Dr. Linn."

"You go . . . can't miss work . . . please . . ." The words struggled to come out. "Fine. Just let me sleep."

She opened her eyes and noticed he'd dressed already in shirt and tie.

Carrie raised her head and tried again to clear her mind. He needed to work, but she knew he needed a little show of strength in her to actually leave. "Jason, I'm just tired. It's not like I need help, just sleep. Come home for lunch. I'll be fine till then."

Worry creased his features. He was holding her hand.

"Take a drink of water, and then I'll go."

A drink, a kiss, another round of hesitation, and then she could let the weariness overtake her again. After he left, she wished him back. Jason's presence brought a refined comfort. Then she thought of Lauren. How she'd love to have her here today. A few times during her earlier relapse with the disease, Lauren had stayed with her, using her sick days and vacation to lie in bed beside Carrie. They'd watched TV together, and Lauren cleaned house. Sometimes it reminded Carrie of the days after that summer.

Lauren. Where was Lauren? Then Carrie remembered—she'd be in Florence today. It felt as if it'd been a week since they talked. She needed to reach Lauren to tell her she'd meet up with her. They could meet in Florence, or at the Monterosso al Mare, a part of the five-village Cinque Terre. Monterosso al Mare, the scene of the

135

crime, she thought with a slight smile. Shouldn't she smile over the tragic by now? It had been in the Cinque Terre that she'd loved Graham; she probably fell in love with him that very first day. It was also where he betrayed her. And where she humiliated herself and the Benders.

Carrie needed to talk to Jason, get airline tickets, pack, ask her mother-in-law to help with Eddie . . . the list clouded her head. Even the thought of arrangements required more energy than she could exert.

Carrie opened her eyes again.

She couldn't go.

The realization sent a cold chill through her. Her time was past. This idea to leave something behind for Eddie wouldn't be coming true. She might not even have the strength for the birthday party she'd planned for him. The heaviness of sleep tugged at her.

Carrie tried to envision Italy, to walk the village streets again, if only in her mind. But instead, she found herself somewhere else. Where was she? "Hello?" she called out to anyone, unsure of the passage of time. Then she realized it was that familiar seashore again. At least she'd gotten out of bed, Carrie thought, but how had she found this place?

Soft blue-silver light without a sun in the sky.

Her bare feet walked along the pebbled shore; the stones were smooth beneath her feet. The waves made slow turns across the earth, then they slid toward her toes. The coolness sent an exhilarating sensation up her legs. That water. The touch of it reminded her of drinking ice-cold lemonade on a hot day, only better, much better. She looked at her feet, expecting them to look younger, like she was a child again, such was the feeling of each wave.

Another one was coming; she waited, expectant. This one

pushed all around up to her calves and it nearly pulled her in. She wanted to be pulled away. Carrie wished to shed everything she carried and dive into that water.

Everybody needed to know about this beach. She'd bring Eddie here every day after school, they'd fly kites, and she'd take him swimming too. Jason could sit in the sand, look for varieties of birds, or read a book. Lauren wouldn't have a worry here. Her father could come from Portland; maybe she'd get to know his wife and not even mind her intrusive presence. And maybe even, somehow, she could tell Graham, mail him a map of this coastline. It would be like in Italy when he'd hesitated so long before diving in. That long-ago magical night, the water so perfect, even that didn't compare to this place, though she didn't know why. Somehow she just knew it.

Standing on the shore, oh, how she wished to dive into that ocean. The crystal waves rolled toward the beach and slid across her feet. They were nearly soundless in their serenity. She knew beneath the surface, there'd be more sound than above. This sea contained living qualities, as if it could speak or sing to all who swam there.

One step forward, then another.

But something stopped her. This wasn't right for her, or maybe these pure waves shouldn't be disturbed—was that it? And something behind, it too kept her still, though she couldn't pull her eyes from the water to see what it was.

From across the silvery waves, a different sound came. Carrie strained to listen. The sound came toward her, growing louder. The slap of oars. From a wisp of fog came a wooden boat, sanded and lacquered till it gleamed like glass. Two people sat in the boat, the man rowing as the waves carried them toward her. The woman wore a large hat, one corner held by her gloved hand, though there wasn't much of a breeze.

Carrie recognized them.

"I can't believe it—I've wanted to talk to you both for so long," she called.

They smiled and waved.

"Are you coming ashore?" Carrie called again.

Mrs. Bender kept waving, and Mr. Bender pushed hard on one oar so they turned back around.

"Wait! I need to talk to you."

Mr. Bender smiled and called back, "It's okay, there'll be time. There's always time."

"No, there isn't. Please, I want to say something, or ask something."

"Oh, my dear," Mrs. Bender said. "Don't you worry yourself. If you only knew what's ahead. Oh, I can't wait for you to see."

She shouted to them. "Will you forgive me?"

Mrs. Bender stood then, still holding her hat. "The time for forgiveness is here and already gone. We forgave you years ago."

Carrie had so much to say, wanting to explain. The words fell from her heart soundlessly and seemed to take off in the water, leaving a wake that divided the waves until they reached the boat which grew smaller and smaller. When the wake reached the boat, it served as a push onward, instead of bringing them back. Both waved, Mrs. Bender tossing a smile back.

"We'll see you a little later, dear!" Carrie thought she heard.

Awakening brought back bits and pieces. So, it had been a dream. Just another dream. Carrie lay still in the fog between dream and consciousness, but this time she could recall everything. That seashore in silver hues was the place she kept dreaming about. And now the Benders. She'd always wanted to ask their forgiveness, but life kept her busy, and the nagging was easily ignored, or put off for another time. Then she heard they'd died within two years of each other, and Carrie was too late.

"Carrie, are you okay?" Jason asked. How long had he been there? Was this still some kind of dream? "Should I get you to the doctor?"

"I'm okay. What are you doing home?"

"I was worried. Vance told me to work on the applications from home." Carrie felt his finger along the edge of her chin and realized she was crying.

"I'm sorry," he said.

"Sorry for what?"

"That you can't go to Europe. I've been trying to think of every way possible. But I can't, unless you have another remission, and you know I'm believing God for another miracle."

"Thanks. It's not okay. But then, in a way, it is." She felt stronger and more awake, though the pain in her joints hadn't subsided. "I'll be okay. God gives and takes, right? I'm trying to trust Him regardless of the giving or the taking, which of course is easier to say than to do."

"When God takes, He usually gives something in return. But Carrie, I can't think of anything He could give that makes this good."

She smiled. His face was so full of worry. "He's already given me you."

"This wasn't the life you wanted."

"Sometimes we don't know what's best for our own life. You have been better than I could've ever chosen for myself."

"Do you ever wonder what would've happened if you hadn't married me?"

She didn't want to answer, didn't want to hurt him, but he wanted to know. "I have wondered. I have. But for every scenario I imagine, it always comes back that this is the right place for me. I wouldn't trade you and Eddie for anything, or anyone. I just think you got cheated."

"Never say that. I knew in that parking lot you were all I'd want on this earth, even if it wasn't the easiest journey. But I'm sorry about Europe for you."

"It's Lauren's journey, though I'm worried about what it'll mean for her. She thinks she's doing this for me. I hope she'll forgive me once she finds out; I should've told her a long time ago."

8

Jet lag put her to bed and woke her up in the middle of the night. But regardless, Lauren was ready by dawn to get moving and finish this quest. Without Carrie, she didn't have much interest in the allure of Firenze. She'd take a ton of photos on a quick walk through the city to share once she returned home. The Uffizi Gallery was the main agenda.

As she embarked into the world outside her safe little hotel, Lauren wore the tourist costume: sunglasses, comfortable shoes, map, camera, sunscreen. Tourist essentials, though she did try to hide things like the map and camera in her bag so she wouldn't stand out too much. The hotel desk clerk had given her the city guide, showing the easiest route to the famous art gallery.

The streets were already filled with cars and scooters, the sidewalks dotted with morning city dwellers. Lauren joined the mass of people.

Florence, Italy, was a mecca for Renaissance lovers, with its heritage of artists and writers including Botticelli, Michelangelo, Donatello, Dante, da Vinci, and Petrarch among so many others. A settlement since before Christ through its golden age of the fifteenth-century Renaissance, Florence had gathered many treasures. For a while in the 1800s, it was the capital of the Italian kingdom. Lauren had missed Florence when she'd been in Italy before. Carrie had extolled its glory over the years, sometimes while they'd watch a movie or commercial she'd shout, "Look, it's Florence!" Eddie now recognized the city he'd never seen with its red tile domed churches and famous bridges. "Look, that's Florence. Huh, Mom?"

Wandering streets, she tried to decipher the Italian names from the map. Around a bend, she found the river Arno that cut through the city. She recognized the famous Ponte Vecchio, built in 1345— or so the map said. The bridge appeared to have odd and mismatched apartments built into its sides in staggered rows across its span. She read that the structure was the only one in Florence to escape destruction during World War II.

Everywhere, Lauren found photo ops. She soon kept both map and camera in hand, no longer caring if she'd be recognized as a tourist. There was something to read about or take a picture of at every corner.

Ahead of her, a group of travelers chatted loudly—obviously Americans—making their way through the narrow street in a large circular mob. The tour guide held a yellow umbrella high in the air—the guiding compass.

Lauren sat on a bench; the sun warmed the golden city, bringing more travelers and citizens to stroll the river's edge. Flowers, fruits, and vegetables in crates outside of shops, the outdoor cafés, rumble of cars, and people on cell phones. This was certainly a long way from Harper's Bay. A trio of men sang an operatic tune and came toward her with their dark eyes welcoming her as much as their smiles. Lauren quickly moved on. She'd heard about Italian men.

Searching the map, she spotted the Uffizi. She was traveling in the wrong direction.

I'm in Italy. Alone. On a mission, an adventure, a grand quest, if you will. Me.

142

Lauren walked streets that appeared to be thousands of years old. These buildings had seen wars, changing governments, the rise and fall of empires.

Finally, the street she sought and the street she walked on matched. And then she found it. The Uffizi—Italy's greatest art gallery. How she wished for a cell phone to say, "Carrie, I'm here!"

After paying at the entrance, she found a guest book. She signed her name and then added something else as an afterthought.

Lauren Rendell. And Carrie Timmons too.

The Uffizi Gallery held an incredibly vast collection of the most well-known masters. She'd never seen anything like it. Here she could get lost inside the visual creations of Caravaggio, Michelangelo, da Vinci, Botticelli among the many Lauren recognized. Hundreds of years had passed since the artists considered the canvas and palette, never realizing the generations of viewers who'd later examine and appreciate their works forged in the solitude of their minds.

For nearly an hour, Lauren perused the rooms, once called offices or *uffici*, discovering the Gothic, Early Renaissance, High Renaissance, and Mannerism until she realized she'd missed the painting she'd come to see.

Lauren wove back through the hallways and rooms until she reached Room 8. She was surprised she'd missed it, but there it was. Carrie's Fra Filippo Lippi painting, *Madonna and Child with Angels*. She stood before it, her head tilted, and wished for Carrie's presence. And yet, Carrie *had* stood in this place more than a decade earlier and found this to be a favorite. The Madonna was in profile and appeared younger than many of the usual paintings of her. On her lap sat a healthy Jesus held up by a clothed angel pushing from below and another at Mary's side as if to aid her with the child. Softly muted colors and the expressions on the faces gave the painting a heightened warmth and humanity. Lauren could understand Carrie's fondness, and yet how easily she had overlooked it among the more vibrantly painted works.

Soon, Lauren said good-bye to *Madonna and Child with Angels*. She wished to take a picture for Carrie, but photography wasn't allowed in the museum. Instead, she decided to look for a postcard in the gallery store. As she wandered through, a peacefulness settled around her, and Lauren found an appreciative pleasure that overcame her original quest. She was walking through the Uffizi. The world felt a little smaller and more beautiful because of the ages and creations surrounding her.

Lauren smiled. Only a Carrie adventure could turn into not only a gift for her best friend, but a blessing for Lauren as well.

EDDIE STARED DOWN at Bobby P. on the ground before him. "I told you not to say that!"

Then he saw the blood on the corner of Bobby's mouth. He'd really hurt him; his own fist hurt too. Tears streamed down Bobby's face as he jumped up and ran for the teacher. The other kids were staring at Eddie. But it wasn't his fault.

Last year in first grade, Bobby P. called him "mama's boy" for the first time. It was at recess like today, on a day after his mom had helped in class. Bobby P. didn't say it nicely. His mom often called him "my boy." He'd lain in bed that night, staring at the glow-in-the-dark stars on his ceiling, wondering what was bad about being his mommy's boy.

The next time his mom said, "Come here, my favorite boy in the world," Eddie asked her about it. She said that Bobby P. didn't live with his mom, and he was probably sad about that. "Sometimes when people are sad about something, they are mean to other people."

"Why?" he remembered asking.

"No one knows for certain. Maybe 'cause hurt can turn to anger, or we get upset seeing people happy with things we don't get to have. We humans are strange that way."

Eddie tried to understand, but Bobby P. kept calling him "mama's boy." Today, he got so mad, he wasn't sure what had happened.

"Eddie, I need to talk to you." Mrs. Smith's face didn't have its usual kind expression. Eddie realized he was crying, which made him angrier. He wiped his cheeks and tried to keep the tears inside. Across the playground, Bobby P. was being taken to the bathroom by the recess duty teacher.

"Eddie, is something wrong?"

He wouldn't look at her. "No."

"Come on, this isn't like you. Why would you punch another student?"

Eddie didn't want to talk. He wanted to just slide inside himself or run away . . . that's what he wanted to do, run far away.

"Eddie. You know I have to call your mom about this."

The anger welled up inside again. "You can't call her."

"Why not?"

"She's too sick to answer."

The teacher paused a moment. Eddie knew his dad had told the teacher that they needed a conference. He knew it was about what they'd told him last night, that the doctors thought his mom would die.

"Bobby P. was making fun of me," he said.

"What did he say?"

"He said . . . he said . . . that I was a mama's boy." Shame flushed his face and neck, and an aching confusion hurt his stomach as he both wanted and didn't want to be a mama's boy.

"Okay, we'll talk with Bobby P., then, too. It's going to be okay."

But Eddie knew; his mom and dad had said so last night. It wasn't going to be okay. Never, ever.

THE PHONE RANG incessantly.

The news was finally out. Carrie had asked Jason for several months of silence about her relapse and the ominous diagnosis. Sure, the prayers, cards, and promises of help from their church and community friends were great, but so was some peace. She struggled with the sympathetic stares and, most of all, the forlorn gazes at Eddie. "Poor Eddie," those expressions appeared to say. The peaceful time had been nice—people quickly forgot the difficulties of others as life moved along, but now the focus with their looming tragedy had returned.

Carrie felt terrible wishing them away. What if they didn't have these people who cared? How sad that would be. But now the phone was ringing, and it wouldn't give her rest. And she needed rest.

She thought of the look on Eddie's face when they'd told him last night. The confusion, anger, loss—it kept returning to her. How do you tell your son that you're leaving him? She wasn't sure how they had, but there was nothing redeeming or beautiful about it. And the guilt, it was even stronger than her fears. His own mother was destroying his life.

As she lay on the couch, the filtered sunlight through the window warmed her aching muscles. She needed to make phone calls herself, to invite people to Eddie's birthday party. Instead, she ignored the ringing phone until it was Lauren's voice over the answering machine.

"Hello? You've just got to be there. Come on, pick up. The time zone is so crazy, I haven't had a chance . . ."

Carrie dug beneath the couch pillow for the phone. "Hello!"

"Oh, you are there, thank goodness."

"How is it? Where are you? What's happening?"

"Great, at an outrageously expensive hotel in Florence, looking at art from long-dead people."

Carrie laughed even as her mind was zipping through every question she'd been saving. Surely she'd forgotten some of them.

"Did you see the Uffizi?"

"Mission accomplished. But . . ." Lauren paused, then asked, "How are you?"

"Seen better days, but I have a million things to ask."

"And this call is costing me a fortune; I forgot about the calling cards. But before I forget, will you check in on Grandpa?"

"Of course. I'll tell Jason to, just in case . . . I haven't felt the best lately."

"What's the doctor say?"

"No, we're not talking about that. You're in Italy—that's what I want to hear about. I've been so anxious, now I can't think of everything. Were you scared traveling alone? Are you getting around okay? Have the Italian men been after you? Did you take the tour books?"

"Uh, let's see . . . I like it, I think, but yes, a little scared and some anxiety over getting to the hotel, need some chamomile tea but not sure how to ask in Italian, definitely am intimidated by the Italian men, I must admit, and forget the tour guides. Exactly why I don't like being spontaneous."

"But you must love it there, come on, confess."

"I think I do. It's evening right now, the city is quite alive and noisy for being some ancient city, but it is beautiful."

"Did you see it? Did you see the Lippi yet?"

"Yes. I have a print and an art book for you—oh, that was supposed to be a surprise."

"At this point, surprises shouldn't wait."

"That's why I'm in Europe."

"I still can't believe it." Then Carrie needed to ask, "How did you find him?"

Lauren didn't even pause to consider who *him* meant. "This whole thing was on a whim. A tribute to Carrie. So I accessed the wonderful world of cyberspace. It was easy, though I wasn't sure it was really him till I talked to this woman at the hotel—she told me where to find the docks and his boat."

"He has a boat?"

"Looked like he lived on it. A sailboat, I think."

"He always wanted to do that. I'm glad he did. I can't believe you didn't tell me. We'll be talking about all that when you return. How is he?" Carrie felt guilty even asking, but how could she not?

A pause.

"Fine. He's missing his front teeth, looks like he broke his nose, has gained tons of weight and has gone completely gray."

"That good, eh?" Carrie said with a laugh.

"Worse, much worse, but I'm trying to be nice. Did I mention the body tattoo and, uh, the baldness?"

"You just said he had completely gray hair."

"Oh, I did, well, what's left of his hair is completely gray."

"Enough about his terrifying looks . . . he buried the box? I always wondered." Carrie had more questions, but there was something more important. "I need you to do something for me."

"Anything," Lauren said.

"Anything?"

"Oh, yeah, I have to be careful saying that when it comes to you."

Carrie laughed. "Anyway. If you find the box . . . did he give you a map or something?"

"Directions, but there could be a shopping mall on the site."

"No, not if it's where I think. Did he mention a beach, and then a stone stairway and a bench?"

"Yes."

Carrie closed her eyes, pulling her knees toward her chest. So it was where she thought. He wanted to surprise her, yet where else would be more poignant than that bench where the cliffside was cut back—a place of refuge.

"I'm sending something to your hotel in the Cinque Terre. I want you to put it inside the box if you find it. It'll be something for Eddie."

"For Eddie?"

"Yes. I finally figured out what to leave him. I just need to finalize it a bit."

"Let me get this right. You'll overnight something to the hotel. When I find this box you've been seeking all these years, I'm not supposed to bring it home; instead, I'm supposed to leave this new thing for Eddie inside."

"Someday he can go find it. You know, years down the road. Well, wait. Maybe you should get what we left, and just bury Eddie's. I don't know what Graham left in there."

"I'm bringing back Graham's thing—he said it's marked which one is his."

"What did he say it is?"

"Didn't say, only for me to bring it back and send it to him. The two of you are awfully secretive about it. What is your 'secret thing'?"

Carrie closed her eyes for a moment. All this was taking an enormous amount of energy. The past with its numerous layers rushed toward her, and she grappled with what this meant for her present life, and the people she loved in it. "It's just . . . something important. I'll explain, but don't open it." She wouldn't lie, but she also knew she couldn't tell Lauren right now. "It might not even be there."

"Graham said it was there as of fourteen years ago."

"Someone could've found it already or, well, maybe he lied to you—we don't even know him anymore." And yet Carrie did know something of him. There was something she'd seen, a connection between them that couldn't be explained. "Bring back what's inside, but don't you dare open any of it until we're together. I'll FedEx the packet as soon as it's together."

"I have my instructions," Lauren's voice carried the weariness of travel.

"Are you being careful?" Carrie asked.

"How strange to hear those words from *your* mouth."

"Yeah, how did this happen?"

They talked a few moments longer, but as Carrie turned off the phone, she thought of more questions for Lauren. Life would always hold more questions than answers.

LAUREN RETURNED THE phone to its receiver. How much would that cost her? she wondered. Then she chastised herself. Wasn't every call to Carrie priceless?

As she thought of Carrie and home, across the many miles, a feeling of loneliness swept over her. Carrie wasn't doing well, that was obvious.

Wasn't that her favorite pastime—worrying over Carrie and her grandfather too? Worry kept Lauren from living her own life.

The car siren of *la polizia* sounded outside, getting louder as it passed through the narrow roadway. The sound reminded Lauren where she was.

She'd made it to Italy. Alone. If she could do this, couldn't she do more than she'd been doing? Life was short, Carrie would say, but Carrie really tried to live it. How strange that she'd be the one with the shortest life of the two.

First things first, Lauren thought. Dig up a buried chest of secrets. Yes, she could do that. But after Carrie's reaction today, Lauren wondered just what it would mean. What if it opened the past in such a way as to hurt Jason and Carrie, maybe Eddie too?

CARRIE HELD THE phone against her chest. The flowers in the vase, the framed art on the walls, couches and chairs turned at perfect angles for comfort. Her home was a showroom. But what of the dusty backstreets of an Italian village, the sound of a horse's hooves on cobblestone, the feel of water as she swam at night?

A chill slid through her; her favorite blanket not thick enough. The house so quiet, the loneliness for Italy or something indefinable so sharp.

Carrie's body had begun to feel ancient, like some fragile relic that could crumble at the slightest infraction.

She rose slowly with the blanket over her shoulders—that feeling had come over her again. To wander. To seek whatever it was that was missing. The steamer trunk drew her, but she resisted. That pile of letters wouldn't be so easily discarded now that Graham was so heavy on her mind.

Why do I do the things I don't want to do? It had always been one of her favorite Scriptures. She understood the plea of Paul toward heaven. Not an excuse for further fault, but the awed frustration of continued failure. That would be her. Here she was, supposedly a spiritually mature woman, yet her thoughts so easily returned now to some lost love, her doubts quickly rose about her future "on the other side," and her irritation at her body's failure left a dark cloud where godliness was supposed to shine through.

Down the hall, the mirror made Carrie pause. Mirrors were enemies of illness. They spoke a truth she didn't want to know. Her skin was pale; her hair appeared a faded brown color and needed a trim to put some bounce into the limp ends. Carrie had never thought of herself as particularly vain.

She and Lauren joked, "We would've made ugly pioneer women without makeup and hair products." Of course Jason said she was beautiful when she awoke, or with wet, tangled hair after a swim, or pretty much anytime. But that was Jason. There was no getting around it now: she wasn't looking her best.

This must be what it's like to be old, she thought. To still feel the same inside and then look in the mirror and see a strange, tired face looking back at you. And to feel cold, from the inside out.

At the hallway vent, Carrie settled down beside it, the metal warm to the touch. When she was a girl she'd sit on the heater, letting the air fill her nightgown until it puffed out like Cinderella's gown. Sometimes she'd bring her school clothes and get dressed there with the warmth flowing over her. Life had been simple, though she dreamed always of growing up—how foolish to dream such a thing. Her father had shielded Carrie from her mother's drinking until she was old enough to notice. Years later, she'd realize alcohol was behind her mother's late-night loudness, quick temper, and the mysterious meetings she attended and then quit.

The heater warmed one side of her, making her other side feel more chilled. Carrie stretched across the vent, her head on the carpeted floor, the blanket puffing around her like a cocoon. What a sight she must look. Her mother would've enjoyed the scene.

Look at you. A heap on the floor.

Once after Carrie picked her up from a bar, her mother told her, "Don't think you're so high and mighty. This is a passed-down thing. My parents and their parents before them. Someday you'll wake up on the floor. The drink's been passed down like some dark gene; there's no escaping it."

Carrie avoided alcohol for just that reason. She'd live on the edge in other areas, but those pretty drinks with umbrellas terrorized her. All that striving to do good in life, to fully live, to love completely and without condition—hadn't life slapped her in the face anyway? Graham walked away. Eddie would need therapy after all the pain of his childhood. Her love and appreciation for Jason had taken years to develop, too many wasted years. Lauren didn't know how to have another close relationship other than theirs. And Carrie's father had run to another family, become consumed with his new life.

Carrie struggled to live in this world, to find a place, fulfill a calling she never grasped. But now that she was leaving, she couldn't let it go. It wasn't fair that she had to give everything away. Her life would mean so little. And what if this was the end, no life afterward? What if this was all everybody had? Such thoughts filtered in despite her strong faith in Christ. They were quickly dismissed but came unbidden again from time to time.

As she lay on the floor, Carrie remembered Mrs. Bender coming to her room one night while they were staying in the little *pensioni* in Monterosso al Mare. Mrs. Bender was concerned about her newfound relationship with Graham, even though Graham had already come often to meet the Benders.

Mr. Bender had been her father's supervisor for twelve years before retiring to a life of travel. When the couple offered to take Carrie and Lauren on an educational tour of Europe, only Carrie's mother had hesitated, though she soon acquiesced. This wasn't the first or last motherly talk, perhaps because the Benders had no children. Carrie didn't mind. The older woman didn't quite understand the times; it was the '80s and relationships had changed a lot since she'd dated in the '50s, but thankfully Mrs. Bender was the first to admit it. And she did have good advice at times. But this time, Carrie didn't understand what Mrs. Bender was saying. She spoke of the difficulties of life, how dreams didn't always come true, but you had to keep living, and that love would come sometimes in the most surprising ways.

Throughout the years, Mrs. Bender's words would return to Carrie. The moment of Eddie's birth, in that first instant, Carrie understood what Mrs. Bender meant about love in surprising ways—the love for her son was like nothing she'd ever dreamed existed. And by then, she also knew of the pain of life too.

"Have faith in the larger view, my dear Carrie," Mrs. Bender had said. "Have faith that what's before you today isn't all of life. You have to have faith in the larger view, the one beyond this life."

For so many years, Carrie had asked God to show her how to live. Now she asked Him to show her how to die.

9

A light rain had begun to fall as Graham motored toward the marina in Harper's Bay with the mainsail and jib already pulled down, and his space assigned for the Brothers Harbor docks. His rain jacket was zipped to his neck and the hood loose over his head as he steered forward, cheeks stinging from the cool bite in the wind.

Graham called for dock assistance over the radio.

"I'm coming in alone. Is there someone who can grab a line?" he asked.

"Sure. I'll send a man down in fifteen."

The man waiting at the side of the slip turned out to be a mere boy. He stood with hands shrugged into baggy jeans, a chain dangled on the side; his black sleek hair had bangs cut at an angle, covering half of one eye. *Wonder how much help this kid will be?* Graham turned the wheel and put it in reverse before killing the engine and sliding in. The young man took hold of the hull and hopped aboard, scooped up the rope, and hopped back off, tying the front down to the dock before Graham made a move behind the wheel.

"Pretty quick of you," Graham called up as the boy then scurried down the port side to catch a second line, tying the boat securely.

"I've had some practice; my dad's the harbormaster," the kid said, wiping back his black bangs. "My name's Lou."

"Graham," he said, reaching for the boy's hand.

"Where you in from?"

"Just up north," Graham said. "Hey, I need a few supplies. Any recommendations?"

"There's a market up a block, all kinds of shops down Main Street. Or Wal-Mart in Crescent City."

"Have you lived here long?"

"All my life."

Graham hesitated to ask, didn't want suspicion. "I used to know some folks from here. Myles was the last name."

"Don and Cathy Myles."

"Daughter's name might be Carrie?"

"Sure. My dad knew Don pretty good before he moved up north, Portland, I think. Carrie's married to a man who moved from out of town some years ago. Think she was sick for a while. Cancer or something. The holiday lady."

"The holiday lady?"

"I don't really know her, but nice lady. She always had the best Halloween candy."

Graham smiled. "Let me guess, Reese's Peanut Butter Cups?"

"Yeah, and other kinds. She'd give those king-sized ones—all the kids would talk about it and go back there every year. Until she got sick, that is. I remember a few years back, a bunch of people put king-sized candy on her doorstep when she was in the hospital one Halloween. Everybody wanted to give her a surprise, and they had a story in the *Tidal Post* about it. At Christmas she'd put up this really cool manger scene and have a neighborhood open house; seems she did something at Easter too—might be the one who organized the Easter egg hunts. They have money anyway, at least for this area, but not snobby like some."

"Money, huh?"

"Her husband is high up at the bank. Or something. Can't remember."

Strange to hear this boy talk of her. The stability. Carrie with her spontaneous nature. Had that summer changed her so much? He couldn't envision any of it. Maybe that girl he'd known truly was imagination alone. It was presumptuous of him to assume she wouldn't want stability or a life such as she now lived. Presumptuous and egotistical—as if she'd never moved on. A part of him wished she hadn't moved on, much to his shame. Nobody else in this world loved him. It gave him a sort of security to imagine she still did, that someone did.

The young man was asking him something.

"Sorry, what did you say?"

"Just asked how you knew the family."

Small-town talk, he knew, could spread rumors like wildfire. "I was practically a kid when I knew them. Old family friends, probably wouldn't even remember me."

"Well, if I can help at all, you have the number. Here's the harbor rules." He dug into his back pocket for a folded piece of paper. "You gotta use the bathrooms at the end of the dock. No shower or toilet use in the marina."

"Standard California regulations, right?"

"Yep. Can't think of anything else. Just come fill out some forms at the office and you'll be set. Oh, the Brothers Harbor Café has the best fish and chips around—but they're closed for the night. Got a great breakfast too."

"Thanks."

"You have a good evening."

Graham hadn't seen many current movies, and a good restaurant sounded appetizing; clam chowder on Friday nights was a given everywhere along the coast. But this was Harper's Bay. Everything would resurrect thoughts of Carrie, he realized, whether out exploring the town or staying locked inside his boat.

Graham returned to securing lines and buttoning down for the night when Salt's meow brought the reminder of his need of a veterinarian. That was why he shouldn't have a pet. He'd already forgotten he had one, and an injured one at that. Poor cat. Down below, he found Salt already asleep again in Graham's cabin, curled up on his comforter like a white snowball. Only a few bites were missing from the Fancy Feast cat food he'd opened for her. That wasn't like her. He looked down the dock for Lou to ask about a vet. An older fisherman was lumbering from the opposite direction.

The fisherman nodded his head in greeting. "How ya be?" he asked, looking the sailboat over.

"Just fine, thanks."

"Where you from?"

Graham always found it an amusing question that he'd asked himself a time or two—where exactly was he from? "Just down from Oregon."

"Nice little gal you've got there." He nodded toward the boat. "Name's Charles, but everybody calls me Cap Charlie."

"Graham Michaels," he said. "Hey, do you know if there's a veterinarian nearby? I have a little injury down below. Think maybe she got in a fight before we started sailing."

"A fight, eh? What's her breed?"

"I have no idea."

"A mutt, eh?" Cap Charlie grabbed a rail line and put his foot on the side of the boat.

"Are cats called mutts?"

"Oh, a cat. Was picturing a fella like you with a dog."

"Stowaway. Stray."

"You or the cat?"

Graham laughed. "Maybe both."

"Vet's not far. I could drive you in the morn unless we need to call him now."

"I think she'll be okay tonight."

"I needed a few supplies anyhow, and bet you do too. I'll be here with some espresso in the morning."

"Thanks. From both of us."

Graham followed Cap Charlie to the shack office of the harbormaster. He was staying one night, and that was it, he told the man as he filled out papers amid the usual dock chatter of weather, tides, currents, and fishing news.

As he returned to the boat to check supplies, he mentally made a list. He'd especially need extra gasoline to get back to Newport.

Despite his attempts to think of Harper's Bay as just another harbor town, Graham was the impostor in a forbidden setting. This was Carrie's home. He was the intruder. He needed to leave as soon as possible.

Later, as he slid into bed beside Salt, he noticed the cat seemed even more lethargic than the day before. The worry brought a light sleep and also the bother that this cat had encroached so deeply into his life—a cat in his bed, for land's sakes. Graham kicked off his socks beneath the covers and couldn't even toss and turn properly for fear of hurting Salt. He stared at the ceiling, then flipped on the radio with hopes that some familiar song would send him to dreamland.

Something about his phone call to Aunt Fiona kept bothering

him too. Uncle Fergus was buying them a new house. Had bought her a new car. Had Uncle Fergus given up the drink and suddenly changed his ways? Graham knew that couldn't be it, or else he wouldn't still be managing the docks. So why the sudden change in income?

Graham knew nothing of the Irish economy of late. But maybe the boys were bringing in the dough and sharing it with their dad. Or maybe Uncle Fergus wasn't the low man anymore, the brute force. Who said crime didn't pay? That justice prevailed? Good overcame evil? None of that was true, at least in this life.

His parents died because of that man, and now he was living the high life. He should have been rotting in a prison. Thoughts turned to Manny. Why had Graham been such a coward? But Lauren was digging up that past. If he had that tape, he might be able to stop his uncle. All these years, Graham hadn't let it matter.

Now it did.

PAIN ENGULFED HER as if she were in a bubble. Pain was an entity of its own. Singular. Isolated. No one could come inside. No one could hear her, though she could hear them.

Sometimes Carrie wanted to send out a signal: "It's not as bad as it looks." Other times the pain seared so sharply, it seemed to split her brain in halves and quarters and eighths until she wished for any escape. Give her a gun, a window to leap from, water to drown in. Anything, anything to stop it. *God, please stop this. It's much more than I can take.*

From a far distance, she knew Jason was frantic. People were staring and touching her eyes and poking something into her arm, lifting her up, the straps of a stretcher tightened around her legs and chest.

Eddie stood in the doorway. Carrie reached for him, but he ran away.

Time, which she found both fascinating and frustrating, whirled out of context. Everything moved slowly, yet she knew she'd arrived at the hospital. Where was Salvador Dalí now? She could tell him what to paint, images juxtaposed over one another.

Pain, a living entity, walked beside her, clung to her, possessed her. The faces of Jason and Pastor Artie came into focus though distorted; they were praying for her, holding each of her hands. A sweeping of peace fought even as the pain remained.

I'm going to die now, she thought, ready to rise from the stretcher and walk away. Where was that seashore, the living water, and the open sky? The undones would have to resolve themselves. Jason, dear Jason, should find someone to love him more. Lauren might never get over the anger of what Carrie had done, when she opened the box. That made her pause, wish to change it, but she was leaving now and didn't know how to return. Friends and acquaintances marched like a parade taped in 8-millimeter film.

Eddie, Eddie, Eddie.

Carrie knew time had passed again. In trying to get her bearings, she realized she'd been in an ambulance, then the ER; now she was someplace else. With the coming awareness came a crash of aching pain. She could run away from it. Or if she found that secret door of escape, she could run free for a while. She could concentrate and race across the pebbled seashore. She could look at cloud formations and plan her route of flight. Running down. Running up. Leaping, believing, laughing. Near flight, near escape from the crutch of gravity. It was just a leap away. Close, so very close. She could almost do it. If only she could say good-bye. If only she could leave the right message behind. If only she knew how to fly away without really leaving.

Carrie opened her eyes. She stared through waxy eyelids, blinking more than usual to cast away the sting that rimmed the edges. Staring at the television, she watched the antics of a late-night talk show host. There came laughter, hollow and flat, through the speakers, as if the two-dimensional world were animated life. Jason was asleep in the chair beside her, his hands on his rounded stomach, head bent uncomfortably to one side. She tried to reach for him, hand him a pillow, move over to let him share her bed. But her arms were too heavy.

This was not real, she thought. This was not reality; it couldn't be. How did they get here? On what road did they turn to find themselves here, in this moment? And how could it ever get back to good? How could anything ever be good again?

She didn't want life to end this way. Perhaps she'd read too many books and watched too many movies. Where was the purpose, the redemption, the honor? A disease was none of those. Real life was eating away at her, taking over and ending any chance for imagination and dreams.

Yet what made her different? Thousands of people died every day, all over the world in tears and anonymity. Nameless, faceless, some not only forgotten but never known in the first place. She remembered a Thanksgiving the year after her favorite great-uncle had passed away. It seemed the holiday as usual except for a few brief mentions of Uncle Pete. Life moved on. Life would move on, slide right over her as if she'd never been.

She'd told Jason just a week earlier, "I wish there was some climactic event. Something honorable to die for, someone to save. Do you think I could donate a kidney or something?"

"I don't see the doctors letting you do that anytime soon."

Carrie knew there were things left to do; she knew it more and more by the dreams. Or were they realities beyond this life? Her purpose for living wasn't over, at least not yet.

HER HEAD AGAINST the window, Lauren watched the landscape turn from hills with dotted villages to more rugged and mountainous terrain. The train to Cinque Terre took the same route back to Pisa, then continued through Tuscany to the coast. As the train turned north, the ocean came in and out of view. They drew closer to the coastline of the Ligurian Sea, part of the greater Mediterranean. Aqua coves with sandy beaches scrunched between hilltop towns and towering cliffs.

It was nighttime at home. She pictured Carrie asleep in her tall sleigh bed, or maybe she'd fallen asleep on the couch watching one of her independent or foreign films—she always watched them late, after Jason had given up for the night. Carrie would later beg Lauren to watch her favorite ones with her; both Lauren and Jason would roll their eyes, knowing Carrie's quirky cinematic taste did not match their own. Carrie would try to quote favorite parts of the movie and never get them right, getting frustrated and saying, "Just watch it. You'll like this one; I know you will. If I explain the background, what the writer was symbolizing . . ." By then Lauren would be nodding to appease her. Now, as the landscape swirled by, she realized that after Carrie was gone, she'd probably watch every one of those movies and wish for her friend's commentary.

Lauren thought next of Grandfather sleeping after another day of searching the house for the elusive. She wondered about that, what it meant—for the past six months he daily rummaged through the house in search of something.

"What are you looking for, Grandpa?" she'd ask on her visits to his house.

"Something. I'm looking for something."

"What is it? Can I help you?"

"No, it's something I lost, and I'm the only one who will recognize it."

The doctor said he didn't have Alzheimer's or any other physical malady. Said that for his age, her grandfather was "fit as a fiddle"—whatever that phrase meant. Lauren had gone through various stages of concern. Her coworkers, her minister, and Carrie all had differing opinions, from it being psychological, a misdiagnosis, a cry for attention, or that she should ignore it. By the time Grandpa's friends came over for their poker night, he'd put aside the need to scour the house for that missing something.

The train slowed at another village. Lauren was unsure why they stopped at some villages while others passed by—all were marked with white signs over the boarding areas beside the tracks. Names like Torre del Lago Puccini, Viareggio, Lerici, La Spezia. At each stop, passengers got on and off—tourists, children going to school, people in business attire with briefcases, natives who appeared to be from a long-forgotten era, some with baskets resting on their laps.

As the train moved out again, Lauren heard a commotion ahead of her. Suddenly two young girls were in the aisle, leaning toward her with outstretched hands.

"*Mi scusi!*"

Lauren put her hands up, an involuntary reaction. Her purse sat on the seat beside her, close to them. The reminder of pickpockets brought her tugging the purse onto her lap. Still the children begged, hands reaching toward her, the Italian words coming louder and louder.

"*Per favore!*"

Lauren reached into her pockets and found some change. Anything to make them leave.

"There, now go away!"

They scurried on to the next people, who more brusquely sent them down the aisle where they reached their parents. Gypsies, she realized. She'd heard of them, but the encounter left her rattled. *So much for the pleasant train ride along the coast.* Quickly, she rummaged through her purse and backpack, making sure nothing was missing. At the next stop the Gypsy family disappeared from the train car.

The doors closed and the train sped off again. She put her travel bag beneath her feet and kept her coat in the seat beside her to ward off any passengers looking for a seat.

Gypsies—homeless, wandering vagrants. Her heart continued to beat faster, taking her breath. Her throat constricted. Lauren looked around, but no one seemed to notice; she didn't want anyone to notice, and yet, maybe she needed help. Maybe she was having a heart attack. She took a quick gasp of breath. The village outside rushed in and out of view with its church spires, cars zipping down narrow streets. Was there a hospital close by?

Calm, calm, stop panicking, she kept thinking, fighting the physical urge to jump from her seat and grab somebody to help her. Her heart rate finally slowed; her breathing became less labored.

Where had that come from?

How could a startling yet harmless encounter with two Gypsy children rattle her so? Her eyes were watering, and she wiped beneath each in case of a mascara smudge.

But in her thoughts came disturbing words from childhood spoken by other children, teachers, and acquaintances alike.

"You don't know who your parents are?"

"If you can't do your family tree for this assignment, then do your adoptive family's heritage."

"Anyone could be your mother. Even someone like me."

This country, being alone—it reminded her of the past she avoided, tried to forget, tried to believe never existed. Her parents could've been Gypsies like that family. Those girls begging for money—that could have been her life. Lauren didn't know. She'd never wanted to know.

But maybe some things weren't supposed to be forgotten.

10

"R eady down there, Cat-Man?"

Great, Graham thought, holding a cup of coffee. He looked at the white ball asleep inside his laundry basket. "See what you've done to me? Now I have a nickname."

"Espresso orders taken now." Graham opened the doors from the galley, and poked his head out to see Cap Charlie, his gnarled hand held like a waitress writing down an invisible order. "My cappuccinos happen to be well-known in these parts."

"Is that right?" Graham said, smiling at the old fisherman's antics. "Now, I'm quite the connoisseur, have experienced the best coffees in the world. I'm not like your usual small-town critics."

"Give me five minutes," Cap Charlie said, taking the challenge.

Graham cleaned up the galley and added a few items to his supply list, then picked up the laundry basket with his feline passenger inside. When Salt lifted her head and gazed pitifully at him, his worry only increased. He'd hardly slept all night, fearful he'd roll on the cat, or that she'd stop breathing.

"Help is on the way, little gal."

Cap Charlie arrived with a steaming white cup on a little silver platter. A cup of water rested beside it with elongated packets of raw sugar Graham had often seen in Europe. He balanced the tray and stepped aboard as the boat swayed slightly. "A little more wobbly than my giant beast."

"Quite the display you have there," Graham said.

"I've been a-researching Viennese brewing procedures since they be the first coffee makers, you know. I'm planning to tour the best European coffeehouses next year."

"Really?" Graham chuckled, picturing Cap Charlie on an airplane, traveling around Europe. "How'd a fisherman like you become a coffee aficionado?"

"Started with my tour of duty in '42. Been drinking the black brew ever since, but these newfangled espresso machines helped perfect my love of coffee."

Graham chuckled. "Who'd have thought?"

"It ain't proper to drink this masterpiece on the run." Cap Charlie looked at Salt asleep in the laundry basket. "So there's the patient, eh? I think I've got some better transportation for that little fella—you sit back and drink this while I'm gone."

While Graham sipped Cap Charlie's cappuccino, the fisherman found an old cat carrier in a storage shed on the docks. As Cap Charlie checked Salt over with a tender touch, Graham couldn't help but feel concerned about the cat. He shook his head. It was just a cat! Just some stray he'd never rid himself of. Now he'd be paying for a vet bill.

Graham followed Cap Charlie to the parking lot, lugging the carrier in his arms. He could see through the holes that Salt stared with wide eyes at this entombed captivity. Cap Charlie unlocked the passenger door of the Chevy Malibu; one section had been eaten away by the salt air.

"That's no ordinary cat, ya know," Cap Charlie said as he turned the engine over. It roared to life.

"Oh, yeah?" Graham said, wondering what kind of engine the

fisherman had hidden beneath that hood. Sounded more like a race car than an old sailor's land transport.

"Yep, that's right. That boy's surely a little angel cat."

"Really? Hard to believe when he is a she . . ."

"Don't doubt me now, he or she, you still never know about these things. Visiting angels can appear in the strangest creatures. She's a God-sent angel on a mission."

"You've been on the sea too long."

"You're right about that," Cap Charlie said with a chuckle.

The town was another quaint harbor community with cottage-style homes rising slightly up the slope of a mountain while the town itself nestled closer to sea level. Fishing, lumber, and tourism were probably the employment opportunities of the area.

They turned down a store-lined street that housed the local newspaper, various shops, and a hardware store. At the end of the street, Cap Charlie pulled in front of a small building with a sign that read, "Pacific Coast Veterinarian."

"Here you be. I'll come back in half an hour and check on you both. We can get those supplies of yours afterward—I've got me a breakfast date."

"Seems retirement has done you good, Cap Charlie."

"You have no idea," he said with a sly grin.

The antiseptic smell of a veterinarian clinic stopped Graham as he opened the door. Salt meowed in complaint. A few others waited on plastic chairs in what he supposed was the waiting room; charts of dogs and horses covered the walls. A receptionist's desk was to the left. The woman didn't even look up as he approached.

"Yes?" she said, still staring at the computer screen.

"This cat has something wrong with her."

"What's wrong?"

"Well, she's not eating like usual, or moving around. Seems lethargic. And there was some blood on her fur."

"Hair."

"Huh?"

"Cats have hair, not fur."

"Okay. Then the blood on her fur, I mean hair, is so thick, I couldn't see any injury." Graham couldn't find the words to describe this correctly.

"Name?"

"Michaels, Graham Michaels."

"No, your cat's name."

"Well, she's not actually *my* cat. She's a stray that kind of stuck around . . ."

The woman sighed with impatience.

"Salt. I call her Salt." Graham looked behind him. Since he was the only entertainment in the room, the few people on plastic benches were watching him.

"Salt. Okay. And your name?"

"Graham Michaels," he said. He should be in Oregon right now, not in Harper's Bay, not with a cat that wasn't his, not in this smelly veterinarian's office. He should take this stray straight to the animal shelter and leave town.

"Take a seat. One of the docs will see you in a bit."

"All right."

Graham found an empty chair and put Salt's carrier between his feet. A whisker stuck from one of the holes; then he saw her pink nose.

"Your cat's name is Salt?" a boy next to him asked.

Graham wanted to say it wasn't his cat. He didn't like pets. Since his dog as a boy, he hadn't had one pet except for a gecko that traveled on his boat around the Hawaiian Islands for two months

170

before he put it back on land and sailed on. Graham glanced over at the kid; his legs dangled without touching the floor. Cute kid with two bottom teeth missing.

"Yep. Captain Salt should be her name."

"How come?"

"'Cause I live on a boat and she seems to rule the roost now."

"You live on a boat?" the boy asked in amazement.

"A sailboat, not a big one, but big enough for me, and now Salt."

"I have a dog named Pepper. Salt and Pepper; funny, huh?"

"Yeah."

Graham looked beside the boy to a woman who simply stared ahead with a cardboard carrier in her arms. The woman and boy obviously weren't together.

"What's wrong with Pepper?" Graham asked. "And where is he? Is he really small and in your pocket?"

The boy chuckled. "No. My dad is with him and the vet. He has a sore on his leg that he keeps biting, and he needed his shots anyway. We almost didn't come today, but my grandma came for a visit, and she's paranoid about him not having his shots. She said he could get a disease and give it to us, or we could get sued if he bites someone on accident, or, well, Grandma comes up with every bad thing that can happen."

"Paranoid, eh?" Graham said, knowing this boy probably didn't even know what the word meant. He'd no doubt overheard his parents talking about "paranoid Grandma." Leaning his back against the wall, Graham sighed, trying not to breathe in much of the vet scent.

"My mom is at the hospital; that's why we almost didn't come here. But Grandma, you know . . ."

Graham's head lifted, meeting the boy's eyes. Deepest brown and filled with worry. "Is your mom okay?"

"No. She's going to die."

Several people looked their way. The boy didn't seem to notice. He simply looked back down and began swinging his legs. Graham hadn't been around kids much, but enough to know how blunt they could be about things adults would never speak of.

"What's wrong with her?

"They think it's PRMS, or Progressive Relapsing Multiple Sclerosis." The boy spoke casually, then smiled. "She says MS really stands for 'misunderstood superstar.' My mom's funny."

What to say to that? Then a thought stopped him. He glanced around the room, then back. It couldn't be. Surely, there was no way. Graham looked more closely at the boy. Carrie had dark brown eyes, but so did millions of people. The two other people in the waiting room were either looking at the boy or looking at Graham. A woman gave him a sympathetic expression. "My name is Graham," was all he could think to say.

"I'm Eddie." He put out his small hand and Graham shook it. The waiting room lapsed into silence; even the receptionist was quiet, though after a moment she returned to tapping the keys of the computer. Graham tried to guess the boy's age—maybe six or seven? He was bad with ages, but remembered the five-year-old girl of a woman he'd dated briefly, and Eddie seemed older than her.

Just then a man in a white coat walked out, picked up a chart, and said, "Salt."

"That would be us," Graham said, hesitating as the boy watched him.

The doctor glanced at the woman with the dog carrier. "Miss Melfie will have that prescription in a few minutes for you."

"Thank you," she said, standing and giving a sympathetic glance toward the boy.

"I'm Dr. Rooks. Let's take Salt down to an exam room."

"Sure," Graham said, picking up the carrier. Graham followed the man, looking back, wondering again about the boy and his mother. The coincidence was too great. How could this be Carrie's son? And yet, she had a boy—seven years old, hadn't Lauren said? A boy named Eddie, named after a favorite uncle. In Harper's Bay. Mother dying. He said she was in the hospital, but if it was really serious, why were they at the veterinarian? Graham had a sudden urgency to find out. This had to be Carrie's son. How could it not be?

As they walked down the hall, they passed another examination room. From the corner of his eye, Graham saw a black puppy being petted and calmed by a middle-aged man. He turned back but noticed Dr. Rook waiting at the next doorway.

"Right this way," he said cheerily. Graham walked inside and set the carrier on the sterile examination table.

"So what do we have here?" the vet asked, gazing at the chart. "Salt, a stray, so she, or he, hasn't had shots?"

"Not that I know of. She was pretty scroungy when she showed up."

"Well, let's take a look. And the note says she has an injury?"

"I discovered it last night." Graham explained the cat's change in behavior and appetite, and the injury on her chest. As the doctor pulled her from the carrier, Salt meowed and looked at Graham as though he were a villain.

"Well, she is a she," the doctor said with a smile.

"That's good to know, I suppose."

"But it seems she got into a fight or something, probably a week or so ago. This lump here is an abscess. It takes a while for the infection to show up. I'll have to lance it and put in a drainage tube."

173

Graham grimaced at the thought. Salt writhed in the doctor's hands, trying to scratch free.

"I'll get my assistant in to shave some of this hair first. Then we'll give her a little something before doing the procedure."

"She isn't going to like that. She's quite proud of her looks."

"I bet. That's one good-looking stray. Maybe you should've named her Angel instead of Salt."

Graham frowned instead of joining the vet's smile. "I've been told that before."

But the doctor was again gazing at the paperwork. "Your paperwork says you're not a local?"

"No, sailed in last night."

"Oh, are you planning to leave soon?"

"As soon as possible—why?"

"Well, to be safe, I'd like to keep her for observation. No extra charge, just figured it'd be best to observe her for a bit."

Graham sighed. Salt had calmed again and rested on the cool table with her head tucked down. Not her normal prideful look.

"Okay," he said.

"Great. So, that's all. Take this chart to the receptionist in front."

"The doc will make you better, okay? You crazy cat." Salt opened her eyes, then closed them again. Graham hesitantly walked away. He didn't have the presence of mind to look into the other examination room until he reached the waiting room where the boy, Eddie, still sat.

"So, what happened?" Eddie asked, jumping up when he spotted Graham and looking for Salt in the carrier. The room had cleared out except for the lone kid. Graham wondered why the father would leave him here, trusting that he wouldn't get kidnapped or something. Things like that happened all the time these days.

"They're keeping her for the night."

"Surgery?"

"A pretty easy one. She'll be okay. What about you, no news?"

"Nope."

"Excuse me, I'll take the chart," the receptionist said. Her head was tilted, holding a phone between her cheek and shoulder as she reached a hand toward Graham.

"Sure." Graham handed it to her, just as she started talking again. He glanced back at the boy, who looked so small sitting on the chair. For a second, he had the image of himself sitting alone on a chair in a hospital in Ireland. He couldn't remember why he was there except he was bandaged and waiting for his aunt to fill out papers pertaining to either his injury or his parents' deaths. *Where did that memory come from?*

"You can pay when you pick her up," the woman said then.

"Okay." Graham took a step toward the door.

"So do you live around here?" Eddie asked.

"Nope. Just a visitor."

"Oh. I live here. I was born at the same hospital my mom goes to. Well, sometimes she goes to other hospitals; once she stayed down in the city for a long time."

Eddie stopped talking and again stared at his shoes, knocking them together.

Graham was trying to think of a question that wouldn't seem too nosy. Already he was staying too long; he knew he should leave when a man walked from the hallway, a sleepy puppy in his arms. "She's all fixed up," he said cheerfully to Eddie. The boy didn't leave the chair; his gaze remained cemented on his clapping shoes. The man frowned, then continued to the counter to check out.

"So this is Pepper?" Graham asked the man. The puppy's leg was bandaged.

"He has a cat," Eddie told the man, presumably his father, "named Salt."

"Is that right. Well, isn't that funny?"

"His cat has to stay overnight."

"That's sad," the man said, then waved to the receptionist. "Thanks, Mindy. And thanks for keeping an eye on Eddie for me."

"Sure thing. We'll put that on your account. You take care now, okay? Give Carrie our love."

"I will."

A wave of heat flushed over Graham. The truth pierced through him. Graham quickly walked outside; the cool coastal wind felt good on his face. Outside, however, he had nowhere to go. Cap Charlie had yet to return. Graham walked down the street and sat on a bench to wait. A few moments later, he heard the boy and man coming his direction.

"There he is," the boy said. "You forgot this."

Eddie lugged the cat carrier. The puppy still rested in the man's arms.

"Thanks," Graham said, standing up again.

"My son says you live on a boat?"

"Yep."

"New to town or passing through?"

"I didn't mean to come here."

"Really? The Lord can be pretty mysterious sometimes."

Graham wondered at that, wondered if this guy would still say so if he really knew. "That he is," Graham conceded.

"Do you need a ride somewhere?" the man said.

"We have a car," the boy said.

"I'm waiting for my ride, thanks."

"I'm Jason," he said with a hand outstretched.

Graham hesitated, then said, "You're married to Carrie?"

Jason looked surprised, but not suspicious. "Yeah, do you know her?"

"The receptionist mentioned her name." Graham quickly added, "Eddie says she's in the hospital."

A shadow seemed to cross his face—sadness, that was it. "Yeah. Running some tests and observation. A little dehydration, medicines not quite working right, some things like that. She should be home soon, Lord willing."

Graham didn't know what to say. He thought about lying, making up some story, saying he was someone else.

"My name is Graham. Graham Michaels."

The man reached out to shake his hand, no hesitation at the name. Graham could slip away, run—not walk—to the boat, and sail off.

"Nice to meet you," Jason said. "Are you leaving soon?"

"They're keeping my cat overnight. Then I'll head out. But nice meeting you. Hope your wife gets better." It was strange referring to Carrie as this guy's wife.

"Yes, we all hope that."

The boy stared at his father as he said it. Eddie had said his mother wasn't getting better; Graham regretted saying such a thing.

"Safe journey," Jason said.

"Bye," Eddie said, looking back at him forlornly.

What did this all mean? Such coincidences didn't just happen.

"Wait a minute," Graham said.

"Sure." Jason's quizzical expression made Graham doubt what he was about to say.

"You aren't going to believe this. I don't, really. I wasn't intending to come here. I was out in my boat. I was going to keep going. I . . . how do I say this?" Graham looked at Eddie, not wanting the boy to be listening so intently. Jason seemed to realize this too.

"Eddie, sit here with Pepper."

"I don't want to," Eddie said with a frown.

"Just for a minute."

The boy sat on the bench and grudgingly took the leash as Pepper raised her head and whined. She wagged her tail and rested her head on Eddie's lap, but Eddie didn't seem to appreciate the gesture.

Jason took a step away and Graham turned his back toward the boy. "This is going to sound . . . well, I know Carrie. Or rather, I did a long time ago."

"Oh." Jason seemed pleasantly surprised and then the look drained away. "Oh. Graham. *The* Graham."

Graham's stomach made a strange twist, sorry to see this man's face fall, but also disturbingly happy Carrie's husband knew of him. Then guilt for that happiness too.

"Dad, can we get an ice cream?" the boy asked, pointing to the ice-cream shop window decorated with bright lettering and colored cones.

Jason didn't seem to hear until Eddie asked again.

"Sure, yeah."

Graham wondered what could be going through the man's thoughts, and whether he should keep explaining, but he wasn't sure what he could say.

"Would you like an ice cream?" Jason asked.

Graham glanced behind to meet Eddie's expectant gaze, then back to Jason's sudden expression of camaraderie, which made Graham utter a surprising "Yes." Eddie cheered and zipped down the street to an outside table, leaving the puppy on the bench.

"It'll give us a chance to talk," Jason said.

Graham's defenses immediately rose until the pat on his back. Who was this guy who could so easily welcome him in?

Carrie's husband, he reminded himself.

THE TRAIN STOPPED at Monterosso al Mare, one of the five villages of the Cinque Terre. Late afternoon in Europe brought the usual siesta time. Lauren dragged her luggage behind to a rappity tune as wheels clamored down the cobblestone street. She was hungry, but cafés and storefront doorways were closed up tight until evening. The map printed from an Internet site wasn't the easiest navigator to the *pensioni,* but after several times up a narrow street that curved between stone buildings and beneath a small bridge, Lauren spotted the sign to the small hotel that clutched the edge of the sea cliff.

Quaint and completely old-world, the Italian inn appeared something from an age gone by. Lauren pushed open the heavy wooden door to slide inside. The lobby was painted with murals of the Italian countryside and ocean scenes with velvet-covered chairs and a huge vase overflowing with fresh flowers. Lauren approached a deserted front desk. She rang the bell several times before a robust Italian man came barreling from a corner alcove where he'd been sleeping. He cleared his throat several times before his loud voice interrupted the quiet.

"*Buon giorno,*" he said. "Reservation you have?"

"Yes, *grazie.*" Lauren handed him the printed paper.

He gave her a fatherly smile. "Only you?"

"Yes. Only me," she said, thinking how sad that sounded for such a romantic setting.

After filling out a paper and turning over her passport again, the man helped Lauren get her luggage into the miniature elevator. On the third floor, there were only three rooms—the *pensioni* must have been a large house at one time. She opened the door after several tries with the key and entered a cozy room decorated in gold and burgundy. The room's balcony overlooked a rocky beach and the expansive blue Ligurian Sea. A warm breeze brought in the delicious scent of food cooking.

Lauren had been in this village before, though this wasn't the *pensioni* she'd stayed in when catching up with Carrie and the Benders and meeting Graham for the first time. Lauren was glad to be in a different hotel than that one. The restaurant in the Hotel Royal, on the other side of the village, was the scene of that heart-breaking final night with Graham.

Closing the balcony doors, Lauren sat on the bed with the weight of travel heavy upon her. She shouldn't sleep, though the villagers were relaxing in the warmth of the afternoon. Only for a few minutes, Lauren decided, she could close her eyes that long.

It was dark when she awoke. Her stomach complained loudly. From the balcony, Lauren could see people walking the esplanade along the beachfront. The village sounded more alive at seven thirty in the evening than when she'd arrived that afternoon. Lauren felt intimidated going out there after dark. But her water bottle was empty. The only food she had left was a half-eaten protein bar that had backpack lint all over the open end. Hunger and thirst finally sent her outside.

Within minutes, Lauren saw she was underdressed. Many of the older women strolling the narrow shops and walkways wore skirts, blouses, and nylons; the older men wore slacks and dress shirts—nicer than what some people wore to church back home. Tourists and youths backpacking the country were easily identified by their casual attire.

Rich scents drifted around her—from Italian cuisine to perfumes or colognes of other strollers, some kind of orchard tree, and a waft of cherry tobacco from a man with a long pipe, sitting at an outdoor café. Lauren merged with the others, forgetting her hunger for a time and enjoying the anonymity of such a stroll. At an outdoor stand, she bought a bottled water and a huge slice of thin pizza. Two young Italian men smiled at her in that flirtatious way true to stereotype. Lauren quickly continued on until the narrow streets opened along a stretch of walkway above the beach. Elderly couples, families, young men in small groups, and young lovers holding hands—it seemed the village pastime to parade along the walkways in late evening.

An empty bench invited her to sit. Lauren took a bite of the flimsy pizza, which tasted nothing like its American counterpart, but she liked it all the same. The village lights reflected across the gentle waves, and Lauren thought immediately of Carrie and her first days of meeting Graham in this very village. As her gaze moved upward into the brilliant night sky, it was Eddie's words she recalled as she spotted a W-shaped constellation.

"I think that's Cassiopeia," Eddie had told her. "It looks like a big *W* like in my name; did you know my real name is Edward?"

Lauren smiled at the memory. It had been the summer before when Eddie stayed the night with her so Carrie and Jason could have a weekend away. She'd been nervous, unsure quite how to care for him overnight—it was one thing to take him to the park or for ice cream. She feared he'd get bored, cry for his parents, or not go to sleep. When Eddie spotted her old telescope, they decided to set it up in the backyard—Lauren hadn't done that since she and Carrie had slept outside as girls.

"Mom says Cassiopeia is in the Milky Way, and the Milky Way looks like milk spilled across the sky with stars shining through it."

"You're a pretty smart kid."

"I'm a genius," he said in a serious tone that took Lauren aback a moment. She spotted a slight grin at the corners of his lips. Eddie was so like Carrie.

"Oh, yeah? Well, Mr. Genius, who was the first president?"

"President George Washington."

"That's right."

"Ask me who painted the Sistine Chapel."

"You know about the Sistine Chapel?"

"Mom and I have a book all about Italy. Someday we're going to visit there together. After she goes with you again, when I get bigger."

"Maybe you should come with us."

"Dad said it's a girl trip this time."

"That's true," she said, thinking it would be harder having a child along, even if that child was Eddie. "Who painted the Sistine Chapel?"

"Michelangelo. Ask me something else. Harder."

Lauren tried to think of some trivial fact, one she'd know the answer to or was too vague for an answer. "How old is God?"

Eddie's smile could be barely seen in the darkness. "He doesn't have an age. He's like time or like counting numbers—no beginning and no end."

Lauren thought a moment over his answer. "Who told you that?"

"Dad."

"God is like time or like counting numbers . . ." She considered both, how a person could count ahead or in the negative for an infinite number, never ending, never beginning. "That's weird."

"I know. Dad also said that people should believe in God because of dirty jokes, and some other reason. Oh, yeah, because of how people don't like death."

"What?"

"Dad was saying how people around the world have these things after people die; he called them something, like we have funerals. But everybody does it. 'Cause people aren't like animals—we don't like things to die. We don't know what to do, or how to live. He said it's something like 'cause we have inside of us a ghost, or not a ghost, but that's what I thought of 'cause of the Holy Ghost—oh, yeah, a spirit. We have a spirit that will live forever and ever, but our body holds our spirit here on earth, so it's sort of like being in jail, or . . . Dad said like when I hold a balloon and if I let it go, it'd fly away. Our bodies hold the spirit. And something like the spirit inside us doesn't understand stuff on earth. So we think it's strange, like how fast time goes by. I don't really get it, but that's what Dad said; he said it better than me. Weird, huh?"

"Uh-huh. Okay, and dirty jokes?"

"Oh, that's the funny one. He said you don't see animals telling naughty jokes, do you? Or birds or bugs. They don't laugh over stuff like poop. They don't get embarrassed either. He read about that in some book from some famous guy." Eddie sat on one of the lawn chairs she'd brought out for their stargazing. "Dad said it's sort of like being a bird stuck in a turtle shell." He chuckled at this.

"A bird stuck in a turtle shell." Lauren wondered if she was really so dense as to not understand that spiritual symbolism.

"Yeah, 'cause we are immortals, you know like my *Super EX* cartoon has immortals that live forever. We're immortals, but we're stuck in a mortal body. A bird in a turtle shell."

"That's pretty interesting, I guess," she said, a bit mystified yet strangely intrigued by the idea too. Eddie started laughing then, a deep giggle that sent him bent over at the waist.

"What?"

"Can't you just imagine two little birds and one goes potty, then the other starts laughing and falls off the tree branch? It's like a cartoon."

"You are one crazy child." But she thought about that. Could such basic life experiences and human behavior reflect a more philosophical battle between spirit and body?

They returned to stargazing, until Eddie said, "I wonder how they made this telescope. How does it make things closer?"

"Maybe you better ask your dad."

"Could we look it up on the Internet?"

"Sure," she'd said, though they ended up having ice cream and watching a movie he'd brought over, something with giant ants that he couldn't believe she'd never seen before. Lauren still hadn't looked that up on the Internet, and Eddie, always full of questions, had forgotten to ask again. Maybe she'd do that and surprise him when she returned. She also needed to read that famous guy whose philosophy of death and dirty jokes Eddie had tried explaining.

The Italian night sky held the same constellations as the California sky. Lauren ate the last of her pizza as she sought the patterns and images, thinking that people had stared upward for thousands of years like this. She pictured Galileo, Plato, or the apostle Paul looking at these same stars from this very country. She felt infinitely small in the scheme of eternity, yet in the same moment infinitely connected and known by the God who made all of this.

She thought of that comment about death. Losing a loved one was something a person never got over. Lauren would never get over Carrie. Who else knew her so well? Every major life event included Carrie.

Lauren was completely divided by time: tomorrow she'd be digging up a piece of the past. Might it not help her best friend on her future journey? Might it not help them all in some small way?

Her pizza finished, Lauren now stood to walk the rocky shore-line where her best friend fell in love for the first time. And on that same beach Lauren had found Carrie on a rainy night with a bleed-ing hand and a broken heart.

11

Graham kept reminding himself—*this is Carrie's husband and son.*

That fact didn't mix so well with their visit to the ice-cream parlor. Before ordering, Jason made a call from his cell phone in his car. By the worry creased into his expression, Graham wondered if he'd called to check on Carrie. When Jason saw his son, he pasted a smile back onto his face and said, "So, what flavor do you want, Eddie?"

A mixture of guilt, wariness, and suspiciousness pulsed through him. Graham's green pistachio was closely inspected by Eddie until he offered Eddie a few licks.

"Dad, it's kind of weird, but good. You should try it too."

Graham and Jason both laughed at that.

The puppy slept in Jason's white luxury car parked in front of the ice-cream shop.

Jason asked questions, but nothing intrusive. Nothing direct or deeply searching as if he was hunting for information. Graham wondered what the guy knew exactly. Did Jason know he'd broken promises, that he'd abandoned Carrie their last night together? Or did he only know he and Carrie had spent a summer in Italy? Any of it would make most men uncomfortable, yet here they were chatting over ice cream like old friends.

"Where did you learn to sail?" Jason asked. Though he had

checked his watch a few times, Jason seemed genuinely interested now, as if asking about some strange habitat or a new scientific discovery. Leaning forward, Jason absently took bites of ice cream while processing what Graham told him. Graham guessed his favorite reading was *National Geographic* or something similar.

"I learned in Europe. I started on a charter boat as a crew member. Learned everything there, then bought a small boat for myself and took short sails on my days off. Pretty soon short trips became long trips, and I entered the sailing subculture."

"Interesting how there's a subculture for just about every sport, activity, and hobby."

"And religion," Graham said without thinking, then remembered Jason's mention of God.

"True, very true, though I don't suppose that was God's plan. I doubt the Creator of all things would want His creation thinking of Him as a hobby or extracurricular activity."

"Hmm, maybe not," Graham said, shifting in his chair.

Jason must have noticed his discomfort as he scratched his head. "Sorry, I'm a little distracted today and have a tendency to launch into faith. I sort of need a lot of faith, especially lately. I'm in this men's group at church, and we get into all kinds of debates and conversations."

"Sounds interesting."

"Oh, it is. We figure what's the use of being a Christian if you don't really look at faith from all angles and examine all philosophies."

Usually Graham felt wary around overtly religious people. Plus, this was Carrie's husband. But there was a genuine care in this man that stunned him. Graham wasn't sure he'd ever encountered someone like this. Maybe Jason's religion was the reason he could have ice cream with his wife's old boyfriend or whatever he'd been to Carrie.

Graham wasn't in the business of sharing his heart. But Jason seemed like someone who'd accept a person as he was, despite beliefs or background—maybe that's why Carrie had married him.

Their ice creams dwindled and Eddie piped in, "You could have dinner at our house tonight. We usually eat out when Mom is in the hospital, unless Grandma comes and cooks."

"I need to get back to my boat," Graham said quickly. Already his emotions were so tangled he couldn't understand them. What did he feel for Carrie anyway? Anything? Everything? He had no idea. What remained of *them* since that summer? And what should he feel with her son and husband sitting across from him? Was it right to feel anything? Yet after that summer, and now knowing she was truly dying—even Eddie knew—part of him did want to see Carrie, did want to say good-bye or make amends. There was even a curiosity to see where she lived, what she'd filled the rooms of her house with, what made her Carrie now. He'd wondered that before, even asked her that summer what her room was like back home.

What's on your walls? What kinds of books are on the bookshelves? Tell me everything about your room, so I'll know more about you. I want to know everything about Carrie Marie Myles.

Graham's eyes met Jason's curious stare. "So . . . will you tell Carrie you saw me?"

Jason hesitated then. "Yeah. You aren't leaving without seeing her, are you?"

"Well, I wasn't planning to see her. Didn't plan to be here; didn't plan to meet Eddie, or you, or Pepper."

Jason hesitated a moment, then said, "You need to see her."

His surety only heightened Graham's uneasiness. What would it be like to see Carrie again, and with the encouragement of her husband? Jason must not know Graham had betrayed Carrie, left her crying and hurt on a rainy night in Italy. Surely he wouldn't be so kind if he knew the truth. Graham glanced over at Eddie, who seemed lost in his own little world, drawing his fingers through the drips of ice cream on the table.

"Carrie . . ." Jason glanced at Eddie, then back to him. "Well, the doctor's aren't real hopeful." Jason's direct eye contact confirmed what both Lauren and Eddie had told him. "And she's struggling with the things from her youth. Nightmares and such. We haven't talked much about it, but I know it's there. She doesn't want things left unresolved, and I've been praying she'll have peace about this. And now, here you are."

Chills prickled down Graham's back as Jason spoke with such confidence. Perhaps this was a God-planned encounter. But if so, what did that mean for the rest of his messed-up life?

"I continue to pray for a miracle of course, that God won't take Carrie from us yet. But, whatever God's will, I know having some resolution about her past would make both life or leaving more peaceful."

About this time, Graham noticed Eddie turn around in his chair to pick up dead leaves from an outdoor plant and drop them down like parachuting men. But from the tilt of his head Graham knew he was absorbing every word. It reminded Graham of his own way of eavesdropping when adults didn't realize it. Here Eddie was, in the midst of an ongoing tragedy, unlike his own swift calamity— was either any less painful or devastating?

"Okay, if you think it will help," Graham said quickly, ready for the subject to change. He added, "I wonder how Salt is doing?" Just as he expected, Eddie turned right around.

"Are you sure you don't need a ride?" Jason asked.

"Oh, I nearly forgot. No. I think that's my ride across the street."

"Carrie should be released in a few days. Why don't you stop by the hospital tomorrow? I could pick you up."

"It's okay—I can get there. What time?"

And so it was set. Graham would be seeing Carrie, tomorrow.

Cap Charlie had fallen asleep in the car and awoke with a start when Graham hopped in. "There you be. Ready for some supplies? Where's that angel cat?"

"Keeping me here for another night," he said with a shake of his head. What did that say for God, and planning, and unexpected encounters?

He'd believed in God as a small boy. Sometimes he'd acknowledge guilt; "backslidden" would be the label of his grandparents' church. It was the rest of life that complicated matters. He wanted to walk the straight and narrow, but what did that exactly mean? Was it a bunch of rules to follow? Don't drink, cuss, swear, or chew. The Ten Commandments. Never judge someone else. Was Jesus really the Way? Not even many of the Christian churches he'd attended seemed to believe Jesus was enough. They added His "follow Me" with statements and creeds of faith, guidelines, profiles to exemplify, instructions to not stumble, and ministries to do all toward becoming one of God's elite.

Faith was the most simple and the most complex of puzzles. All Graham knew was that a week earlier, he'd successfully outrun the past. Now, he found himself with nowhere to run.

12

Was Graham in Harper's Bay? Carrie asked herself from within a strange fog.

Or had it been a dream? Jason coming to visit and telling of their meeting, somewhere in town, some ordinary place that surely indicated fiction, not reality.

She reached out her hand, wishing to feel Jason's firm hold. And surprisingly, there it was.

"You're here," she whispered, unable to fully find her voice. She wanted to cry for the relief of Jason's presence. For all the years of thoughts of Graham, this was the man who'd stood faithful. How she didn't deserve him. He so easily loved her.

"Yes, I'm here. I'm always here."

"I think I've been sleeping," she said, opening her eyes slowly. She saw the IV bag drip in a steady rhythm. Her eyes were so heavy.

In the fog when Jason said Graham was in Harper's Bay, he had lain beside her in the hospital bed as he did most nights and they'd talked, or rather Jason talked. He'd brought pink lilies, so if they were there, then it wasn't a dream. She turned toward Jason, who was rubbing his face, and past him to the vase of pink lilies visible by the light of her roommate's TV.

"Graham is here," she said rather than asked.

"Yes, so you do remember," Jason said, leaning forward to gauge her reaction as her eyes lost their strength to remain open. "I was worried how you'd react."

She wasn't sure how to react, but thought of the letters so recently found again; she'd nearly tossed them out on several occasions. Jason knew of the letters bound in twine and stuffed in the steamer trunk. Once he'd told her to keep them, saying that some eras of our lives were meant to be remembered as a marker of God's journey.

That summer. All that had happened would be thought of in simplistic terms. Young love gone astray. First love. A tragic love story. And even those were more than most would give it. It happened one summer. Nothing. Forgettable. Momentary. Over. Unrealistic. Fantasy. Love lost.

For her, Graham Michaels had been everything for a time. And yet, it later became more than just him. More than a love for a season. That summer and the letters she'd written weren't so much a testament of love gone wrong, but as Jason said without really knowing, it was more the journey to discovering Christ's love. For it was the loss of Graham that brought discovery of a love unending— the only one that never disappointed. But how did all this work together now that Graham was here? And Lauren right now in Europe, digging up the box, a box of dual secrets.

"Carrie, are you okay?" Jason leaned closer.

She nodded but didn't have the energy to face it all, didn't have the strength to untangle the strands and find a solution. A day at a time. Or a moment at a time. Until she left this world, she'd face the next moment and see what it held. Troubling though, so many potential problems were rising up just when she wanted to make peace, ask forgiveness, and find some way to say good-bye to those she loved.

"I think I'll sleep a little more," she said. "Is Eddie okay?"

"Yes, he's just fine; no worries."

"How many days till his birthday?" she asked, feeling a cold panic rise. "I have to be home for it, Jason. No matter what."

"I know; don't get yourself upset. Why don't you sleep, and I'll get something to eat and check on Eddie." Jason bent down and kissed her on the forehead. "Carrie. Don't worry. I'm here. You'll be home for the party, and we can decide if you want to see Graham or not. But . . . well, it might be a good thing to see him, before, well . . . Let's talk later, my love."

She held his hand for a moment longer before letting him go, giving a slight smile, a reassuring smile. And then she fell down, down into the fog. Inside that place, she tried comprehending that Graham was here. Jason and Eddie had spoken to him. Jason, remarkable as ever, was able to put aside his own feelings about Graham and try to do the best for everyone else.

Only slivers of Jason's earlier conversation could be conjured— was Graham simply passing through? She didn't want him to see her like this. She'd missed him for years, imagining if it had ended differently. Then there was the praying, sometimes with utter selfishness that God would bring him back to her, other times in peaceful surrender that His will had been done. The warring forces of want and logic and eternal thinking.

These had not fully disappeared with her marriage, bringing a deep guilt for some time.

If she could only keep her love for Graham a pure thing. It seemed there were people a person should love her whole life. Even if the love wasn't returned.

"Awake in here now?" the night nurse asked, coming by to check her vitals and IV. Had more time passed her by?

"You tell me if I'm awake," she mumbled, which made the nurse chuckle.

"I'll have to check your vitals and then give my opinion. Let's hope this new prescription does a better job than the last one."

"That's the hope," she said, wishing to be alone with her thoughts again. She watched her roommate's television with muted sound as the nurse took her blood pressure. With the dividing curtain, only half the screen could be seen—enough to view some alien talking with a human on the futuristic show.

After the nurse moved on to her sleeping roommate, Carrie sat up in bed for some water. Her mouth was dry and her lips chapped despite how Jason would apply lip balm whenever he visited. The clock came into focus, and she added the nine hours. It was morning in Italy. Lauren would be in the Cinque Terre. She might be still in bed, gazing at the dawn as it woke the town on the Ligurian Sea, listening to the shop owners and schoolchildren as they started their day, the cars driving the winding coastal roadway, the train on the track coming through. Children laughing and chattering in Italian as they headed off to school. Would it be a sunny day today? It had been all sunshine when she and Graham had been there, except for those last few days.

A protective worry rose up as Carrie imagined the scene of Lauren alone in Europe. At times the Italians could be intimidating, the men aggressive, and fewer people knew English there than in other parts of Europe. Lauren might have transportation trouble at the train stations or airports. A dozen bad scenarios clouded her thoughts. Lauren shouldn't be there alone. *What was she thinking?*

And yet, Carrie hoped her best friend would allow the beauty and challenges to do whatever work they needed on her. For years, she'd taken as her mission to break Lauren out of her careful mold. Many times, Carrie had gone too far, infringing on who her friend was, trying to force her out of a shell that was hers to stay inside. Now who was out of her shell? Lauren was in Italy, and she was in a hospital bed, biding her time toward death—life over, the inevitable end before her.

Carrie pushed the button to sit even farther up. Her head wasn't fuzzy anymore. And there were the lilies, filling the room with their sweet scent that couldn't quite overcome the hospital smells. Her roommate snored on the other side of the thin curtain as the nurse moved on to finish her rounds.

Carrie longed for home, staring at the IV drip that would re-hydrate her. *Hurry, hurry*, she wanted to tell it. Her son's birthday was only days away.

Carrie tried to resurrect every detail of the village that had been like a fairy-tale world to her. They'd made reservations in that *pensioni* where she'd stayed with the Benders. The quaint rooms and breakfast area, she remembered waking in the large bed and realizing that meeting Graham hadn't been a dream. She'd see him again that day. Everything about the village included memories of their time together, but the village itself was something from a story-book. The ancient streets so narrow and curving. Old men sitting at tables, talking with boisterous expressions. Red geraniums overflowing window boxes, in colors brighter than the flowers here. Would the enchantment be gone now? Without Graham and the perfection of those days, how could it not be a disappointment? But Lauren would be visiting without such memories. She'd be climbing that stone stairway without knowing their magic. What a perfect place Graham had chosen for the box. He'd gone back, fulfilled one promise. Some-how it endeared him to her even more. More than it should. More than she wanted it to. He always seemed a bit broken; she'd known that from the beginning. Hadn't she believed she could fix that, that love would heal all wounds?

Graham had given her bits of information about his life in Ireland. She knew he'd been in a pub when a bomb exploded, killing his parents. She knew there was more than he'd told her. Scars beyond her understanding, especially as a girl of eighteen. Carrie had been ignorant of what pain could do. She'd lived a happy life until that point. Life was vibrant, love unending and unconditional. Why wouldn't everything work out? Why couldn't every dream come true? Life was about possibility and changing the world. How could a long-ago past destroy the future?

But in years of sifting through memories, Carrie caught the little things Graham said that she'd ignored. He didn't know if he could love. He didn't want to need or be needed—this was his fear. And she marched on without understanding him.

Carrie knew she shouldn't fight the sleep that again came to take over. Sleep was either consumed by dreams or it stole the little time she had left.

A sudden fear came over her. Was she leaving Eddie a destiny similar to Graham's? Would the loss of his mother as a child be the barricade against living a complete life? What would Eddie remember? A mother in bed, constantly ill, hospital rooms, needles and IV bags, bottles of medicines? The smells of childhood would be antiseptic and medicinal except for her favorite perfume, Givenchy Tempore, about which Eddie always commented when she wore it. He'd breathe in deeply as if taking her into memory. "That's my mom," he'd say. At least there were those small graces amid the bad.

Could it really be possible that Graham was here?

Now that she was awake, it seemed more impossible. Yet it had to be true.

How could her life be ending, just when the answers she'd wished for were finally being found?

THE MORNING LIGHT warmed Lauren's face, and the sound of the sea filtered into her consciousness. The light and scents were all different from the seaside village she'd spent her life in. There were towering pines, fog, and rocky shores. Here was the scent of rich soil and vineyards, balmy winds, and ancient streets. Lauren wondered if Carrie remembered which room she'd stayed at in this hotel. When Carrie awoke, could she imagine life holding both the joys and the pain back when her future was wide open?

Slowly Lauren unfolded from beneath the cozy down comforter. Today was the day.

Lauren would find what was left of Carrie's past. The idea of it seemed fictional, something from a movie, an idealistic plan—even a newspaper account was much more appealing than what this reality would surely bring. There were complications to consider. For example, how would she dig up the box? How big was it? Where was it exactly, as in, its *precise* location?

Courage was required. Lauren was tired of strapping on some faux courage to make it through each day. All she wanted now was to sleep awhile, hide out in the room, or scurry on home.

Again, hunger got her from bed and to the shower. Her dark hair was easier to style; her natural curl wasn't frizzy in this weather.

Downstairs, she was greeted by a kind-looking older woman who offered breakfast.

"*Si, grazie,*" Lauren said. "Did a package come for me—Lauren Rendell?"

"A package?" The woman didn't seem to understand.

197

"A letter? Package. Mail." Lauren realized she was using her hands to gesture and folded them in front of herself.

"Ah, mail. No mail."

Lauren found a small table by the window and wondered if she should wait to recover the box until she had Carrie's delivery for Eddie. Minutes later, the woman returned with tea and a plate with prosciutto, cheese and tomato slices, boiled eggs, cantaloupe, cucumbers, and hard rolls. The food, the hot tea, the quiet of the room, and the sound of waves on the beach outside had a tranquil effect on her. It surprised her that the anxiety could drift away if she let it, that she could be in a foreign country and feel the peace of the moment.

After breakfast, Lauren wandered up and down steep path-ways, along tiny streets with pastel-colored houses clinging between the rugged coastline and the sea. Bright geraniums overflowed from window boxes. What would life be like here?

As Lauren turned a corner, she recognized the village *piazza* with the fountain gushing water in the center. Sitting on the edge, she imagined the millions of invisible footprints along these stones. Her own were here from over a decade earlier, and Carrie's and Graham's. And thousands of others had walked here, in good times and bad. She thought how Carrie always sought to understand time and the meaning of life. Didn't all the philosophers find agony in such pursuit? Artists dedicated years of unfulfilled work toward cap-turing a moment of time. It reminded Lauren of a debate with Carrie over Salvador Dalí's work.

"He fascinates me," Carrie said, admiring the book she'd bought of his work.

"I think he's weird," Lauren had said. They were at Carrie's house, planning their trip to Europe. Carrie was trying to fit in a side trip to Belgium to view one of her favorite Dalí pictures—

Impressions of Africa. The trip was already being shaped and reshaped; something had to go. And for Lauren, one Dalí picture was worth the cut. They could already see other works of his all over Europe.

"Weird is interesting," Carrie had said, gazing at the surrealist images.

"He would self-induce psychotic hallucinations to create those bizarre pictures."

"He led a rather unconventional life, even for an artist, I'll give you that."

"I read he really wasn't that good. One of commercial success and hype, but not really a master."

"So you've taken up reading about artists, have you?"

"Anything to discount this," Lauren had said, seeing a picture in the book of an elephant with tiny, elongated legs. "To say it nicely—yuck."

"Yuck to you, not to me. An artist dissects the world around him. He studies it from different angles and layers and in different shades and viewpoints. What he puts on canvas, or paper, or shapes from bronze, is all an interpretation of what he sees or feels. Perhaps this was meant to evoke disgust in you."

"Then he was successful. But art shouldn't disgust a person. It should make you feel good."

"That's quite some Western thinking there."

"Oh, is it now?"

"Most of us within the American pop culture, and I am including myself here, we desire anything that makes us feel good. That's why we have so many problems like addiction, obesity, greed. We think everything should make us feel good, and that feeling good won't harm anybody else, not even ourselves."

"So let me get this right. By looking at disgusting art like Dalí's, our society would be changed, a countercultural revolution, and all things bad would be decimated?"

"Oh, you have a wicked tongue sometimes. Of course, there is no simple cure. But art has value even when it disturbs us, perhaps even more so because it disturbs us. It makes us think beyond ourselves. Can create compassion, if we let it. Can cause confusion that will lead us to seek more solid answers. Remember Jesus' parables, they disturbed people more than inspired. The people went home and had to figure them out."

"Please do not tell me you're comparing Dalí with Jesus."

"Of course not, not really. I just think he saw time too clearly."

"Who?"

"Dalí."

"Back to him, eh?"

"Dalí was haunted by the subject of time, and of memory."

"As in *Persistence of Memory.*"

"Yes. He understood that a human life was fleeting, and he wrestled with that fact—at least that's what I think. And surely something in the past haunted him, or many somethings. I can appreciate *Persistence of Memory.*"

Ah, Lauren thought. Nothing else needed to be said for them to both know what they spoke of. That summer. The defining age for them both.

"Back to his issues with time. Is that so original? Every writer, poet, and artist seems to create his or her struggle with time. It's simpletons such as myself, thank you very much, who aren't consumed by it; we just live instead of stressing over the ticking clock. You should try it sometimes. Mindless existence isn't as bad as it sounds."

"I'm sure you have the perfect quote for this."

"Let me consult my extensive mental files . . . *like sands through the hourglass, so are the days of our lives.*"

They'd both laughed at the soap opera reference and returned to planning their trip. Belgium and the Dalí painting were cut from their itinerary.

"I'll see it some other trip," Carrie had said with confidence. How could they expect that even the current trip they'd planned would turn out this way? Or months later, Lauren would walk the same rocky shoreline of that summer. But this time, alone.

HIS BEDROOM DOOR shut tightly and his desk chair against it, Eddie counted the days on his calendar. Usually, his mom would be marking off the squares with him until his birthdate square. Instead, she was in the hospital. Even when she was sick before, she'd been home for his birthday.

Tonight Dad wanted him to visit Mom. Eddie didn't want to. He didn't want to sit in the waiting room, or walk around her bed and watch her try to stay awake or fight off the hurt. They'd taken her away in the ambulance; now she was hooked up to tubes again, and she wasn't saying anything to make it funny.

Grandma made her *famous* lasagna, which always made Eddie wonder how lasagna could be famous. He'd laugh to himself, thinking of a hunk of lasagna in a tuxedo or on the front of a newspaper. When he told Grandma, she gave a fake smile. She only laughed when she watched *I Love Lucy*. He'd rarely seen her even chuckle any other time.

Dad stayed a long time at the hospital. Eddie was tired, and Grandma wouldn't let him play his Game Cube, saying kids nowadays played too many electronic games. Instead, she wanted him to read, but his head hurt. Grandma watched her show in faded color that didn't have any cool giant monsters or anything.

As Eddie peeled at the edges of his fingernails, he saw a photo of him and his mom on his small desk and stared at it a long time. Did she wonder where he was? Was she sad he hadn't come? She seemed far away, though Eddie knew the exact path to get to her.

Earlier Grandma had told him to take a bath and scrub extra good since it was church tomorrow. Before he could follow her instructions, she had stopped him.

"Look at your fingernails. Let me see them."

Eddie had stared down, seeing them as if for the first time. How often did he look at his hands? Dirt was evenly distributed in a perfect line on each finger tip.

"Do you have any fingernail clippers?"

Eddie stiffened and sat on his hands, hoping their absence would make Grandma forget and let him go take his bath.

"Let me see those fingers," she said, prying one open. "This is exactly why I'm needed at a time like this. The details. Everyone forgets the details."

The clippers seemed to appear from nowhere, then the sudden snap.

"See, that didn't hurt."

Eddie stared at the half-moon nail she dropped in his palm. It was a severed part of him, resting in his hand. Like an ear, or a toe, or an eyeball.

"Put it back," he said. Then a panic filled him. "Grandma, put it back."

Something his own body had grown was broken off before him. He picked up the fingernail as his stomach did a flip and then a flop. He ran to his room with his grandma calling behind. Mom and Dad wouldn't like that, would say he was being disrespectful, but it wasn't nice of Grandma to do that to him. Fingers curled and clenched against his palms, Eddie tried not to feel the tingling pain along the edge of the missing nail. He jumped on his bed and slid his head under the pillow, hoping Grandma would leave him alone.

I hate her. The thought popped into his head. Eddie felt worse for having such a terrible thought.

His head beneath the pillow, Eddie thought of the man with the white cat named Salt . . . Graham was his name, or Mr. Michaels as Dad said to call him, until the guy said, please, not Mr. Michaels. Eddie liked the sailor guy. He was nice. And he had a cat, which seemed much easier than a dog. Graham lived on a boat and just pulled off the ropes and sailed away to wherever he wanted to go. Eddie wished he could do that. He'd go far away, though he didn't know where. Mom always talked about Europe; she'd been there a long time ago.

Grandma came in later while he pretended to be asleep. After she tucked in the blanket over him and turned off the light, he got up, pushed the desk chair in front of the door, and flipped the light back on. The calendar said Mom had three full days to get better before his birthday. She wasn't going to make it; he just knew it. It wasn't her fault, but it wasn't fair either.

If only he could go away.

Eddie thought of one of his favorite stories. He had it on CD and sometimes listened to it before bed. In the story, a mouse named Reepicheep takes his little boat, a coracle, to the end of the world. That's what Eddie wanted to do. Auntie Lauren was in Europe right now. That Graham guy went anywhere he wanted. His mom was going the farthest away and wouldn't be coming back. Maybe Eddie would make his own coracle and go out into the ocean until he reached the end of the world. Then he'd get to that other place like Reepicheep did, and over there, he'd meet his mother when she arrived.

Eddie knew he couldn't really do that. But still, he thought he'd listen to the story of Reepicheep anyway. It was better to imagine.

WITH A LIGHT backpack on her shoulder and Graham's instructions in hand, Lauren walked along the beach. Her heart started pounding at the prospect of what awaited. It might not even be there, but she needed to know. The rocky sand crunched beneath her feet. Lauren felt like a burglar about to do something wrong. An elderly couple walking along the beach gave her a long look; surely they'd sensed her nervousness and become suspicious.

The stretch of beach was longer than she remembered. The sheer cliffs jutting toward the sea broke up the long rocky coastline. Even with the tide still high, she could get from one beach area to the next.

Not wanting to appear too much the treasure hunter holding a map, Lauren sat on a craggy boulder to get her bearings, all the while her heart racing in anticipation.

Back in California, Graham's instructions had appeared so simple to follow—then she'd wanted to get on the road and away from Graham. But now, gazing up at cliffs and this long stretch of beach beside it, she tried discerning the directions. With her back to the village, it seemed she should continue south down the beach. There'd be a first rocky outcropping—this was where Graham had met Carrie, he told Lauren; then she knew he regretted the telling. Two more outcroppings, and then she must walk away from the water and along the cliff until she found a stone stairway.

The sun shone warmly as Lauren continued down the beach. The waves made gentle slides toward her feet. The shoreline was littered with gifts from beneath the surface: seaweed, broken shells, softened pieces of driftwood. She found a path and walked inland toward the sea cliffs.

And there, rising from the beach, was a stone stairway winding up along the cliffs. Her fear dissipated for a moment. This was it. For fourteen years the box had waited, endured the seasons, the promise of a year broken again and again. Abandoned. Deserted. Forgotten. Lauren found it ironic that she would be its liberator.

Putting her foot on the first step, Lauren looked back a moment. Nobody around.

Graham had told her, "Follow the stairway leading up the cliffs. Partway up, there's a stone bench. It has a great view of the sea and the village below. It's a bit of a climb."

Lauren started up. No one came from above or below on the beach. The climb was steep, but the steps were wide, and the rock wall could be held for balance. How she wished Carrie or somebody was with her. Yet, it did exhilarate her, this adventure all alone. The cliff towered above. She was getting out of breath and realized she needed to get back on an exercise program when she returned home.

Pausing a moment, Lauren looked out at the view. The beach held hues of yellow and orange that contrasted sharply with the stark blue Mediterranean waters. The village roofs were coming into view above some lower outcroppings. She continued up, wondering if this was the right stairway.

Then around a corner, she saw it.

A bench made of a long rectangular stone sitting atop chiseled stone legs. This had to be it.

Upon reaching the bench, Lauren sat down a moment. She quickly bent down, kneeling on the stairs, and began to gently wipe away the layer of top soil. Then she encountered rock. A wind swirled up and lifted her hair from her shoulders. Lauren stopped a moment and considered what she must look like. The image actually pleased her. It wasn't the typical safe Lauren. She had chosen to do this. This was for Carrie, but now, it was for her too. The adventure had become her own.

Lauren reached for the backpack to pull out a large spoon borrowed from breakfast. Using the knife, she tried digging into the ground. It was hard, but pieces could break away. At the very center beneath the bench, she dug the deepest and a large chunk of slate stone broke away. She started pulling more rock and more earth from what became a fairly deep hole. Then she struck something hard, something that didn't sound the same as the knife against the rocks.

This had to be it.

13

"May I help you?" the hospital receptionist asked.

Graham nodded, more to himself than to her. "I was looking for a patient."

"The name?"

It was the first time he'd said her full name in years. "Carrie Myles."

The woman began tapping at the keyboard.

"I mean, Carrie Timmons."

"Thank you. Yes, she's in room 312. Take that elevator there."

And just like that, Graham was entering an elevator and on his way to see her. He hoped to find Jason first before facing room 312, estimating he should be finished with church by now.

Graham had picked up Salt from the vet first. Dr. Rook said Salt should be fine, but it would help if she wasn't jostled around too much. The boat's motion might be too jarring or make the cat sick. Maybe he could stay a few days longer, the doctor suggested. Graham wasn't sure if that cat was an angel or a devil in disguise. But she did look pathetic with shaved hair, not fur, and a tube draining from her chest.

Cap Charlie had loaned him his car to run the errands after giving directions to the hospital. Now he was here. All the things he rehearsed to say fled his thoughts. Was he dressed up enough in his usual faded jeans and black long-sleeved shirt? Maybe he should've brought a gift, or flowers, or a card. What kind of gift was appropriate for this bizarre reunion? Graham regretted not bringing something, even if only for Eddie.

As the elevator opened on floor 3, Graham stood alone until the doors closed again. A sharp ding interrupted the quiet inside the elevator. He could easily reconsider, return to the ground floor, hop back in the borrowed car, and be out of the bay and in open sea by noon. Something told him to stay, see it through; for once in his life, stop running.

He walked from the elevator, looking both ways. There was Eddie in the waiting room, playing with a little blue dinosaur on the coffee table.

"Hey, how's that dog of yours?" Graham asked, approaching the boy.

"Hi." Eddie hopped up from the floor and smiled widely. "My dad said you were supposed to come today. He said you knew my mom when you were younger."

"Yes, I did," Graham said, feeling strangely guilty.

"My birthday is almost here."

"It is? Are you having a party?" Graham immediately regretted asking.

"I don't know. I think my dad forgot."

"I'm sure your dad didn't forget."

"Mom never forgets stuff like that. My dad is really smart, smarter than my mom, she says. But he forgets things that she doesn't."

Graham didn't know how to respond, so he asked, "Is that your dinosaur?"

"Yep," Eddie said, and Graham decided to sit down with him. Anything to avoid the coming reunion. "My mom bought this pack of dinosaurs, and we picked him out as our favorite. We both like blue."

Eddie sighed and leaned back, his feet dangling, arms crossed, and a deep concentration covering his face. He said, "Life is just hard."

"Yeah, you're right, life is hard, but good too," Graham replied in a forced somber tone that threatened to be exposed. "How did you figure that out at such a young age?"

"'Cause my mom is going to die."

Graham leaned back against the cushion too. For a moment, he pictured his own mother. The years of missing a mother flashed across his memory in a moment.

There were few answers. But there were moments of beauty. Wasn't that hope? Wasn't it faith that more beauty would come? Wasn't faith also the desire for those glimpses of beauty to be real and for eternity? Graham closed his eyes, uneasy with everything surrounding him. So this is what it was to face the past, the unresolved, and hidden fears. No one ever said it was easy. And yet who could think it would be this hard?

"Is your dad in with your mom?" he finally said.

"She's not doing very good today. They don't want me to go into her room right now, so Grandma Stella is coming."

Graham considered this, wondering just how bad she could be. From Eddie's expression, he wondered what the boy thought or what his imagination was picturing. He knew this from his own childhood—not seeing his parents' remains had brought the worst images. He still couldn't watch those investigator dramas that showed what bodies looked like after death.

"Sometimes it's better to just hang out with your dinosaur." Graham wished for a way to make Eddie feel better.

"When Mom was sick before, she'd say sometimes she wasn't

really in the hospital room. That when people had to stay outside, it was because the hospital workers didn't want us to know she'd escaped again."

"Escaped, eh?"

"Yeah. She said she was off flying around somewhere with her special flying powers." The boy's eyes moved back and forth beneath furrowed brows. "I don't believe that anymore though."

"Hmm. Well, you never know. We are talking about your mom. Once when she was younger, I thought I might have seen her flying."

"No, you didn't."

"Really," Graham said. "I wasn't sure and have always wondered. Now, I think it might be true."

"Well, Mom has always wanted to fly," Eddie said, now a slight smile on his lips.

Graham felt competing compulsions to either rub the top of this kid's head or to simply lean back from the draining weight that came with this boy.

He sighed wearily. "So where would your mom be, if she was flying around right now?"

Eddie sat straighter, the smile a little wider. "Oh, let me think. Maybe she'd fly all around the world. Or maybe she'd fly to another planet."

Graham thought for a moment, then said, "Maybe she's flying close to the ocean waves above some dolphins."

"Yeah," Eddie said, a detective considering a case. "Or, hmm, maybe she's flying next to an airplane; maybe she sits on the wings when she needs a rest."

They both chuckled at that image.

"Maybe she got sick of hospital food and flew to that ice-cream shop and is eating a banana split right now."

Eddie nodded. "With lots of hot fudge on top."

"And caramel," Graham added.

"Whipped cream all over it."

"And three cherries on top."

"No, ten!"

A memory stirred and Graham said, "I know, she's at Dairy Queen eating a Dilly Bar."

"She loves those, and she could fly through the drive-through part."

A voice interrupted them. "Edward, what are you talking about, and who are you talking to?" Graham turned toward an older woman who stared at him as if he were a child kidnapper.

"Is Mom okay?" Eddie asked, jumping up.

"Yes, yes," she said.

Jason walked up behind her. "You made it."

"You know this man?" the woman asked, still suspicious.

"Yes, Mom. Graham, this is my mother, Stella. Mom, this is Graham."

"Dad, can I see her now?"

"She's sleeping finally; the new medicine gave her a bad reaction. They're trying yet another one. But she asked what you're doing and said you better get your room ready for some new toys with your birthday so close. I almost forgot."

Graham watched Eddie's smile replace the concerned expression. "Will she get to come home?"

"It'll be a few more days." The worry returned.

"Sorry you came all the way here," Jason said. "Are you hungry or anything?"

"I could take Eddie down to the cafeteria—all our talk about banana splits and Dilly Bars has made me hungry."

211

"Me too!"

"I'll come along too," Jason's mother said, suspicion still in her eyes.

"Carrie loves Dilly Bars," Jason said, a hint of sorrow in his expression. "I'll stick around here a bit longer, if you don't mind."

As they walked the corridor back toward the elevators, Graham was struck by this peculiar turn of events; here he was walking along with Carrie's son and her husband's mother.

"And how do you know Jason?" she asked pointedly.

"I knew Carrie a long time ago," he said casually as the doors opened.

"And now he's all of our friend," Eddie said. "Come on, Graham, jump in the elevator; it feels really weird."

After sitting down with their trays of food from the cafeteria, Graham was faced with Jason's mother.

"Who told you about Carrie's illness?"

"Lauren."

"Oh, so you know Lauren too?"

"Yes."

"Did you know Lauren is off in some foreign country?"

"Yes." Graham dipped and twirled his soggy fries in the ketchup.

"How long have you been in town?" Grandma Stella sat with arms crossed on the table, taking occasional bites from a small salad.

"Just arrived."

"When was the last time you saw Carrie?"

"Oh, years ago. Over a decade."

Grandma Stella wasn't easily charmed. Thankfully, Jason saved him just as the older woman asked, "How exactly did you meet Carrie?"

Jason set a tray on the table with a grilled cheese and fries.

"There wasn't anything for me to do up there, and I realized I'm hungry too."

Grandma Stella folded her napkin over the remains of her meal. "Well, Jason, if you don't need me after all, I did have a meeting at my church,"

"Of course, Mom," Jason said.

"Then I'll be departing now," Stella said, standing and kissing Eddie on the top of the head. "Jason, I talked with Mr. Michaels here, and he doesn't seem like a serial killer," she said with a dry smile.

"Thank you." Graham didn't know what else to say.

"Certainly. Nice meeting you."

After she left, Graham looked from Eddie to Jason and absently asked, for lack of other conversation, "Is there anything I can do?" He wondered if Jason was inwardly thinking, *Get the heck outta here, that's what you can do.*

"Really? Thanks."

"Yeah, anything. Not like I have much going on till Salt's ready to sail."

Jason appeared thoughtful a moment, then said, "Oh, well, I forgot to ask my mom, and I would normally say nothing. But, well, there is something. I wouldn't ask, but I may not leave for a while . . ."

"What is it?"

"Could you check on our dog?"

SHIFTING AROUND CARRIE were the noises and movements of the hospital room, strangely mixed with the rhythmic flow of waves upon the shore. As one would grow louder and more apparent, the other would fade. Then the other would take precedence and drown out the first.

At the moment, it was that silver sea again. Carrie became more aware of it, seeing the colors and feeling rounded stones beneath her bare feet. She walked toward the water, no longer as hesitant, feeling at home here now. The line between water and horizon appeared close, much closer than at the seashore she'd always known. Was this some small planet her mind had concocted? She knew this was a subconscious experience, except it seemed so real. More real than anything, more than what she'd normally describe as reality.

As the first waves wrapped around her feet, she felt that jolting sensation of elation, tingling up her legs, drawing her ever deeper. Each wave became tiny fingers drawing her in. She took a few more steps, looking outward to the deeper waters. Somehow Carrie knew there would be nothing as luxurious as swimming in there, going out into the open sea. The horizon was the goal and drowning not an option. The water would be buoyant, or maybe not completely, but even beneath the surface she'd be able to breathe. The current would pull her in, helping her across. All this she knew as truth, though she didn't know where that truth came from. Another step like refreshment, as all-quenching as the most pristine waters, like living waters; yes, that was it. The water itself seemed alive.

Eddie.

And as she reached to dive, she knew from the place of truth it wasn't quite time. Go back, something told her. Go back.

Eddie needed her here a little longer. And she didn't want to leave him. Carrie hoped whatever kept her with her son, it would last a very long time.

14

Lauren's hotel room was locked shut; she'd even closed the thick drapes covering the balcony doors. In the lamplight of the fading afternoon, Lauren stared at the small container.

The box of secrets was much more diminutive than she'd imagined. Maybe she pictured more the typical treasure-chest size—whatever that meant. But bigger for sure. The metal box was decorated with ornate designs and about the size of a VCR tape.

She hadn't opened it yet. The seal seemed nearly welded shut. The task was too difficult to accomplish on the exposed cliffside.

The original plan she'd formulated was to find the box, open it, replace the contents with whatever Carrie wanted to leave for Eddie, then close it all back up and head for home. But none of that plan worked.

Nothing had arrived from Carrie.

When Lauren called, no one answered at Carrie's house. While on the phone, she tried her grandfather too.

"Grandpa, this is Lauren. How are you?"

"Well, fine, just fine. How is your trip to Europe? Are you getting some relaxation in?"

"I wouldn't call this trip relaxing. You sure sound good."

"Well, I'm still looking for that thing I lost, but I'm also having a visitor today."

"A visitor?" This worried her. Already she wondered about his mental health over the something he sought that he couldn't remember. Now a visitor? "Who is it?" Lauren asked, fully expecting some answer to worry over.

"Mrs. Mabel. She's coming for some of my chili."

Lauren chuckled, both that the sweet elderly woman down the street was visiting, and that after all those years, he still believed his chili tasted good. "Well, don't run her off too quickly. Maybe you should've started her with some coffee or tea and finger sandwiches."

"We've done that the last two days. I figure if she likes my chili, she might be a keeper."

"A keeper, what does that mean?"

"It means when you're my age, you can't waste a day. And that grandson of hers comes along too, our chaperone, Mrs. Mabel says. Isn't she funny? Lauren, he's a right fine boy, he is. He works from home and keeps an eye on Mrs. Mabel. Seems to make good money drawing buildings or something. You should ask him on a date."

"Uh, whatever happened to all the propriety you and Grandma taught me?"

"Again, life is short, and we've got to be a little more lenient on propriety and a little stronger on pursuit."

"Has Carrie or Jason checked on you lately?"

"No, they haven't. The e-mail prayer group from church sent out some emergency about our Carrie-girl. Guess she was taken to the hospital."

"What happened?"

"I tried calling, but they wouldn't give me any information. And no one in the e-mail group knows either."

After she hung up from her grandfather, a sense of panic to get home filled her. But that box sat on her bed, a secret wanting to be told. Taking the butter knife, Lauren went to work prying into the edge line and hitting the top of the knife with the hard sole of her walking shoes. The wedge began to work, but her forehead was getting damp by the time it popped open.

The lid opened on hinges in the back. The inside was lined with red velvet in surprisingly good condition. But nothing else was in there.

The box was empty.

"THIS IS A cool car," Eddie said from the passenger seat.

Graham drove with Eddie beside him in Cap Charlie's '70s Chevy Malibu with dented front fender and paint faded beneath years of California sun. *The hillbilly has arrived,* Graham thought with a chuckle as they turned into an upper-end subdivision, worthy of a banker's life and status. The houses rested on large tree-dotted lots in a sloped section of town. A few had views of the ocean, and trail markers pointed down paved bike and walking paths toward the great Pacific Ocean.

"It would be fun to fix up a car like this," Graham said. He'd often pictured settling down in a harbor town, moving into a house that didn't rock and turn around all day. Maybe get an old classic car and a sea-weary boat to fix up in a workshop. The idea of seeing something restored beyond its original design appealed to him somehow.

"It would be fun to paint it like Sonic the Hedgehog," Eddie said with a chuckle.

"Sonic—I love that cartoon."

Eddie had begged Jason to let him ride along. Graham didn't want any part in this, really, but he had volunteered to help out, and it did get him away from that hospital. Hospitals only brought memories of Ireland; the sounds and scents brought a vivid sense that could incite panic in him. And now they were heading to the Timmons house in the late afternoon.

"Turn here; this is it," Eddie said, pointing to a driveway between stucco posts. The driveway wound up the hill, and the cream-colored home was impressive, he had to admit. A momentary thought: *Had Jason sent him here to remind Graham of all he could never have given Carrie? Did the man want him to see their lives and understand how happy they were, how happy Carrie would be if not for this illness that destroyed her from the inside out?* They were a family, this reminded. Was it all a veiled reminder before Graham saw Carrie again? But Jason's concerned expression for his wife had not been an act. He'd apologized several times about asking him to check the puppy, explaining, "My mother wasn't sure if she closed the front gate when she left the house. And with that injured leg, I just worry Pepper will get into trouble."

Graham cast aside his insecurities and suspicions as they pulled in front of the house. There was an alarm touch pad in the entry; Eddie knew the code. Front door with stained glass in the window, a tile entry, high ceilings, decorated perfectly. Decorated in a sort of Italian style, he knew there was probably some fancy name for it. Tuscany Chic, Italia Moderna, whatever. So this was Carrie's style. It did remind him of her, if not more refined and mature than when he'd known her.

I could've never given this. I couldn't live this either. It's all for the best, for her, for me, for this guy who loves the heck out of her.

Graham walked through the entry feeling like he was betraying Carrie. Surely she wouldn't want him here, looking at framed old maps of countries around the world—a large one was of Italy, and only he knew of all the memories she had there. He stopped for a moment before a narrow table against the wall, an array of framed photos captured the lives of the people who lived here. It was the life after him. Eddie at various stages of life. Jason and Carrie's wedding.

How strange to see her again. He had photos on his boat of this woman as a girl of only eighteen. Her hair changed in different photos; her face didn't hold as much soft innocence of youth—instead, she'd grown more beautiful. Even in the one with her in a hospital bed, pale and hair messy, Carrie's smile remained and brought his own smile in return. He continued through the house. This was her life, where she made coffee and read books and watched movies—did she still paint? This was where she surely felt safest—her home.

If years ago he had found her . . . If he'd never purposely hurt her. If they'd gone back for the box after one year as promised. If he hadn't been raised by grandparents who never really wanted him. If Uncle Fergus hadn't carried that bomb into the Irish pub.

The thoughts could drive him insane.

"That's Florence, Italy," Eddie said, coming up behind him as Graham stopped at a picture on the wall.

"Yes, it is. Your mom likes Europe."

"Especially Italy. She said it's where she discovered pretty things."

"What . . . what does that mean?" he asked, surprised that Carrie would speak highly of the country where sorrow had also come.

"She wrote something on the picture about it," Eddie said, before skipping off to the kitchen.

Graham looked closer in the low light and jumped at the words, as if she were speaking them to him. *Remember the beauty.*

He had questioned if there was anything left of the Carrie he knew. Seeing her words on the matting, Graham knew there was.

She could remember the beauty. Only Carrie could so completely do that—find a silver lining regardless of the pain.

Eddie walked from the kitchen with two oatmeal raisin cookies in his hand. "My grandma makes good ones," he said. "Want some milk?"

"Thanks. We need to check on your puppy. Remember, that's why we're here."

"Oh, yeah. Pepper's in the back, silly dog," Eddie said with a grimace.

Through the living room and out the back French doors, Graham saw the covered patio, fenced-in swimming pool, and a hot tub by another set of French doors that he assumed must be the master suite.

"Is there something else wrong with your dog?" he asked, needing to focus on why he'd come so he could quickly depart.

"Just that she's a dumb dog."

"You know, they say that there aren't really any dumb dogs. Only dumb masters." Graham winked at him.

"No, she really is dumb. She doesn't learn any tricks. She eats everything she's not supposed to eat. She steals my dad's newspaper every morning. And that's just the beginning of the list."

"Has anyone tried to train her?"

"I have. Lots of times."

"And you're still trying?"

"I gave up."

"Can I try?"

"I guess."

Graham spotted the puppy chewing on something in the corner of the lawn. Then the black lab scratched her neck with a back leg.

"Hey girl," Graham called.

Pepper popped up, surprised. She wagged her tail so hard it jiggled her whole body.

"Come here, come here, girl."

Pepper jumped up, ran off, ran back, jumped again. Graham tried to pet her, but the energy seemed too much, and she sprinted back and forth around the yard.

"Oh, you're a wild Pepper, aren't you?" Back to Eddie, he called, "You're right. She needs some work. But I think she's pretty smart."

Eddie walked up beside him, hands on his hips, doubt creasing his brow. Graham held Pepper's face between his two hands.

"Look into those eyes. Do they look dumb to you?"

"I don't know," Eddie said with a quick shrug of the shoulders, then turned away.

"Seems to me she can practically understand everything we're saying. What a sweet girl you are."

Graham scratched Pepper behind the ears, causing her to immediately roll over, legs sticking straight out.

"Oh, you like that. Eddie, don't you love a good back scratch?"

"Yeah."

"So does Pepper."

"My mom is the best back scratcher."

Graham thought of that for a moment, picturing this little guy stretched out with his back hungry for a good scratching. He remembered his own mom teasing him. She'd scratch one little spot and then stop until he'd beg her to scratch all over. Since childhood, he'd never had a proper back scratch. His fingernails didn't reach or have the proper length for premium touch. Such a realization brought an old longing back. That's what this boy did to him, brought conflicting thoughts. Conflict between his own lost childhood and the coming loss for another child. Conflict between the encounter of Carrie's present and a past he'd walked away from.

As Graham continued petting Pepper, they sat on the patio

chairs and watched a few autumn leaves make a lazy fall toward the swimming pool.

"How big is your sailboat?"

"It has a little bedroom in the front and one in the back, a kitchen in the middle, and a head, or bathroom, too."

"Where is it?"

"Down at the harbor."

"Can I see it someday?"

"Sure."

"Maybe I could stay the night there tonight."

"Uh, probably not tonight." Graham wondered what Jason would think if Eddie asked him about this.

"Do you have a pirate's hat?"

"No, but I have a pirate eye patch."

"Wow," Eddie said with admiration.

Graham knew women were often intrigued by his lifestyle, but that often was his ploy to garner the request: "Maybe you'll show it to me sometime." To which he could oblige. But Graham had avoided kids for years. Not intentionally really. His life just didn't involve them, and maybe he was too busy to be bothered. Or too selfish.

"We should probably get going."

"Do you get tired of living in it?"

"Once in a while. But usually I really like it. Not many people can just pull anchor on their house and sail off to the next town, or even the next country."

"That's what I was thinking. You could take your house around the world."

"And I have."

"Wow," Eddie said again with a faraway expression on his face. "Does your boat have a name like the *Titanic* or the *Queen Mary*?"

"The *Salt Garden*."

"That's a funny name."

"It was given to the boat before I came along. I thought of changing it, but a sailor said it's bad luck to change a boat's name, and then the white cat showed up, and it just seemed to all fit. Sometimes things work out like that. They don't make sense; then suddenly things fit into place."

"I know what you mean," Eddie said with that serious expression that made Graham want to chuckle. Graham wasn't sure where his sudden wisdom had even come from. The boy commented, "It's kind of like your boat is your cat's garden, in a way."

"Guess you could say that."

Pepper sighed with contentment, her head on the ground, large eyes looking up at them.

Eddie dug his foot against the concrete, then stepped over to scratch Pepper's head. "She is kind of cute."

"Be patient with her."

Graham suddenly wished this boy were his. He thought of the life he'd missed, of feeling his child's hand within his own. If he hadn't made one mistake that led to the next mistake and the next . . .

"I think you might be all of our saving grace, Eddie," Graham said, unsure what that fully meant, but believing that maybe through this child something of redemption could be found. Only how— that was the question.

"What's that mean?" Eddie asked.

"You know when Sonic the Hedgehog saves Amy?"

"Yeah."

"I think you might be a lot like Sonic."

"I just wish I could save my mom."

"I do too."

"But, if she goes to heaven, doesn't that mean she's safe forever and for always? That's what she says, but I don't know if I believe it. She doesn't want me to be sad."

"That's where I hope my mom is too. And my dad." He said it with a slight smile, but a surprisingly sharp pain pierced through him.

"When did your mom die?" Eddie asked.

"When I was eight."

Eddie sat on a patio; he kicked his feet back and forth, watching them. A slight wind in the tall backyard trees was the only sound in the darkness. Finally Eddie spoke. "I'm seven. I'll be eight in two days."

"I know."

"Were you sad when your mom died?"

"I still am."

"I'll be sad forever too," Eddie stated.

"You'll miss her your whole life. But that just shows how much you love her, and how much she loves you."

Eddie bit his lower lip. Graham wondered what would it have been like to contemplate the coming of his mother's death? His parents' deaths had come to him in such a wave of shock and horror. But would it be worse to see the bomb being built, trying to ward it away, watching its placement, and seeing the countdown of numbers? Carrie's illness was the ticking bomb right before their eyes.

Graham bristled from the closeness this boy brought, like someone slicing deeper and deeper inside. It always brought the instinct to leave. For him, love was drowning in a deep pool, with silence and a few ripples to mark his falling in. No one could hear, no one could help, no one cared to. It was love after all. Love was a little bit of death without the chance to grieve, without reason to grieve—or so people believed at first. It was vulnerability with carelessness delivering near-fatal blows.

In the end, love made secrets that no one cared to hear. It created a loneliness that no one could touch.

Graham believed one thing—he had not survived love. How would this child?

15

Going home.

Lauren changed her plane ticket to the earliest flight back to San Francisco. For once, she didn't care what it was costing to get home. There'd be a long journey in the next twenty-four hours, she'd gone home from Europe before with a barely coherent Carrie at her side.

A train had brought her to Milano Malpensa, then a flight straight to D.C., then another to San Francisco, then a small plane to Harper's Bay. The airport bustled with anonymous people from anonymous places heading to anonymous destinations. She was one of them. Everything was unraveling all at once. There might be little left when she returned.

She took a moment to figure out the airport pay phone to call home. Carrie's cell phone went straight to voice mail. On a whim, she decided to try Carrie's house—Grandma Stella might be there with Eddie and have some information.

Somebody had to know something.

"Wanna see my room?" Eddie said, holding a gallon of milk in his hand after they'd returned back inside the house. Pepper looked in great condition; his food dish was refilled and fresh water supplied. Graham was ready to go.

"Are you supposed to drink from the milk carton?"

Eddie smiled sheepishly.

"Don't try pulling anything over on sly Graham, now," he said with a smile. "We better get you back to the hospital."

"I don't want to go back. Come see my rock collection. I have one rock that has real silver in it."

Graham glanced at the large round clock, then realized he had no excuse, nowhere he had to be except for checking on Salt. Eddie hurried down the hallway, glancing over his shoulder to see if Graham was following. At Eddie's bedroom door, Graham gazed into the little world of boyhood that had been cut short for himself. This would've been waiting upon his return from Ireland. His parents said he'd have his own room to decorate. He'd have his dog. He'd go to school and maybe even get to ride his bike there and back. Graham took it all in, what Carrie had provided her son. Posters on the walls of planets, the blue Sonic superhero, and a rock chart. Eddie had a motion lamp and Lite Brite game that Eddie turned on for him; boy's clothing littered the floor. From a bookshelf with books, toys, and pictures, he picked up a small baseball mitt.

"I take that to watch Barry Bonds and try to catch one of his homers."

"Giants fan, are you?"

"Yep."

"I like the Angels."

"No way! The Giants are the best. Barry Bonds hits the ball into the San Francisco Bay; I've seen him. My dad takes me to a game every year."

"What about your mom?" he asked, wondering why he asked.

"She goes sometimes. If she's not sick."

"She's been sick a long time then?"

"Yep," Eddie said, so easily that Graham recognized something of the masking in his tone. Hadn't he used that same technique over the years?

"Your parents are dead?" a guy asked him during a party at his apartment. They were passing around a pipe, and the attention turned his way.

"Yep," he'd said as easily as Eddie.

"An orphan. That's wild, Graham is an orphan." The announcement to the others. Was it supposed to be funny?

"Hey, do you wish you had parents right now?" Graham had lifted the glass pipe, bringing home the point. He was the one they came to. Didn't he have the money, blood and guilt money that it may be, from insurance and an occasional "gift" from family in Ireland? He had his own apartment when everyone else was still asking permission to go out. Wasn't he the lucky one?

Eddie broke into his thoughts. "My mom wants to go to the moon."

"She does?" Graham thought that sounded exactly like the Carrie he'd known.

"She has a whole list of things she wants to do, but she won't get to do them all. The list is in this giant suitcase that was her grandfather's. Mom keeps a bunch of neat things in there. It's like a big treasure box."

That reminded Graham of the other box probably now discovered by Lauren in Italy.

"Wanna see it?" Eddie asked, hopping from the bed.

"See what?" he asked. Eddie zipped beneath his arm and down the hallway. "Hey, we need to get going."

Graham turned off Eddie's lamp and Lite Brite, then went down the hall in search of the boy. In the farthest room, Graham found him. Eddie somehow had pried open a large steamer trunk and was looking through it.

"Wait, hold on. I have a feeling you're not supposed to be in here."

"Mom shows me stuff in here all the time."

"Well, you need to have your mom here; and I need to go check on Salt now."

As he stepped over an old baby blanket, something caught his eye. There discarded on the floor was a pile of letters wrapped in brown twine. There had to be at least twenty letters, maybe more. But what caught his notice was the name across the front of the top letter. *To Graham Michaels.* They were letters for him.

He stood up quickly, knowing what a terrible invasion this was.

"We need to go, Eddie. Right now."

The phone started ringing as if he'd been exposed and someone was calling to confront him.

"Let's put this stuff back."

"I'll get it," and Eddie was out the door with Graham left alone in the room, the letters at his feet. He felt a terrible desire to slip them into his jacket, or at least pull one from the stack. They were for him. And would one missing even be noticed? What had she written? What had she said to him? Quickly, he pushed everything back inside the trunk and shut the lid. He needed to leave this house, and now.

Graham nearly collided with Eddie on his way back into the hallway.

"It's my auntie Lauren. She wants to talk to you."

"What are you doing there?" Lauren practically yelled. A few travelers turned her way. Even after Eddie had said they had a friend at the house named Graham, she hadn't believed it. Thought surely he'd said *Grandma,* though he repeated himself several times.

"It's a long story," Graham replied, sounding distracted.

"I can't believe you'd show up in Harper's Bay. What is going on?" She was standing and wished for a cell phone to pace back and forth.

"I'm checking on Pepper. Carrie is in the hospital. I don't know what's wrong really, something about her prescription not working or something. Eddie was tired of being at the hospital, so Jason—"

Lauren's mind tried to comprehend this. "You know Jason. You know Eddie. You're in Carrie's house. You know Pepper? How did this happen?"

"Hey, you came to my boat and got this snowball rolling, and here we are—avalanche." Graham sounded annoyed at her accusatory tone. But so what that she'd found him, how did it get this far? Jason must be frantic, and Carrie, what must Carrie think of it all?

Graham then said, "I haven't even talked to Carrie."

"Well, don't until I get there. Does she know you're there?"

"I think so; well, I don't know for sure."

"Okay, all right." Lauren was on a sinking ship and needed to think clearly on what to do next. "I'm at the airport in Milan. Just don't move in or anything."

"Yeah, that's funny. Hey, don't you have something to tell me?"

"Like what?"

"Like about a box."

"Oh, that."

"Well?"

"I have some questions for you about that," she said.

"Why?"

"Because the box was empty."

Graham was silent over the line.

"Well, not exactly empty," Lauren corrected.

"What does that mean?"

"I thought it was empty at first, then I found a note. I'll show you when I get back. I'll be home tomorrow, or today for me and tomorrow for you . . . whatever, just don't let anything bad happen before then."

"How do I do that?"

"I don't know. But I'm sure you being there hasn't been good. So just hold on."

16

Graham wasn't sure what Lauren expected of him. And he wasn't volunteering for anything else. His one offer to help out had backfired. Now he carried the image of Carrie's house in his thoughts, and the knowledge of the letters—letters he now wanted to read. Carrie could easily find out he knew about them. Eddie might tell Jason about showing him the old trunk. Or if Carrie went home, surely she'd notice that the papers and items had been quickly shoved back inside.

That night, he couldn't sleep again. It was like an insomniac's marathon lately. The comforting sounds of the harbor tried to lull him to sleep: the gentle rocking and taps of the boat against the dock, the water against the hull, the occasional foghorn with its lonesome cry. Everything brought loneliness, as if he were lost and forgotten in the belly of a great fish.

Eddie would be sleeping now with his moon and stars comforter, maybe the lava lamp turned on. Jason had called after Lauren, asking Graham to stay at the house since he was coming home. Graham spent another fifteen uncomfortable minutes in the living room, chatting with Jason, then he gave his cell number to Jason in case they needed help the next day—guess that meant he had volunteered again. Saying good night to Carrie's husband and son in their house had been the perfect awkward ending to a very awkward night. It was altogether worse now picturing the home. And the letters.

She'd written him. Written many times. Were they words of anger and accusation? And why had she kept them all these years?

Graham wondered how he'd gone so quickly from the free-spirited sailor to a person of obligation and guilt. How had this complicated web pulled him inside?

Cap Charlie woke him. "Hello, down there. I've got a cappuccino with your name on it."

Graham opened the hatch and peered into the foggy morning. "Thanks. Wanna come down?"

"Sure, if I can fit. It's a might smaller than my boat."

"Yeah, try living this way."

"You tired of it yet? Land isn't so bad."

"Sometimes I'm tired of it."

"Life be short, Cat-Man. Speaking of cats, how is your little angel?"

"Keeping me here longer than I'd like."

"Maybe you're supposed to stay. Ever thought of that?"

"Might have crossed my mind a time or two, though I can't understand why."

"Sometimes there be no understanding the way things ought to be."

Graham chuckled. He'd learned over the years that fishermen and sailors alike had wisdom to consider.

As they continued talking over Cap Charlie's perfect cappuccinos, Graham's cell phone rang. It was Jason saying that Carrie was doing better.

GRAHAM MET JASON in the same waiting room. This time he held a Hot Wheels car and a potted geranium, which he handed over to Jason instead of presenting it to Carrie himself.

"She knows I'm here? Does she want to see me?"

A hesitation, then Jason said, "Yes."

"What was that—are you sure?"

"She doesn't look the same, you know, as when you last saw her—just know that."

Graham leaned against the door to room 312. She was in here. He was supposed to be going in. He even had the mother-in-law's permission now—for some reason, Grandma Stella liked him. What was stopping him?

The last time Graham saw Carrie . . . he didn't want to remember that, but it came unbidden anyway. She was hurt, her hand bleeding. And he'd left her there. Alone. Walked away. How quickly he'd betrayed her.

"I have a confession to make," she had said only the evening before.

On that evening, he didn't know how quickly it'd be over. With her confession statement, he'd responded serious-like. "Unfortunately, if you want to confess, I believe the village priests only speak Italian, or Latin. Or so they've made me believe."

"You've been to confession?"

"Daily since meeting you."

"What?"

"Kidding. I'm kidding."

"Good, you had me wondering what you'd be confessing."

Then Graham had become thoughtful, honest even. "I actually have thought of such things. I mean, I guess you make me think of getting my life together, the parts I've ignored for a long time."

"Like what parts?"

His mind flashed back in time. "Like about God, and who I'm supposed to be for God. And Ireland. I wasn't very brave when I needed to do something important."

"Graham, you were a child. You can't be expected to do some noble, brave thing as a child."

"If you only knew . . ."

"Tell me." She knelt before him and took his hands in her own, pressing their palms together.

"I can't. I let my parents down. I betrayed them."

"I don't believe it. You can't blame yourself for anything that happened when you were eight years old."

"I don't usually, but then, part of me does." Suddenly he wanted to run from it again. It hurt too deeply, brought such shame. "How did this become my confession time? You're the one with a confession to make."

Graham could tell she didn't want the subject changed. She wanted to ask and understand. But he felt sympathy in the air. And he didn't want her sympathy.

"Go on," he encouraged.

She leaned back to sit cross-legged on the floor, then took a breath and said, "Well, you know I love you."

"I guess," he said, embarrassed but pleased. Carrie had told him before that she loved him. But loving and being in love were different; he didn't ask which one she meant. He just accepted what she gave, no questions asked. There had never been the intense moment, the announcement like a proposal of love for him. That first night when they swam, she first spoke with the words "I love this." She'd whispered, "How can anything be this perfect?" From that night on, Carrie simply spoke what was there, without pomp or drama. She didn't mask her words or try to pry something from him. It came as naturally to her as pointing to the sky and commenting on a sunset.

She'd say, "I simply love you," looking at him as if he was truly something to love and admire. Or other times, kidding, "If I didn't love you . . ." Then the casual and easy expression, as if it came easily for her, "Because I love, that's why." Carrie didn't then wait with paused expectation, the need for reciprocation. She simply gave, didn't require any word or affection in return. She believed in them, and it made him believe too. Or nearly. Whenever they were apart, he'd begin to doubt. Nothing was this easy. Love required pain too. Everyone he knew said life was terribly hard, and always would be. She seemed to believe they could make it work somehow. Not until the last week had she begun to worry. He'd seen the traces of it, especially since Lauren's arrival—a reminder of reality and that the suffused world they'd lived in for the past two months wouldn't last forever. And he was leaving with Mrs. Preston, not for long, but the change brought fear to them both. Not that Carrie doubted much. Carrie didn't consider anything other than happily ever after.

"I think I need you," she said then.

And with those words, he realized his own need. And his own love. He'd surrendered sometime along the way. All he needed was to see her face, and the doubts and fears would melt away.

Taking a step toward her, suddenly a loud blast shattered the quiet. Carrie jumped; Graham pressed his hands over his ears.

"A car backfired. That sounded like a bomb." Carrie looked out the window then turned back toward him. "Graham? Are you okay?"

He couldn't move; it was as if his heart had stopped.

"Graham, are you okay?"

Rigid all over, he felt nauseous. He stood, tipping the chair over with a crash. They both jumped.

"I'm fine," he said, but thought, *A bomb, yes, it sounded just like a bomb.* And the sound and the sickness that filled him transported him instantly back. The sickening loss and confusion and pain as if it had just happened.

It was a sign, he thought. Surely. Or if not, at least a reminder of reality. Their mutual need. His sudden dependence upon her to feel alive. He felt a false sense of invincibility with her; she herself possessed a seemingly unending amount of it. Yet it was a lie. He knew what fake security produced—a swift and shattering dose of pain.

The next morning, the rain would pour down the window with her standing before it, and him already knowing what he was about to do. She didn't know of the change within him, didn't know it was their last good moment together. All night, over and over, Graham kept seeing his mistake, realizing how foolish he'd been to let down his guard. He nearly told her everything about Ireland, and the secret of Uncle Fergus might put Carrie in danger also. And how well did he know her? What did she know of love, of pain, of living in the world? Carrie was idealistic and too dreamy for him. It would never work. How did his carefree summer in Europe turn out like this?

Graham knew the break must be swift. First, he needed a Judas. And immediately he knew who that Judas would be. Somehow he always found them out, so easily identifiable. Lauren didn't like him; she didn't trust him, wanted to be rid of him. This was her chance. All she had to do was bring Carrie to the restaurant that evening, and he'd be gone from their lives.

His arm around the Italian girl, Graham hoped the girl wouldn't slap him before he did what needed to be done. He flirted with her; she flirted back. Within minutes of meeting her, he couldn't remember her name. Graham felt sick the entire time they talked. He'd been drinking all afternoon, as much as possible. Only that would give him the reckless strength to do this. He tried to not check his watch. Then from the corner of his eye, he saw Lauren and Carrie. The Benders were with them, which brought further regret.

But what did he care? What did he care for any of these people? This was what happened when he let himself get dragged in. Commitment. Responsibility. People counting on him.

"Graham, what is going on? We were supposed to meet." He'd expected sudden anger from Carrie, not innocent confusion. Hurt.

"Carrie, this is . . . what did you say your name was again? Oh, it doesn't matter."

"Graham. What are you doing?"

"Having some fun. Is that so wrong? Come celebrate with us."

"Celebrate what?"

"I'm leaving tomorrow."

"Tomorrow? I thought we were burying something. I thought we had plans."

"Plans changed. Mrs. Preston is returning to the States, but I'm going to Greece to work on her brother's boat, learning to sail."

"You aren't coming back?"

"How can I pass up Greece, learning to sail?"

It escalated from there. Lauren and the Benders were already seated at the restaurant. Carrie, in confusion, walked out but soon returned. Her hair and dress soaked, mascara running in lines down her face, mixed with the tears.

"Why are you doing this?"

"Because it meant nothing. I need to move on." Graham took the Italian girl's hand and walked right past her. The crash turned him back. He wasn't sure how it happened, but the patio doors had shattered, covering Carrie with glass. Screams. Their eyes connecting. Then Lauren beside her, the Benders too. Blood. Her hand was pouring blood, and she didn't seem to notice. Carrie only stared at him with such shock and hurt—an expression of pain he'd never quite gotten over. Then she escaped out the patio door toward the sea. He left the Italian girl on the front porch. A fear swept over him. The sea was dangerous, and he pictured her climbing their cliffs in this weather. He ran to find her, take her back, beg forgiveness.

Lauren reached her first. He saw them on the beach in the rain; Lauren wrapping her hand. And he knew it was as it should be.

It was the last time he'd seen her. That was their good-bye.

And now, here he was at her hospital door. Pushing the door open, he braced himself for the worst. It was like walking into a funeral parlor to view something tragic.

"Graham." Her voice. How strange to hear Carrie's voice again, and it sounded so familiar and calming.

She appeared small, sitting up as the bed hummed with the automatic lift, adjusting the blankets over her pale hospital gown. Carrie. Her smile, and eyes, and small little nose. An unexpected emotion rose within him. Sure, this certainly wasn't her most glorious moment. Her hair, a bit straggly, fell down below her shoulders, perhaps a bit of makeup, though her paleness and weight loss were evident. But it was her. She smiled a weak smile, but that smile nonetheless.

"Carrie," he said, and all fear fled as he approached her. It seemed many decades had passed, and they were meeting again as old people. Usually he imagined himself as an old man all alone. He felt like that already. But sometimes he thought of various coincidences that would bring them together. Imagined meeting decades later, and wondered what it would be like then. The mistakes of life would be worked through, and they'd spend the last golden years making each other coffee, watching the sun set over the sea, reminiscing over the things they'd missed in each other's lives. Such had been his thoughts.

"I wish you weren't seeing me like this. I mean, I wanted to lose a few pounds if we ever met again. But then, I wanted to look fabulous, show you what you missed out on. This isn't quite what I had in mind."

He laughed—only Carrie would say the exact truth, not dance around and pretend things weren't as they had been. Her presence became a sudden comfort.

"You look great," he said, taking a few steps closer.

"And you're a bad liar."

"You look terrible, how's that?"

It made them both laugh.

"Do you want to sit down?"

"Sure." He pulled the chair up beside the bed.

"How strange that you're really here. There you are. Are you happy?"

"Right now I am."

"You are?" She smiled again.

"Yeah," he said, surprised. In a way it was wrong to be happy sitting beside someone on her journey toward death. "At this moment, I can say that I'm very happy."

"Me too," she said. "I can't tell you all the times I imagined meeting you. There've been thousands of scenarios."

He wanted to take her hand; it appeared cold and small resting on the sheets so close within reach. He'd press their palms together and marvel at the years and distance and how their hands were joined again. Instead, he noticed the scar and remembered that night again; he was the cause of the jagged scar on her hand.

"Does Jason make you laugh?" Graham couldn't help asking, knowing it was completely unfair. She didn't answer at first.

"He's not perfect, but he's been an example of what God intended people to be. He's loved when I didn't love back. He's given his life without expecting anything in return."

Graham didn't want that answer, but he could see it—Jason was that way. His faith in God was lived in sincerity. "It scared me."

"What did?"

"Needing you, and wanting you to need me." How strange to realize they could speak as old friends.

"Why are you here now? Not that I'm complaining." She turned her head, resting a cheek against the bed, her legs pulled up. Her hair was messier, and he could easily just reach out and smooth it. Graham realized it had been a long time since he was comfortable enough with someone for even the simplest of touches.

"The boat turned south. A compelling. Wasn't there an open invitation? You'd always welcome me back to your life no matter what happened?"

"If only I had a life to welcome you into. You waited too long."

"You'll beat this," he said, and the lie brought a sudden urge to make exiting small talk and get out of there.

She smiled with her eyes closing. "And then he was gone. Once again gone."

"What?"

"I expect at any moment to open my eyes and find you've disappeared. Death talk makes you uneasy, I understand. Graham, what exactly is your purpose then? That compelling brought you back for a reason."

Who was he kidding? She could see through him as she always could, see him in ways he could hardly see himself. Everything about her, regardless of the changes time and illness had made, still felt familiar with such immediate relief. Who else on earth knew him? Not the day-to-day him, but the inside person.

Here he was, Graham realized, reaching for the one he'd nearly destroyed. He wanted to get the answers from her, even in her hour of need. *You tell me my purpose. I don't know. It's always about me, my selfish needs. I'm lost; do you know how to help me?*

"It was for the best," he said. "I just want to say I'm sorry for how it happened."

"Was it best for you, or for me?"

"Well, I don't know. For you, that's for sure. You've had a nice life, it seems."

"Yes. I found home, right where I couldn't see it. In front of me."

Graham nodded, though he couldn't deny he really wished to hear how she'd never gotten over him, how she wished he'd never left, all that baloney of love songs and cheesy romantic movies.

"What was it all for?" he asked, not really meaning to, but needing the question before them.

"What was that summer for?" He nodded, and she closed her eyes a minute, turning away. "You changed my life, Graham. Made it richer even if I got lost for a while, thought I couldn't live after losing you. That last day was a great awakening. My life had been spared pain for so long. You'd known only loss since you were a boy."

"And so I hurt you."

"I should've listened more. Afterward, I remembered things you'd said. Your doubts that I discredited. I hadn't experienced anything then. But for all the what-ifs, it would've all ended here anyway. This illness, you know. We all have a number of days. So I haven't spent mine as well as I could've. None of us do. But you, I want the least amount of regret for you. Do what you need to do."

"What do you mean?"

"I never asked the secret you left in that box."

"No, just as I never asked about yours, or looked when I buried it." How strange to be talking to her about this. She didn't seem to know that Lauren had found the box empty. "I almost looked, but I figured I'd done enough betraying. I've only told one other person in my life." Then Graham wondered about that. Could that one person have gone and found it?

"I need to talk to you about what I did. Lauren needs to know, I'm sure of that now. And . . . and I wanted Lauren to put something back inside."

"Lauren's on her way home."

"Already?"

"I talked to her last night."

"Then I didn't do it." Her crestfallen expression confused him. "What didn't you do?"

She closed her eyes, shaking her head. "I can't believe it. I'm too late."

"You aren't too late for anything," he said, not knowing what else to say.

"I wanted something put in the box, for Eddie, for the future. The last thing."

"Hey, hello in there?" Graham said. She opened her eyes. "It isn't too late. It'll be okay. We'll work it out. Someone will take that box back, Jason or Lauren . . . or even me. One of us will do it, I promise." Even as Graham said it, he wondered if she'd believe him. He wondered if he should believe himself.

But this was different. This went beyond life, beyond love in the romantic sense, the marital sense even. There was something of eternity here between them, and in a promise to give something to a boy, a boy much like himself.

CARRIE HAD SO much to say to Graham. Years of dialogue, ages of stories. It was as if they were nearly one person—or two sides of a coin. So alike, and yet so completely different. Their lives had viewed completely different worlds. Now, here, they faced each other again.

She wanted to know if she'd been wrong. Was it sin, failure, obsession? She hadn't really carried the torch for him; there was a life to prove it, and yet, had he ever left her? Was a little part of "laying down your life for your friends" also holding a bit of love for someone whom everyone would say to forget?

God, I have to know. Don't I need to know?

Relief flooded over her. Surely the past proved that she shouldn't trust Graham or his promises. But she did anyway. She told him her part of the secret left in the box, and her fears at Lauren's reaction. A part of her wished to know what he'd put in there so many years ago. She wished to ask a million things, to know everything about him. But once again, the energy drained away like a leak in an air mattress.

"I have some things for you too," she said. "A postcard of a painting that reminds me of you. And some old letters I never sent. After I'm gone, I'll have Jason give them to you."

"Carrie," Graham said, and she marveled at hearing him speak her name again. "What's it all for?" he asked again.

Another of the questions without answers, she thought. And yet, Carrie knew with a peaceful settling inside that it was okay; the answers were unanswerable, at least in this world. But she'd know in just a little while.

She said with eyes closed, "Maybe everything is really all about eternity."

17

The loud tinny engine of the small plane from San Francisco to Harper's Bay still rang in her head. Lauren had been breathing recycled air on the different planes and in the airports so that the first blast of fresh sea air nearly sent her to her knees in relief. Home.

Lauren wanted to slide beneath her comforter and be left alone for two or three days, then reemerge ready to face reality. No chance of that.

First stop, her house. There she could drop off her luggage, the box, and find out where Carrie was and how her grandfather had coped without her daily visits.

Lauren took a taxi, another thing she'd never done in her hometown. Who had she become, anyway? Some spontaneous, new, adventure-seeking person who dug up buried treasures, ate pizza along an Italian seashore, and jaunted to foreign landscapes by herself, no less.

This was not her. And yet, Lauren couldn't deny a sense of accomplishment even with the mess she was returning to. The women at her office were going to be shocked. She'd actually pulled it off—souvenirs bought in the Milan airport were proof she'd gone.

The house smelled musty. Her plants looked wilted. The fish

had survived and stared at her arrival with bulging eyes. The recorder blinked with eight messages: coworkers with questions, who didn't believe she'd actually gone somewhere on vacation; several salespeople; and someone at church wanting her to do something.

Is this all my life consists of? Lauren thought, realizing a week ago she hadn't cared.

Picking up her phone, she dialed her grandfather first. No answer. Then Carrie and Jason's house. No answer there. Carrie's cell phone went straight to voice mail. Had everybody disappeared? Next the hospital; the switchboard said Carrie was there and rang her room. Jason answered.

"How is she?"

"Okay, I guess, considering. The doctor should be in soon. Are you home?"

"Yeah, I gotta check on Grandpa, and then I'll be there."

"Oh, sorry, Lauren. I forgot to stop by or call him, Carrie even asked me to."

"No problem. You've had your hands full, I'm sure."

"You have no idea."

That made her want to ask, but Lauren figured she'd find out soon enough. As she picked up her purse and jacket, her open bedroom door lent a perfect view to her tall queen-sized bed with its thick comforter, electric blanket, jersey knit sheets, and down pillows. Walking away was like leaving an oasis without water in the canteen.

She found her grandfather's house empty.

A woman from church who did home nursing and housework was supposed to come daily. But what if Grandpa had done something like fire her? Or he could be lost, wandering somewhere. She spotted an empty coffee cup on the table. The liquid inside appeared fresh. She touched the coffeepot and felt its warmth. He had to be close.

"Grandpa?" she called, wandering the stuffy rooms.

There was a knock on the door. "Hello?" a voice called.

"I'll be right there."

"Did you lose a grandfather?"

It was the guy down the street who cared for his grandmother. Grandpa had tried setting them up a few times.

"I did lose a grandfather."

The guy—she couldn't remember his name—was clean-cut and wore jeans and a button-down shirt. He smiled and extended a hand. "I'm Bruce, and you must be Lauren."

She shook his hand. "Yes, I am."

"Your grandfather's down at my grandmother's house, having scones. She only makes scones when your grandfather is coming over," he said.

"Okay." She was at a loss for what that meant.

"Would you like to come over?"

Lauren paused, still confused. "I have a friend in the hospital. Will you just tell my grandpa I'll be back later?"

"Sure."

As Lauren drove off to the next location, she recalled just how good-looking the grandson had been. And close to her age, she'd guess. How strange was all that?

LAUREN HANDED JASON a steaming cup of coffee, such an involuntary action, she realized. How many cups had they handed the other during the last few years? The hospital didn't feel foreign; they'd been here so often it seemed nearly natural, if not for the constant reminder of death and illness.

After arriving, Lauren followed the usual routine, checking the floor waiting room, then down to the cafeteria where Jason sat alone. Lauren heard the medical updates, and after the years of transferring such information, the impact of his words struck her. This was real. Carrie was dying. The feared diagnosis had come. They sat across from each other in silence, both imagining the coming weeks and months, and then the years ahead when Carrie would be gone. Lauren went for coffee refills; it was something to do.

"And where's Eddie?" she finally asked.

"Getting a ride over after school, though he didn't want to come," Jason said. A slight annoyance came through his tone. "He refuses to see Carrie in the hospital this time. I don't know why."

Lauren found it interesting, wondered what Eddie was thinking; that little guy was always thinking more than an average seven-year-old should. Taking a sip of coffee, Lauren then broached the other subject. Graham.

"So, I can't believe you let Graham see Carrie." Lauren was also irritated that Graham hadn't done as she'd asked.

"Yep, I did." Jason said it easily enough, but she detected a faint betrayal of his real emotions. "I suppose, if we weren't all losing Carrie, I'd be pretty worried about now."

Lauren hadn't let herself stand in Jason's shoes. It hadn't crossed her thoughts when she jaunted off to find Graham Michaels. And yet, how could she be so blind? Jason knew only a fraction of the power of that first love, and that fraction was more than enough. And here, in walks Graham—over six feet tall, slender, and sure of himself, handsome, and, the clincher, a full head of hair. Jason seemed to read her thoughts.

"Yep, I'd be heading to the gym and checking out Rogaine." He rubbed the top of his head.

Lauren laughed at the twinkle in his green eyes.

"Jason, he broke her heart. You healed it."

"Some things can't be fully healed," Jason said softly, perceiving more than she'd realized. "At least not in this life. He's the one I feel sorry for though."

"Why?"

"He's more lost than all of us."

Lauren couldn't speak for a moment. Her immediate protests were lost as she realized this truth. It was part of what kept Carrie worrying and caring, praying even, for Graham all those years—the knowledge of how lost he really was. And now Jason could see it and care for him. She saw Jason with new eyes, new respect. She wanted to say, "And you're the best of all of us" but knew he'd get embarrassed and brush away such words.

"I'm trying to be okay with the idea that he's here. It's not the easiest, despite my logical brain usually being the strongest. I'm not wanting my wife to rehash old memories when this is the last I have of her."

"Jason. Don't you know?"

"What?"

"You've given Carrie the very best of life."

"What are you talking about?"

"If you only knew her life before you. When she was about to destruct with her mom, who came through for her? Who is here for her now? Who does she know to believe in, even if sometimes none of us say enough about how heroic you are? You gave her security, a home, a family."

"I'm nothing special."

"You're more than you realize."

Lauren hoped Jason would let himself accept some of what he'd given to Carrie. He'd granted her a life when hers was falling apart. He was the hero of Carrie's story.

LAUREN PEEKED INTO Carrie's room, hoping not to awaken her.

"You're back," Carrie said with a weak smile.

Lauren instinctively covered her mouth. How could someone deteriorate so rapidly? Carrie had shrunk smaller, her cheekbones protruded, her face pale. She was younger, but older too at the same time. Lauren walked inside, sitting on the bed carefully, afraid of hurting her.

"Yes, the great adventurer is back."

"I just closed my eyes and here you are. Well, sort of."

"Doesn't seem like that to me."

"How was it?" Carrie said with a wan smile.

"Far," she said, thinking of the journey, wondering where to go from here, and feeling extraordinarily tired. "But good too."

"And did you find it?"

"Not really," Lauren said with a sigh. She wanted Carrie stronger before fully explaining. "We'll talk about it, but there's something else first, or rather someone else . . ."

Carrie nodded, then winced in pain a moment. "I saw him. Graham. He came here this morning maybe, or yesterday."

"I'm sorry I opened this all up, and it was all for nothing too."

"Lauren, you don't understand. All the unresolveds are finally being concluded. I can't tell you how good that feels. We need to talk, Lauren," Carrie said. "About the box."

"Yes, we do." Lauren hated the suspense of telling her that the box was empty.

Just then, footsteps came quickly down the hallway.

"Hi, Mom," Eddie said with hesitation. Jason was behind him.

"Lauren, guess you're back just in time to take our girl home."

"She's going home?" Lauren was shocked; Carrie didn't appear in any shape to be away from medical care.

"Yep," Jason said, but there was something wrong in his forced cheerfulness. "They're bringing in a wheelchair."

Turning to Eddie, Lauren asked, "Hey, where's my 'Hello, Aunt Lauren, I sure missed you'?"

"I sure missed you, Aunt Lauren. Were you gone?"

"What?"

"Just kidding," Eddie said, and his old laugh returned.

An hour later, Lauren stood at the glass window of the hospital pharmacy. Carrie sat in her wheelchair, and Jason walked beside her. Eddie's head popped up from behind as he haphazardly pushed the wheelchair down the hallway.

"I'm getting out of here," Carrie said in a weak attempt to cheer from the wheelchair. Eddie pushed faster when he spotted Lauren, and let out a warrior whoop, which then started them both warrior whooping, much to Jason's chagrin.

"We're going home, we're going home," the two took up.

"No more obnoxiously bright fluorescent lighting," Carrie said as cheerily as she could.

"No more stinky, stinging hand washing before every meal," Eddie shouted.

"No more needles."

"No more bad waiting rooms."

"No more grouchy nurses."

"Yeah, no more grouchy nurses who don't like our pranks."

"Yeah, no more grouchy nurses who don't like our pranks or our laughing at night."

"Yeah, no more . . ."

But for all the cheering, Lauren and Jason weren't joining in. He caught her eye, acknowledging her thoughts. No more hospital.

There was nothing more for them to do.

MOM WAS HOME. Eddie woke up knowing this fact immediately. There was a different feeling in the house when she was home, even if she was still asleep. And tomorrow was his birthday. She'd made it home just in time.

Crawling like a spy on a mission, Eddie crept to his parents' bedroom door. It was open just a crack. From the kitchen came the sounds of Dad making coffee, but he knew Mom was still in bed— she said her best sleep came right at dawn. Mom's door creaked slightly, but the lump in bed didn't move.

For a second, her stillness startled him. What if she had died in the night? It could happen, he knew. Then he saw the blankets make a slow rise up and then down. Poking his head up, there she was, funny with her face all sleepy-looking. Her mouth was open a little, hair all over the pillow, her hands tucked under her chin. That's what she probably looked like when she was younger like him.

Lifting the covers ever so slightly, Eddie slid one arm, then a leg, then all of him beneath the blanket. Mom didn't move. He lay there frozen-like, wanting to laugh, but he didn't want to wake her either. Mom didn't smell her good smell. This was how she smelled in the hospital or when she was taking medicines.

For a moment, he closed his eyes and imagined her not here anymore. He didn't think God would take her, believed if he prayed enough, God wouldn't. Resting close to her, Eddie heard the steady rhythm of her breathing. The cold slipped from him all the way out

his fingers and toes. After adjusting the pillow, Eddie further snug-
gled down into the pillow and closer to Mom. At times like this, he
felt little again, and even with his birthday and turning eight, right
now he wished to go backward. Back then, he'd sneak into bed with
his mom and dad all the time in the early morning. Sometimes he'd
even crawl right in the middle, especially when he woke up cold
after kicking off all the covers. Now the warmth and steady breathing, the comforter pulled over, and the down pillow all made him
sleepy. His eyes drooped and that weird sensation flowed over him,
that feeling of drifting away. Then Mom jerked her arm from
beneath her cheek, nearly hitting his face. Her eyes moved rapidly
beneath her eyelids, giving her a scary expression he couldn't tear his
eyes from. She appeared like one of those creatures from the old
movies he liked to watch. Her mouth closed, her eyes continued
moving. He wondered if she'd stopped breathing; maybe he should
get Dad, or call 911. Her arm moved again, just a quick jerk, then
stopped. She rolled onto her back.

"Mom, are you okay? Are you awake?"

"I had a dream that I was swimming," she said, half-asleep still.
He wondered if she was really talking in her sleep like she sometimes
did. He and his dad had tried listening sometimes, sneaking close or
asking questions to see. Once she said, "Let's tie the giant down with
shoestrings," which made them laugh.

"You were swimming? Your eyes scared me; thought you were
Frankenstein."

"Frankenstein? Oh, I've been meaning to tell you, but you figured it out," she mumbled. Now Eddie knew she really was awake.

"I've known for a long time, Mom."

She smiled at that with eyes still closed. "What a strange dream.
I remembered it clearer this time. I think that's the same dream I
keep having. Or maybe the same place. Strange."

"You keep dreaming about the same place?"

"Yeah, I guess. But this time brought back some of those other dreams. It's this really amazing coastline. But different colors than our beaches. It had different colors than here, or anywhere, I can't even describe the colors. It was a place I've never seen before. But it feels familiar. Or like somewhere I've always wanted to go."

Eddie was quiet, listening, thinking about what she was saying. She seemed to have forgotten he was there, which happened often when she was in the hospital or taking medicines.

"You were swimming there?"

"Huh?" she said, her eyes fluttering open. "Yes. Hey, come over here."

She pulled him closely; he fit so perfectly against her that he could nearly imagine once being in her tummy. "I'd forgotten that part. Yes. I was swimming. The water felt so good, better than any water I've been in. It was like the air, but wet, and so swimming was nearly like flying, I suppose. Don't you sometimes wish you could stay inside a dream?"

"Yes."

"You do?"

"Sometimes. Once I dreamed about this big balloon that took me around the world. And another time I was almost winning a race when I woke up. Was that a dream you wanted to stay inside?"

His mom didn't respond for a moment. "Sort of. But what a better surprise to wake up and find my old snuggle-bug not thinking he's too big for snuggly-buggly."

"Oh, Mom. I am too old for snuggly-buggly," Eddie said with authority. He couldn't help the smile on the edges of his firm expression.

"You are? Let's see about that." She reached her arms around him before he could escape, and he sort of let her anyway. She couldn't hold him very tightly, and he didn't want to hurt her feelings. It was pretty fun too.

"Did your dream make you want to go swimming?" he asked her. Mom loved to swim. She often said she wanted to move where it was warmer so she could be like a fish and swim all the time.

"It sure did. But it wasn't the same—the water seemed different in the dream. I think I've watched too many sci-fi shows lately. My hospital roommate was watching some marathon of the *Twilight Zone*; oh, guess you wouldn't know what that was."

"Classic sci-fi, Mom." She smiled at that. "Guess we can't swim until next summer."

"Guess not," she said, her voice sounding funny again. He turned over. Mom's hand covered her face, fingers around her forehead. "Are you ready for your last day as a seven-year-old?"

"Are you okay, Mom?"

"Could you go tell Dad I need my medicine? Then we'll talk about your party."

"Sure." Eddie jumped back out of bed. Now he wasn't a secret spy, but an agent on a mission to retrieve the potion that would cure the ailing woman. If only he could really find that cure.

LAUREN WALKED DOWN the dock, looking for Graham's boat. Hadn't she done this before? If felt like years ago. She saw the bags of groceries before recognizing the sailboat as his. Cases of Dasani bottled water. Plastic bags with oranges, apples, and pears. A loaf of bread. Cat food. A stack of used books.

She tilted her head to the side, reading the authors: Tom Clancy, John Irving, Graham Greene, John Steinbeck, John Grisham, Dave Eggers.

Groceries told a lot about the person. So did books. A fiction reader, well, didn't that just figure? No self-help books like Lauren would recommend.

He bounded from below deck and stopped short upon seeing her.

"Oh, you. Didn't know you'd returned from retrieving things that don't belong to you."

Her arms crossed at the chest. "I still can't believe you're here."

"It wasn't exactly intentional," he said as he leaned far over the rope railing to grab a plastic bag filled with candy bars and a box of Hostess Twinkies.

"You want me to believe that? If I'd known you'd show up in Harper's Bay, I would've never looked for you."

"As if I was looking for you to find me. I don't expect you to believe me, but it wasn't my plan to be here. Jason called it a God-planned encounter or something like that. Wanna hand me those? Make yourself useful?"

"No," she said, firmly planting her feet on the dock. Who did he think he was? "Jason has never wanted to know the whole story of that summer. He just loves Carrie; that's all he needed to know. If he knew how you treated her . . ."

"Pretty amazing guy, that's for sure."

And then Lauren understood the groceries on the dock. "You're leaving," she stated as he reached over for another bag and carried them down the few steps to the galley.

He popped back up a moment later. "Yep. Heading home."

"Why?" She'd meant to ask, "When?" instead of "Why?" How did her mouth have such a will of its own? She didn't care why, only the level of her relief would be gauged by the proximity of his departure. Right now, the relief she'd expected wasn't there.

"Why not? This is what I do, sail away. And you of all people should be happy."

"Yes, you should go."

"Seems we've had this conversation before. In Europe perhaps?"

Lauren felt sick at the reminder. The night she agreed to help him hurt Carrie, though she hadn't known what he fully intended. She thought it was for the best, convinced this was proof of what she suspected of Graham's character. The more time Carrie spent with Graham, the harder a breakup would be. Later, she realized it was her own insecurities over losing her friend that prodded much of her criticism against Graham. "That was different, and Carrie forgave me a long time ago for my part in that. When I met you, I thought you'd probably hurt her. But I didn't realize how much . . ." She wondered what all to tell him. "How much it all would hurt her."

He was silent a moment, then said quietly, "It can't be changed; the past can't be changed. Or the future for that matter. She's dying. And even if she wasn't, what is the purpose of me being here?"

"Does there have to be a purpose?"

"Doesn't there? It's pretty pointless otherwise."

"Hasn't her life meant anything to you?"

"Our being together was another mistake I made. She would've been better off to have never met me. But I do have a few promises left for her, ones I intend to keep this time."

Then for a brief moment, Lauren let herself see him as Carrie saw him. Not as the hated wretch image she'd clung to whenever thinking of him in the past fourteen years. She saw a glimpse inside of him, to the boy who'd lost something great, to the man who only knew to run. She believed there was beauty in every person. The beauty could be harmed by life choices, by the feeding of evil. She glimpsed this, his beauty. His vulnerability and longing for something greater. This was what Carrie had seen so long ago. She'd loved him because of it. She couldn't get over it.

Just as quickly, Lauren closed off her understanding. She thought of the pain he'd caused them all. How Carrie had struggled to love again, to truly believe in Jason's love. The anger welled inside her. She held back angry words, spiteful and intended to hurt to his core. But what could hurt him? He already saw his own failings. He'd accepted them, perhaps wallowed in them. But at least he didn't delude himself like most people. Did Lauren see her own faults?

"Maybe you should quit running from yourself. Is it getting you very far? Or are you feeling sorry for yourself, drowning in your own mess?"

"What about you?"

"This isn't about me."

"It's about all of us, wouldn't you say?" He stood there with one knee on the hull, his arm resting on it. "We all have our own pain to deal with, and how we do that is for each of us to figure out."

"'Life is pain. Anybody who says differently is trying to sell something.'"

"What are you talking about?"

"It's a line from *The Princess Bride*."

"How poignant." But he smiled, and then she did. The animosity between them fell away, though Lauren wasn't sure how.

"Show me what you found in Italy."

"Okay," she said, opening her purse. "The box was there, but the contents gone. Except for this." She held out the laminated paper. She noticed his long fingers shake slightly as he took it.

G, you know what needs to be done. M

For a moment, he turned away to read it. "Nothing else was there?"

"Nothing."

"Manny," he whispered.

258

"Who?"

"My cousin. He visited me the winter after I left Italy. I told him about the summer, everything—I was drinking quite a bit for a while then." A shamed look crossed his face as he sat on the bench. Lauren felt awkward still standing there. She grabbed the railing and stepped aboard.

"Do you know what this means?" she asked.

"Not really. I wonder when he got it. I suppose I know what he's telling me—that I need to do what I couldn't do."

"And that is . . ."

It seemed he suddenly realized she was there again. He stood and held on to the wheel, staring back at the paper.

"Who is Manny?"

"My cousin in Ireland."

"So can you call him?"

"He's dead."

Lauren stared at him. This wasn't some silly prank. This was serious.

"But Aunt Fiona . . ."

"Who?"

"My aunt in Ireland. She might know something."

GRAHAM STARED AT the paper, his cousin's handwritten note—words from beyond the grave. The many injustices it spoke of. And they rested upon him. And him alone. But even if Graham had the cassette tape, after all this time, it might not be enough to get a conviction for his uncle. Then what? His remaining family members would hate him, and Uncle Fergus would walk free. His own life would be in danger.

"Can you call her?" Lauren asked.

He jumped downstairs for his cell phone, adding the hours to know what time it was in Ireland. His aunt should still be up, but what if Uncle Fergus answered? He dialed anyway.

"Aunt Fiona?"

"Well, if it isn't my nephew again, and two times in one week."

"I have a question for you. Did Manny ever tell you about Italy?"

"I thought that might be what you were asking about when you called the first time."

"What do you mean?"

"What Manny said to give you."

"Manny said to give me something?"

"He told me if you e'er asked, and he weren't here no more, I was to give you something that belonged to you. I have it in me little safe here, and have never opened it all these years. Nearly did when Manny died. But he said it was fer you and you alone."

"That's what I need. And Aunt Fiona, you can't tell anybody about this. Okay?"

"Is this about Manny's death?"

"It might be. And my parents' deaths too."

"Graham. Listen to me, lad. Whatever happens, no matter what 'tis, you do what be right. You do the right thing." Something in her voice indicated she suspected it was Uncle Fergus, he thought. But Graham couldn't be sure. "What be your address?"

"My address?" He looked around. "Can you FedEx it?"

"Use this address: 444 Ruben Street," Lauren said, peering in from above deck. "Carrie's house. Tomorrow is Eddie's birthday; we'll all be there."

He got off the phone and turned to see Lauren bent down on the top step. "She has it, then?"

"It'll be here tomorrow."

"Eddie could use a good-bye before you go. It's his birthday tomorrow, and he wants you there. You'd be surprised how much that boy likes you; it sure surprised me. But you should leave. You really should go."

"Are you usually this manipulative?"

"When I have to be."

"Yeah, and I'll leave the package for you to retrieve, right?" Graham slid the case of water beneath the bench seat. His eyes rested on the ship-in-the-bottle he'd owned since childhood, and he thought of Eddie's last birthday with his mother alive. "After tomorrow, I'll be ready to go."

Lauren backed up, and Graham started putting a few groceries away. He went back up the ladder, expecting a continued discussion. The silence amplified Lauren's absence, stopping him at the top step. Gone.

Man, she could irritate him. *'Cause she tells me the truth.*

Did Eddie need him? How could he? The boy had a lot of people in his life. What did he have to offer? Or maybe Graham needed Eddie.

He'd only met Eddie a few times. Just some kid. Some kid who reminded him of himself. Some kid whose mother he probably once loved, maybe still did if he could define exactly what love was. Some kid whose childhood was being stripped away—just like his. Some kid. Only a kid.

Why couldn't Graham stop thinking about him?

There were different versions, and all meant *need.* So often, any version of "need" became the last words he'd hear, especially when dating. And then he'd be gone, sometimes leaving without a good-bye, other times escaping as the jerk, womanizer, cheater, among the nicer variations. He didn't let it matter, those words they called him. As long as he was gone.

For a few years, Graham had known where he was going. Everyone told him he'd go far, had the looks-and-brains combination going just right. He had more potential than he used. He decided to give in to it, use it all up; every drop of potential would fuel him onward. Sailing was put aside as a hobby. He worked a corporate job at a yachting company. Success, money, love, or at least any kind of substitute if not the original.

"It won't make you happy," an old sailing buddy told him. The guy was always on some spiritual quest or another and fully believed the only way of finding contentment was to "find peace in the moment and seek the eternal way."

Graham observed that the people who said such phrases usually had never enjoyed the worldly treasures. Money did make him happy. Success didn't keep him up at night. He'd slept with a smile on his face. It felt good for many years. It offered happiness, enough to make him work long hours and weekends.

At least for a while.

Hadn't he always been conflicted? At one moment fueled by his own strength, another moment fearful he'd be unmasked and the childhood he'd lost would be revealed. At age thirty-two, he couldn't understand it. His childhood had ended at age eight. More than two decades had passed since then, and still those first eight years were like a lost land he yearned to reclaim.

Graham heard a car engine start, surprising him that Lauren hadn't already driven away. And he should be glad. But a strange loneliness settled upon him like a weight upon his chest. No one would beg him to stay. He knew no one wanted him here, not really. Maybe Eddie did, but of course, he couldn't know of adult complications.

Carrie would probably be relieved. She was surrounded by people who loved her. The last person she needed was him.

He should've never come. Right now he'd be having dinner at the café, maybe playing a hand of cards on the *Tempest* with Jasper and his buddies. He liked older people. They were always offering advice, always a bit envious of his youth, and always had time for a gruff affection.

It was selfish of him really. How conceited was he to believe his presence would make a difference in Carrie's dying days? But then, what else would move him? Conceit, vanity, arrogance, pride. They were his shelter. Sometimes he believed in them more than anything else.

Manny was another voice from the past, and he said the same words Carrie had spoken, "Do what you must do." Part of him agreed. Justice was needed. Was that why he was here? All of this an elaborately planned scheme to get him to face what he'd been fleeing since he was eight years old? A divine plan. As if someone had been praying for him for years. Someone like Carrie.

18

The late night like so many other late nights. Carrie realized how often she'd just expected such nights to be, not considered them a gift. The sounds of a home at rest, the sighs and creaks of a house, the refrigerator's occasional hum, a car coming down the street, a train on some distant track. The scent of a cake cooling on a rack that Lauren had helped her bake. Comforting knowledge that people she loved and people who loved her were in that same house and in that same town. She'd lived it without being thankful. Always she wanted the next journey; she longed for things not found; she dreamed of something to come. Now it was all leaving her grasp.

Wrapped in the blanket, Carrie looked at the four postcards on the coffee table. Carrie held each postcard in her hand.

Impressions of Africa by Salvador Dalí

In the surrealist painting, an artist—Dalí himself—worked on a canvas, seeming to reach out of the painting. In rich colors, the dreamlike sequence in the background with strange contorted figures, the face of Dalí's wife, a guitarist playing in a boat marooned in a desert landscape. This Dalí postcard, Carrie had kept for years, had planned to give it to Graham but never had the chance.

The Broken Pitcher by Edward-Adolphe Bouguereau

The peasant girl with a broken pitcher at her feet so recently purchased from her trip to the Legion of Honor museum in San Francisco.

Next, she found the one Lauren had given her along with a print she'd purchased in Florence. Carrie realized they needed to talk soon—Lauren hadn't mentioned the box since her return.

Madonna and Child with Angels by Fra Filippio Lippi

Last, she had not a true postcard with print, but something much more authentic. Eddie had seen her Bouguereau and made his own picture that size.

Sailboats on the Sea by Edward Timmons

As she considered each, Carrie realized how they comprised such a history of her life and the people within it. Tomorrow was her son's birthday. Life was failing. It was taking all her strength. She needed to answer the essential questions for her son, before time was gone.

What were the most important things she'd discovered about life? Love, and only love. As simple and as intricate as that. The Great Commandment. Love God and others. Everything else fell within those boundaries. How to tell Eddie this? How did something abstract help him? Love didn't take away the sorrow of living; in fact, it only increased it. There were hurts so deep that would not be hidden scars. She would carry them with her, always. With paper and pen, she began her final attempts.

Dearest Eddie,
    I wish I was strong enough to live a long life for you.
    I've had people to love and to be loved by.
    Places that have granted the most perfect of moments.
    I hope you'll have cried over somebody, because love isn't anything unless it's hurt you.
    I hope someone will cry for you, because you're worth it.
    Already I have cried for the loss of you. But I will also rejoice.
    Someday you'll dive into that hidden silver sea, and I'll swim out to greet you.

It was too much and not enough. But somehow, it would have to be.

WAKE UP, CARRIE told herself. *Get up. It's your son's birthday. There's a cake to finish and decorations to hang. He'll be waking up in an hour or two.*

Every year of his life, she'd kept the same tradition. This year she planned to make a sailboat cake, since Eddie talked so much about Graham's boat. Jason had bought a little plastic one and blue food coloring to transform white frosting into a wavy sea.

But then away she went again, Carrie didn't know where; maybe she couldn't remember; maybe there was an entire existence in that sleep world. Perhaps it was where she came near the water that separated one dimension from the other. A short swim across. Maybe she walked along that shore, gazing back a moment, sad to not be putting on a birthday party for her son, but also knowing that once they all swam across it would be okay, more than okay. Were there seashells in the sand? Could she hold them to her ear and hear, not the sound of the sea, but the promise of what waited across the waters?

A longing came, nearly an audible call from the liquid diamonds, beckoning in a whispered tone. She stared across, suddenly thirsty, suddenly too warm for life in the air and earth. Someone waited for her across the sea. Carrie knew who He was; she'd known Him a long time, but in this moment she *knew* Him more clearly and couldn't wait to be there.

Her toe touched the water, the tingling exhilaration ran up her leg. A pause, then she bent to dive in. And stopped. Something . . . the One across the sea stopped her. The Voice in her ear, a whisper grown louder—soon. Soon.

Carrie awoke with a start. The dream—what had it been now?—flitted away. It was a good dream, but what was it? Gone. But something told her it wasn't gone for long.

Fatigue weighed her down, but Carrie got out of bed and headed for the shower. She turned the water on cool when normally she liked it scorching hot. She hoped the cool would revitalize her, help her be strong enough to finish that cake. Last year had been a dinosaur, the year before a volcano with red-frosting lava; the year before that was an orange Elmo face. Carrie's crafts might be failures, but she could make an acceptable cake. Eddie always loved them.

Jason was sitting on the edge of the sunken tub after she got out. "You have to stop worrying about it."

Carrie sat in her thick robe beside him. "Worrying about what?"

"The party."

She sighed, her head falling to rest on his shoulder. "For the past week, I've worried about being well enough for this party. I want it to be a good one for him."

"But you're in pain; it's all over your face. Also noticed you didn't take the painkiller as prescribed."

"I'll sleep half the day away."

"Exactly. Eddie will understand."

"No, he won't. He'll try, and he'll be brave, but he won't understand. Jason, this is the only mom-thing I'm good at. I haven't been a great homemaker, don't make the best meals; I'm always behind on laundry. I know all about my failures. This wasn't one of them." *Until now,* she thought. "I need to know that you won't assume things about Eddie. Ask him. Find out. He is such a different child than you were."

"He's more like you."

She smiled. It was true. "And you know me. You pay attention and don't just assume things I'll like or dislike. Do that for Eddie. I want to know you'll be doing that for him when I'm not here to remind you."

Jason wiped his face with the back of his hands. "Okay. I'll do that for you."

"Do it for him."

Carrie again leaned her head on his shoulder. A jolt of pain shot through her hip, causing her to bite her lip hard. She was losing this fight. But what mattered today was that she give her son the last birthday party she'd ever attend.

PULLING IN FRONT of their house already crowded with other cars, Graham put the Chevy Malibu into park and stared at the place. The fog had burned off early that morning, and now a warm sun shone on the tile roof and perfectly landscaped yard. A heaviness came over him that wouldn't subside. Along with the aching knowledge he'd soon lose Carrie after finding her again, Graham felt what awaited this boy who today celebrated his eighth birthday. Now the weight of a past had caught up with him too. What did he do now?

He knew one thing and hoped to tell Carrie today. Hoped it would give her some peace, and also redeem himself a little after what he'd done to her.

Grabbing his gift with mangled wrapping paper, he headed toward the door. Jason opened it with an already tired expression on his face.

"You made it," he said, surprising Graham with a hug and slap on the back.

"Yep, and you're surviving this mayhem?" Graham asked as a girl with a party hat scurried by.

"Do I have to answer that?"

"Is the birthday boy around?"

"Backyard, amid utter chaos and loving every minute of it."

Graham walked through, passing parents and noticing Lauren talking with some people. He opened the French doors and felt more comfortable with the craziness of children playing some kind of game.

As Eddie ran by, Graham waved him over.

"You're here! Everybody, this is my friend Graham," Eddie shouted to his friends and the other adults on patio chairs. A few waved back, but most of the kids ran on by.

"Happy birthday, little man," Graham said, handing over the gift.

"Can I open it now?"

"Sure."

"Cool!" He knelt on the lawn and ripped the paper apart. "No way! I love it!"

Graham smiled as Eddie held up the ship-in-the-bottle, turning it over and staring inside. He'd marveled in much the same way when his father had given it to him.

"For the future sailor."

"Thanks so much." He wrapped his arms around Graham's legs.

A sudden authoritative voice interrupted. "Eddie, it's not time for gifts yet."

Graham turned to face the intimidating Grandma Stella. "My fault. Sorry, I forgot about party protocol; it's been so long since I've been to one. I told him to open it."

"Okay, then," Grandma Stella said, still frowning slightly. Then her sense of hospitality kicked in, "Come choose either soda or tropical punch. We also have several kinds of pizza."

Following her toward the patio, Graham saw Eddie showing his friends his gift and telling them to be very careful with it. Grandma Stella handed him a plate at the table and pointed out the ice chest. Never one to turn down food he hadn't cooked, Graham took three pieces of pizza and grabbed a Cherry Coke before looking for a place to sit. Lauren had joined the outside festivities and was watching him. He wandered toward her.

"So where's the harassment for me being here?" he asked.

"I thought you'd left," Lauren said with a trace of sarcasm.

"My boat broke."

"Figures."

"Yeah, I can't be noble enough to stay, or selfless enough to go. So I'll say that my boat broke. It's really a lie."

"I know. You're just afraid I'll get that FedEx box before you do." She smiled slightly. Graham noticed she appeared exhausted— the feeling seemed to be going around.

"Perhaps a peace treaty? At least for today," he said, sticking out his hand while balancing the plate of pizza, his soda stuck into the crook of his arm.

Her hesitation was long, but she finally reached out and said, "Truce."

"Where is Carrie?" Graham asked, worried at how Lauren would interpret his question. But he wanted to talk to her.

"Back in bed. I was with her for about an hour. She's upset that she can't handle too much of this. After the party, they're taking Eddie to dinner, so I told her to get some sleep."

They watched as Grandma Stella rounded up the children to play pin-the-tail-on-the-donkey. Eddie carefully took his new gift into the house.

"So, no husband and kids running around for you?" Graham asked, looking for something other than Carrie's deterioration to discuss.

"Nope," she said in a crisp tone.

So he'd picked exactly the wrong thing to ask, and the awkward silence between them was worse.

"What do you do for a living?"

"Insurance."

"Ah," he said, nodding his head as if that told everything. He had no idea what to ask next. "No prospects for a nice girl like you?"

Lauren frowned, and Graham felt a strange kinship to this woman who never had liked him. Her best friend was leaving her, and considering the years between Italy and now, he couldn't imagine what such a friendship would be like. Let alone how hard it would be to lose such a thing. A strange protectiveness rose in him, nearly like a brother would feel for a stubborn sister. A sister. Over the years, Graham imagined having a little sister to play with and protect. She'd annoy him with her girlie things, but secretly he'd like playing Barbies and baby dolls despite his protests to the contrary. It looked fun setting up those little rooms of Barbie stuff. His little sister would brag about him to her friends and look up to him as if he were a superhero. Even as an adult, there came a strange loss for the sibling he'd nearly had. In the strangest moments it would come, a missing of something, as if he'd misplaced something of great value without memory of how to reclaim it.

He set the plate of pizza beside him and rubbed his chin. "There has to be someone of interest."

"Well, a guy who lives down my street. But, I don't know." Lauren stared out at the kids playing their game. "Maybe. What about you?"

He nearly smiled at the way she turned the conversation his way. She was probably good at that, keeping people at a distance. "I've been mostly a drifter in the last few years." Graham glanced at her. "Guess some things have stayed the same. You and I are still polar opposites with Carrie in the center."

Lauren smiled slightly. "After the past week I've had, maybe we'll gain something for all the differences between us."

Italy. Graham wondered what it had been like for Lauren, returning. Had the village changed? What memories would be there for her compared to his own? He thought about asking, but wasn't sure he wanted to know, and the images were already surfacing painfully. Having Lauren beside him, after just arriving home, was the undeniable proof that the village with its memories did in fact exist. He'd sought so long to push it away as mere memory.

Through the open French doors, Graham heard the doorbell ring. He watched Jason come from the kitchen and open the front door. It was a FedEx man.

"I think my package arrived." Graham set his drink and plate of uneaten pizza on the table. Lauren followed him inside. Everyone else seemed consumed by the activities as Jason turned to find Graham.

"It's for you. Delivery from . . . Ireland?" His expression questioned him.

"Thanks," was all he said. Graham wanted to take the package and go, but Lauren was there and surely wanted to see the contents. "Where should I open it?" he asked Lauren.

He followed her into a room that looked like a den. The party had helped with his discomfort at again being in Carrie and Jason's house, but now going into a quiet room, the reminders returned as he saw a family portrait on the shelf and thought of Carrie so close by, yet alone and upset.

"Want me to open it?" Lauren asked, pulling his attention back.

"No, but thanks," he said drily. The cardboard tab opened the top of the white FedEx box. Inside, Graham found a card and a thick manila envelope.

The card was from Aunt Fiona.

Dear Graham,

Manny left this in my care many years ago. He told me if you asked, to give it to you, but only if you asked. I never opened it, but hope it will help you.

This is a hard place to live, and it has many sad memories. But it is where I am to be. Someday come visit your aunt and cousins.

My love and wish for blessings,
Aunt Fiona

Graham noticed she didn't mention him visiting Uncle Fergus, only her and the cousins. Her words seemed an explanation of sorts. Perhaps Aunt Fiona was neither the clueless wife nor the disguised accomplice. She too could be pulled into a web without a foreseeable escape.

The manila envelope bore no name or other words distinguishing it as important. He opened the clasp and poured out the two separate contents. One set of papers wrapped in a rubber band had the name Lauren on the front. Graham handed it to her.

"I'll give this to Carrie."

"No, they're for you. Think before you open it; you might not want to do so here. But Carrie put these papers inside the box."

"Then why give them to me?"

"Because they're for you."

"For me? But I thought it was something important to Carrie. Like a family heirloom or something like that."

"It's something important to Carrie. You're important to her. She found this information over that summer, before you arrived in Europe. But then, you told her you never wanted to know. She put it in the box, thinking in a year, when we recovered it, maybe you'd be ready. Well, you know what happened after that."

"What is it?"

"Carrie just told me at the hospital. Lauren, it's your past."

Lauren stared at him, then at the papers. He feared what this might unleash. But the past and its secrets were unraveling so quickly, there was nothing to do but watch and see how it turned out. Picking up the other envelope and the card, Graham said, "I gotta run."

"You aren't going to share yours?"

"I think I'll want to be alone for this. You will too."

As he left the den, Graham spotted Eddie carrying a piece of cake down the hall, his steps silent and exaggerated. Carefully, he set the cake in front of a bedroom door, then turned to run away when he spotted Graham.

"For my mom, when she wakes up."

A sick knot formed in Graham's stomach. This was the boy's

last birthday with his mother. "Hey, happy birthday. Maybe you can come out to the boat. I might be leaving pretty soon, so I'll see if maybe you can visit in the next few days."

"Okie dokie, artichokie."

BACK AT THE docks, Graham closed the doors, feeling anxious about the contents he now possessed. The padded manila envelope rested on the galley table, reminding him of a bomb like the one that had changed his life.

Inside, he found a short letter written on white stationery.

G. I took this to do what you couldn't. After returning to Ireland, I realized some fights are ours and ours alone. This is yours. I will have my own, but not this one. However, if you someday choose to stand up and do what should be done, I have now included other evidence to assist. Affectionately yours, M

Among the papers, Graham picked up the recognizable object. He'd wrapped it in plastic that had aged yellow and begun to disintegrate. It took time to unwrap. He needed a knife to cut it away. Fourteen years ago he'd bound it, wishing to keep it from destruction even though he didn't intend to return for it. How poignant. How like him. His life was all about keeping secrets alive, living with their pain, holding them close. And yet, he didn't want to face those secrets, didn't want them shown in the light. Yes, it was always about what he hadn't done. The promises he hadn't kept, and the dark secrets he held like a knife to jab his own chest.

From the bound plastic, the cassette tape and cover emerged. At eight years of age, he'd written clearly over the tape cover the sure warning. DO NOT TOUCH. DO NOT LISTEN. DANGER!

So here it was. He wondered if the recording had been preserved. Before listening, Graham started sifting through the papers and other tapes Manny had included. One paper appeared to be a receipt for bomb-making materials. The receipt included his uncle's name.

Then Graham fully understood. Manny had gathered enough evidence to convict Uncle Fergus of the pub bombing. Perhaps he'd planned to take this to the Irish police, or he might have gathered it instead for Graham, giving him the choice between complacency or justice for the murder of his parents. The cause that was Manny's own to stand against had cost Manny his life. Now Manny was gone. Graham didn't want to be the hero. And yet, wasn't this, at last, his first glimpse of redeeming his decades of cowardice?

Part of him wanted to run from it, take the whole package up on deck and toss it overboard. He knew what he needed to do. But he wanted no part of it.

Somehow, Graham knew. This had the feel of God all over it.

EDDIE'S ROOM OVERFLOWED with his new toys from the party: a monster truck, a board game called Clue, boxing gloves, a bow and arrow—all kinds of things. He set them in place around his room. The ship-in-the-bottle rested on his bedside table. Eddie had spent a long time staring inside at the intricate design of the ship, wondering how they'd fit it inside that small opening.

Now he sat on his bed with a sigh. He was eight years old now. His birthday was over for a whole year. The house was quiet, everybody gone and his parents probably asleep. Mom had missed a lot of his party, but she tried hard. And even though she couldn't go out to dinner, it was fun having a take-out Chinese picnic on the living room floor.

He was supposed to be going to bed, but he wasn't tired. He went to the new small TV with a VCR inside of it that Grandpa had bought him, though Grandma Stella was mad—that's why they were divorced, he thought. He popped in a video that had a cool monster even if the special effects for the old movie weren't the best. He still liked it. Grandpa said maybe he'd be like Hitchcock some-day, so he should watch old movies like *Creature from the Black Lagoon* and *The Thing.*

As he lay in bed to watch the show, his eyes began to feel sticky, and he yawned twice in a row. Eddie closed his eyes and pictured the defined outline of his blue dinosaur. Where was his blue dinosaur? Eddie sat up in bed, recalling that he'd been play-ing with it in the waiting room a few days earlier. His mom had given him that little plastic dinosaur. He hopped from bed and started searching his room. What if he'd left it there? What if right now it was in the dark alone? What if someone took it, and he never saw it again?

"Dad!" He called and called as he continued looking; it seemed to take so long before he heard footsteps.

"Eddie, you aren't supposed to be up." His dad looked like he'd been sleeping.

"My dinosaur. I left it at the hospital."

His dad didn't seem to understand the urgency at all. He yawned and turned off his bedroom light. "Eddie, go to sleep. It's been a very busy day."

"But my dinosaur."

"It'll be fine. We'll get it tomorrow."

"What if it's gone?"

"Then I'll buy you a new one, a better one."

"I don't want another one. I want that one." He could picture it perfectly, and Mom would be very sad if he lost it.

"Get back in bed; go to sleep. It's just a little plastic toy. Look at all your new stuff, Eddie, don't be ungrateful."

"Please, Dad, please. He's probably scared without me."

"I'll call the nurses' station and see if they can find it." His dad yawned again. "Just remind me in the morning."

Tears ran down his face; he licked his upper lip, tasting salt. Dad never did things that were really important to him.

He'd go find his dinosaur himself.

CARRIE AWOKE WITH a jolt. Had it been another dream? Yes, perhaps. They were there so regularly now.

As she turned over, she saw Jason asleep beside her. The chaos of parties didn't abide with his nature. Her mouth was dry and cottony. Her eyes ached, as did her entire body, but what was new about that? Sliding from bed, she moved her feet along the hardwood floor until they found her slippers.

In the kitchen, Carrie passed an overflowing black trash bag with cake plates and pizza remnants and wrapping paper. Bits of tape and ribbon, twist ties, and cardboard from opened gifts—the silent, messy house remarked on the activity of the day. And she had missed most of it. Inside the refrigerator, she spotted the remnants of Eddie's blue ocean cake with the plastic boat now missing. At least she'd had the strength to decorate it. How poignant that her last cake for him would be the sea—she hadn't thought of that earlier.

After a glass of water and another round of meds, she crept toward the cracked door of Eddie's room.

"Good night, Eddie. Happy birthday." A sob caught like fire in her chest. *This is the last time, the last year.* She tried to keep eternity in sight, to remember that the days here would be gone quickly, while eternity never ended.

Peering inside for just a glimpse at that sleeping face, she noticed something wrong. "Eddie?"

NOT EVEN HER exhaustion from jet lag and a whirlwind trip to Italy would bring the sleep she desired. Lauren was awake. Her mind found no rest.

On the small table, the papers were spread out like a testament to the past.

The records were in Italian. But it was obvious. Birth records. Adoption papers. The name of her birth parents visible before her eyes.

Lauren didn't know whether to be furious or thankful. Carrie had found these papers fourteen years earlier. The many instances of Carrie asking about finding her birth parents returned to her both before and after that summer in Italy. When they were children, Carrie would make up fantastic stories about Lauren's parents being spies, or that she was kidnapped from a royal family, or that an inheritance awaited her if only they could find her. As they matured, the ideas became more realistic. "You might have a whole family you're missing out on. Your birth parents might be trying to find you. They might miss you terribly."

Carrie didn't understand that for Lauren, the not knowing was easier than discovering some horrible truth. That nobody wanted her. That nobody missed her. That she was a regret they hoped didn't return. As many hopeful and idealistic ideas as Carrie conjured, Lauren considered the worst.

Now, she had the names. That's all she had—simply names.

Lauren stared at them in wonder. Her parents were these names. They were real. As a little girl, she'd wondered who they were until a neighbor heard she was adopted. Mr. Bale would look over the fence when she played and would regularly borrow tools from her grandfather. Lauren always feared him, hated his terrible breath and staring eyes. He'd laughed and said, "You don't know who your parents are? Maybe I'm your daddy, then. Maybe you should come live with me 'cause I'm really your daddy."

Lauren had never told anyone about Mr. Bale's comments, but she never again sought to know who her parents were. What if they were people like Mr. Bale?

Now she had names. Nothing else but names. If she deciphered the Italian words, there might be more. But not much. Now it was up to her to decide what to do with the names. And she didn't feel that old fear. There was too much design. This wasn't the end of a quest, but the beginning. *God, are You really doing this? Is it really this clear? What's wrong with my safe little life?*

God wanted her trust, not just her devotion, she realized. Trust and faith—it was walking blindly sometimes and believing in the One who held your hand.

The phone ringing made her jump. Carrie's number on caller ID; Lauren glanced at the clock, fearing it would be a Jason late-night call. Those were never good.

But it was Carrie's voice, strained and afraid. "Eddie is missing. It looks like he ran away or is trying to find his toy at the hospital."

"I'll be right there."

THE SHIVER CRAWLED from his neck down his spine. Smoke blew from his mouth, and it wasn't funny now seeing how far he could blow his breath. Now it was just cold. The hospital didn't seem all that far on the many times they'd driven there. Maybe he'd turned the wrong way. He stood on a street corner, turning down one way, then the next, then the next. He pulled the ties on his hood even tighter, then inched his hands into the sleeves of his jacket before shoving them into his pockets.

Whenever a car came, he ran for cover. He'd been mad at his dad, terribly mad. Each car might be him, out searching the roads, sorry for not listening to him. But his dad didn't come. How could he not care about his blue dinosaur? His mom had given it to him. No one thought it special except the two of them. Just a plastic little toy. But she'd said it would be their special friend whenever she was sick. Sometimes he had left it with her for the night when she was especially sick. Now it was gone.

None of the cars were familiar. And now Eddie wasn't so mad and hoped to see his dad come driving up. He spotted a telephone on a pole ahead and hurried toward it. But when he picked up the receiver, he heard no sound, and then realized the cord was cut in half.

Then a sign caught his eye. He had to sound out a few of the words, then knew what it said. Eddie put his hands in his pocket. Now he knew where to go.

GRAHAM AWOKE TO his cell phone ringing.

"We can't find Eddie. Have you seen him?"

"Who is this?" he said groggily.

"Lauren." Her voice sounded impatient, which annoyed him.

"What do you mean, you can't find him? It was just his birthday party." Graham saw that it was nearly 1:00 a.m.

"He left a note. When did you last see him?"

"At the party, remember?"

"Did you say something to him?"

Graham sat up in bed, causing Salt to meow from the jolt of covers moving. What was she doing in bed with him? "What do you mean by that? I told him good-bye."

"Did you tell him you were leaving town, or anything like that? Something upsetting?"

"Lauren, I have nothing to do with this."

"Well, the note said he had something important to do, but Jason thinks he went to look for one of his toys."

"Just tell me everything instead of this cryptic message. Where are you?"

"At Carrie's."

"Where is Jason?"

"Driving around the neighborhood, and he went to the hospital too. I'm waiting for the police to show up."

"Should I come over?" He wanted to, but this was a family thing.

"Yeah, maybe. Carrie's not doing so good."

GRAHAM WAS GRATEFUL for Cap Charlie's insistence that he use his car while in Harper's Bay. Peeling out from the harbor, he tried to imagine what could've upset Eddie in such a way that he'd leave. But Graham knew. The boy was losing his mother in slow, awkward steps.

The front door was open a crack when he arrived. Lauren called him toward Carrie's bedroom. They were in the master bathroom. Carrie sat on the tile floor, her back against the cabinet; she'd been crying and looked so pale he thought of calling for an ambulance.

"I can't get her up," Lauren said.

Carrie looked up at him, her dark eyes the same deep pools he'd never forgotten. "If something happens to him . . . Graham. Please help us find him."

He bent down and lifted her from the cold tile floor.

"I want to go look for him," she said, her head resting against his chest.

Graham carried her down the hall despite Lauren's instructions to put her in bed. "We'll set you up in the living room. Get you warm so you can be helpful, okay?"

"Okay," she said, her voice weak and childlike. He set her in the overstuffed chair, pulling the ottoman beneath her bare feet. Her ankles looked so thin, but seeing her feet sparked the memory of walking barefoot on the beach in Italy. Lauren draped a thick blanket over her and tucked it in around the edges of her body.

Kneeling in front of her, Graham took her hands. He rubbed his finger over the scar on her left hand. "Now listen, it's going to be fine. I know it."

"How do you know it?"

"Because I do. So don't worry; don't do it."

She raised her eyes to his in a look that surprised him. She remembered. He did too, those same words he'd spoken just a day before he deserted her. *Don't worry; don't do it.*

"This is a promise I'll keep," he whispered.

A tear fell down her cheek. "Jason is a wreck—he thinks it's his fault. We just talked about him listening to Eddie more, you know, really hearing what he's saying to him. And then Jason ignored him tonight. He called from the hospital where he thought Eddie would've gone. Eddie wasn't there."

Graham's mind was going through differing scenarios. But he

didn't know Eddie all that well. And yet, a part of him did. Part of him knew the interior of this boy very well. "Let's make a deal. We'll find Eddie, and I'll take the box back to Italy and whatever it is you want to put inside for him. But you must calm down, do that praying I know you're good at doing. Is that a deal?"

She wiped her cheek and tried a brave smile. "Yes. Deal."

Then a thought. "I just might know where he is."

GRAHAM RACED DOWN the dock, trying not to make too much noise. He stepped over the railing, feeling the slight rock of the sailboat. Down in the hold a light shone in the galley, and he tried remembering if he'd left it on in his hurry to leave. But Eddie wasn't here.

Then he noticed Salt facing away from him, looking toward his cabin. The cabin curtain was pulled shut. He never closed it unless he was inside.

"Salt, I think I have another stowaway on my boat."

He stepped over her and pulled back the curtain. Eddie stared up at him, a worried expression on his face.

"Hi," he said sheepishly. The red sweatshirt hood covered his head, making him appear even younger.

"That was quite a long walk for you," he said. "Come on out here to the galley."

Eddie followed him and sat on the bench seat across from him.

"Don't tell anyone I'm here."

"I have to."

"Promise you won't. Please!"

"I can't promise that. Your mom and dad are worried sick, Lauren too. Your dad is out looking for you right now."

"So?" he said with a shrug of his shoulders.

Graham didn't want Carrie worrying a minute longer than necessary. "Are you running away, then?"

"I decided to go with you."

"With me?"

"I just want to go somewhere far away."

"Where do you want to go?"

"How about the Great Pyramids?"

"That's a bit far by boat."

"Somewhere then."

Graham smiled at the boy's determination. "How about the Kokomo?"

"That sounds good, wherever it is."

"The Caribbean. It'll take some tough sailing. You'll be gone a long time."

"That's okay."

Graham rose from the bench and crouched before Eddie until they were at equal height. "Eddie, I know you're really sad about your mom. It doesn't make sense. It's not fair that other kids get to keep their parents and you don't."

Eddie only stared at him, but his eyes became rimmed with red. "I don't want her to die."

Graham put his hand on the small shoulder. "I know you don't. None of us do. And you're especially losing out, 'cause I bet she's the best mom in the world."

Eddie cried then; he seemed to just crumble into Graham. At first it was awkward, trying to console someone, trying to be okay with the emotion it required of him.

"You won't have to be brave all the time. No one expects you to do that. And you'll have us here for you, and your mom's love won't leave you even when she's gone. Just don't run away anymore, okay?"

And as he said it, Graham heard his own words as if they were being spoken to him as well. *Don't run away anymore.*

"Okay," was the answer from both of them. Graham knew his time of running was finally finished.

19

The morning was barely a gray softness through the open curtains. Jason lay facing her. Their bare feet entwined; toes moved around the others. He brushed a strand of hair from her face. "I always wished to keep you for myself. And yet, you've never really been mine."

"We don't ever fully belong to one another."

Jason kept his hand on her cheek. "It's a privilege to know each other and have the time we do have. I think it's all some elaborate glimpse of what's to come."

"Lauren has the perfect quote about it. There was one she told me not long ago, a C. S. Lewis quote, from *The Last Battle*. About this only being the prologue of the real life waiting to begin." Carrie's voice was only a whisper. "Make a good prologue for you and Eddie while I'm waiting for you."

Jason nodded. "I'm thankful for every day I've had with you." Carrie watched the tears rise like a tide along the rims of his eyes. They spilled over as he spoke.

She touched his chin. "I've never loved you more than at this moment. And I will love you always."

Their door creaked open.

"Mom, I couldn't sleep." Eddie stood in the doorway, rubbing his eyes.

"Come here," she said, lifting the covers slightly. She backed close to Jason, feeling his body fold around her as Eddie jumped into bed on the other side of her. Her eyes closed, and she breathed in the scent of Eddie's hair. And with a flash of remembrance, Carrie could recall all the dreams of the silver sea. They rolled over one another, over and over until she was again standing there. The smooth stones beneath her feet, the coolness on her face, the living waters drawing her forward. That Person across the waves she couldn't quite see yet.

It wouldn't be today. But soon. This she knew.

Right now, between the two of them, Carrie found a moment like so few moments in her life. One of perfection. A single solitary moment. This was the perfect cocoon in which to transform and change. She'd gather her wings, dive into the water that might really be a sky, and effortlessly swim away.

TURN ONWARD

Eternity: infinite or endless time.

20

Three Months Later

Lauren did everything she'd promised Carrie she wouldn't do. After the expected duties as best friend of the deceased, Lauren closed the blinds in her house and left the phone to the answering machine. She used up her last vacation days and sick days, and she didn't return any phone calls, hoping the world would just leave her alone.

People needed her; she knew this. Eddie might be a lost soul by now. Jason could be a wreck. Her grandfather might be wandering the streets, looking for his missing something. Lauren did care, and something in her kept saying to get up and do something. But a greater something kept her from moving. It was all she could do in a day to feed her fish and get something in her own stomach. Her hair was a grease ball, her funeral clothes wrinkled, the air thick and musty from inactivity.

As another day passed, and then another, Lauren knew it couldn't last forever. But then another day passed, and she still wore her black funeral clothing.

Lying in bed, staring at the ceiling, Lauren thought how she'd held a secret hope God would spare her friend. He could do it. It

291

was childish, unreasonable, impractical. Everyone died. But why Carrie, so young? And when they all needed her most?

The pastor's words from the funeral and all those sayings said at such a time followed her through the days like mischievous nymphs.

To be absent in the body is to be present with the Lord.

She'll want to meet you again someday, if you have a personal relationship with God. Wouldn't today be the perfect day?

She's in a better place.

There will be no more sorrow, and no more pain . . .

She'd heard it before and believed them even. And yet, it didn't help. Death had won.

"Give her back, God. Can't we have her back?"

On one of the days a week after the funeral, Lauren heard someone knock on the door. She peeked carefully through the blinds, having ignored several friends and church members already. But this time she recognized the guy with the grandma—Bruce. He kept knocking, even leaned back against the wall and waited, then knocked again.

"Is everything okay?" she asked, flinging open the door.

"I found these on your porch. Didn't want them to die like the others."

Lauren stared at the flowers in Bruce's hand, then at the two other bundles by her door.

"Your grandfather asked me to check on you."

"Grandpa's checking on *me* now?" Lauren couldn't help chuckling, then she wondered in horror at how she must look. Backing away from the door, she stuttered, "Well . . . thank you . . . For the flowers too. Tell Grandpa I'll call him tomorrow."

"He found it," Bruce said.

She opened the door a crack, trying to smooth her hair. "What did you say?"

"Your grandpa. You know how he kept looking for something?"

"Yes?"

"Well, he found it."

Lauren was stunned. "What was it?"

"Some army jacket that had fallen in the back of a closet."

"An army jacket?"

"Guess inside one of the pockets was a letter from your grandmother. He couldn't rest until he found it. He wanted to tell my grandmother about her, before their relationship moved to the next level."

"Relationship moved to the next level?"

"Those were his words, not mine." Bruce chuckled. "Maybe I could stop by tomorrow?"

"Well, I actually have something . . ." Lauren looked down at her bare feet and wrinkled black dress; no excuse came to mind.

"I'll just stop by and see if you have any flowers left on the porch again. If so, I'll knock, maybe invite you out to coffee."

Lauren smiled. "Okay, maybe."

Bruce smiled back. "You know, sometimes the things we're looking for are pretty close by. Here are your flowers."

A BUZZER SOUNDED, and then the iron gate creaked open. Graham followed the Belfast jailer to the visitation window. Uncle Fergus was already seated at a table.

Nearly twenty-five years had passed since he'd last seen his uncle. Seeing Uncle Fergus in a jail uniform, sitting in a short yellow chair, Graham was surprised at how much less intimidating he appeared. He'd lost most of his hair, and what remained had turned gray. His face showed the years of working in the sun, and his massive size didn't seem so massive now that Graham was over six feet tall himself.

"If it ain't the traitor nephew come to visit," Uncle Fergus said, staring up at him with those same piercing eyes. His hands were handcuffed beneath the table.

Graham pulled the chair up and sat down. An anxious feeling spread through him. He'd thought of this moment for months, really for years, and hoped he could get through it. The prayers from the past could help him now, he hoped. Was anyone praying for him now? His parents were gone, and so was Carrie. But even the knowledge of what they'd given filled Graham with renewed strength.

Setting his hands on the table, Graham then looked deep into his uncle's eyes. "I've come to tell you that I forgive you."

Uncle Fergus laughed uproariously. "Why would ya be telling me that now?"

"Because I finally do."

"So forgive me, my lad, but why this whole trial and testifying. Forgiveness is easy when it's backed by revenge, eh?"

Graham leaned closer, staring Uncle Fergus right in those cold blue eyes. "Not revenge, Uncle. Justice. If you had done this to me alone, it would be different. But you've stolen many lives. And not just in that pub with my father and mother. But Johnjack Kerry. And surely others. Justice for them is why I have to do this. For the baby sister I never got to see, and also for Manny."

There was barely a twitch in Uncle Fergus's expression at the mention of his son's name. Graham felt no fear now, only pity for Uncle Fergus.

"For what you did to me, I forgive you."

"I don't want nothing from you. Not yer forgiveness, not yer pity, nothing."

"Good-bye, Uncle Fergus."

Graham walked from the Belfast jail into a cold Irish day. He had a trial to testify in and would be in Ireland for at least a few months, maybe longer. Graham was under police protection, which drove him crazy, but he could do this. After the burden he'd carried since eight years of age, this was nothing. He would do this.

An hour later, with two officers joining him, Graham carried flowers to his father's grave. It was the first time he'd seen it. And now, he could come without shame.

As he stood there, Graham thought of another boy, across the sea and a continent, who was grieving the loss of his mother. Graham grieved for her too. He'd call him, and send another post-card—there'd been a great exhibit at the Ulster Museum. Maybe when he flew back for a visit, Graham would even share a few parts of the letters Carrie had written to him so many years ago. Or maybe he'd wait. Wait till the boy was older and could under-stand more.

Graham knew something he wanted to tell Eddie. It was a dream he'd had just the night before. He was drifting in his boat at night. The water was calm with diamonds of light moving like the Milky Way over the sea. Then he saw someone out there. Carrie. She was swimming on the starboard side, cutting right through the diamond waters, waving and smiling. It reminded him of a night in Italy. Then she swam to the front of the boat. She called to him, "Follow me, Graham, I'll show you how to get there."

And then he woke up, in Ireland, ready to face Uncle Fergus.

Graham would tell this to Eddie—the boy would believe that it was more than a dream, just as Graham did. For now, Graham not only hoped, but believed, he'd see her again. He'd face what this life was about and do his best to find the purpose assigned him. And someday, he'd follow Carrie across the silver sea.

One Year Later

It was a light and dark day, or so Mom always called such days of billowing dark clouds racing across the deep blue sky. He'd been playing his Game Cube where he'd taken Sonic to the highest level he'd ever reached after beating out the evil Shadow. Auntie Lauren had showed up and called him a video game junkie, but she said it jokingly, like she always did.

"I'm a gamer," he corrected with a smile.

"Kids these days spend too much time playing video games."

"That sounds like something Grandma Stella would say." Eddie laughed at that funny look on Auntie Lauren's face.

"Watch it, fella. I'll whack you with my cane. But you should be outside more, climbing trees, playing hide-'n'-seek, stuff like that."

"It's not much fun playing hide-'n'-seek by myself."

"You can't only have virtual friends."

"I have some real friends too, but they couldn't play today. And let me guess: your mom used to say you watched too much TV as a kid."

"I didn't have a mom or a dad growing up. I had grandparents who were wonderful, though they weren't my blood relatives."

"Huh?" Eddie didn't know this. The grown-ups kept surprising him like this, and just when he thought he knew them. "That's terrible."

Auntie Lauren looked surprised, and he felt sort of bad for saying it. "In a way, but it could've been worse. My grandparents were really great as parents. And I'm going to meet my birth mother in just a few months."

"Where at?"

"She's coming to Harper's Bay. We've been e-mailing for a while now. Maybe you can meet her too."

"Sure," he said. "Will Bruce be there?" Eddie liked Auntie Lauren's boyfriend. Bruce's dog and Pepper were best friends too.

"Probably. Now come outside with me." Auntie Lauren practically dragged him away.

It was nice outside, even if a little cold. The lawn was a bit brittle from a recent freeze. Eddie wrapped himself a little tighter within his coat.

"I heard you got another letter from Graham," she said.

"Yeah, he's funny. He sent a picture of Salt wearing a pirate patch. He said he'd take me sailing with Dad when he gets back."

Eddie noticed Auntie Lauren seemed more relaxed than she used to be. For a while he didn't see her after Mom died. He didn't really care. Well, maybe a little.

"Are you still drawing a lot?"

"Sometimes. Bobby P. says my cartoons are kid's stuff."

"That Bobby P. And even though you're nine now, you're never too old for kid's stuff. That's what your mom would say."

Eddie liked it when people mentioned his mom. Most people didn't, and his friends thought it was scary that his mother was dead, though Bobby P. didn't call him a mama's boy anymore. It was nice when people didn't act like she'd never lived. He thought of her all the time.

Auntie Lauren surprised him by lying on the grass. "Come on, lie here beside me. Let's look for cloud things."

She looked funny in her work clothes, lying there with her hair all fanned out on the dry grass. But he jumped down beside her and started searching the clouds overhead.

"Hey, I see Homer Simpson, right there. See him?" he asked, surprised to find one so quickly.

"What are you doing watching that show?"

"I've only seen the commercials," he said with a mischievous grin.

"Yeah, I bet. Hey, it's Eeyore; I always see him in the clouds."

"Where?"

"Right behind Homer."

"That big puffy one? That looks more like my teacher, Mr. Dominguez."

"Edward, that isn't nice."

"It's true," he said, which made them both start laughing.

A few moments later, Auntie Lauren said, "I miss your mom."

He turned to his side as she still gazed toward the sky. No one said that to him except sometimes his dad. A tear rolled down Auntie Lauren's face and fell into the grass. She didn't even try to hide it from him. Most everyone didn't want to make him sad; at least that's what Dad had said. But Eddie was still sad sometimes, well, a lot of the time. And why would people worry about reminding him of the very thing he thought so often? He still sometimes thought he heard Mom call his name. Then he'd remember.

"I miss her too," he said.

Auntie Lauren wiped her face dry. "Did you know your mom flew once when we were about your age?"

"She told me that story."

"It's true. I was there."

"You saw her flying?"

"Well, not exactly. I actually didn't believe her for a long time."

He wondered, how high exactly were those clouds? Sonic the Hedgehog could fly that high. Supersonic speed. He imagined it, zipping right through like a knife cutting butter. He'd zip through the air, high above the tallest sequoia redwood trees, diving down along the coastal sands, in and out of the crevasses of the rocky islands. Maybe he'd bring his friend Tanner or Auntie Lauren or Graham or his dad. He could picture his dad, smiling wider than he'd smiled since Mom had died, his little bit of hair whipped back.

"Eddie, if we believe, if we really believe, I know you can fly."

For a moment, he thought about laughing, but then he thought differently. "I think so too. Someday we'll fly all around in heaven with Mom."

"I mean right now." Auntie Lauren was already on her feet, pulling him from the lawn. "Come on. Up, get up."

"What?"

"You're going to fly."

"So what do we do?" He visualized Superman's three-step leap and flight. It wasn't something he pictured accomplishing.

"Well, with your mom, we were running around, jumping. Your mom was concentrating so hard it was funny to me. But she kept trying. That's what you have to do. Maybe I can fly too."

"You're going to fall down in those tall shoes," he said, looking at her feet. Auntie Lauren kicked them off and started running around in her stocking feet. Eddie was trying to believe; he really was. But he kept laughing at Auntie Lauren running around the yard, leaping in the air in not-so-graceful leaps. He'd never seen her that way before, so kidlike. When she tripped and fell, he couldn't help laughing until he fell to the ground beside her.

"You have to stop laughing," she said between snorts and giggles. "You have to believe. You can fly, you can fly, you can fly and all that."

"Okay, I'll try. I can fly, I can fly, I can fly." He was still laughing, but then his legs seemed to take over. He hadn't run hard in a long time. The cold air stung his lungs with a rich freshness that made him run even faster. He jumped, landed, jumped again with arms outstretched. And suddenly, for just a moment longer than should be, Eddie felt the pause, a moment of gravity exposed, a second when he was flying.

And he collapsed onto the lawn.

"Did you see that? Did you see?"

"What?" Auntie Lauren asked. She was sitting on the ground.

"I started to fly," he said, looking to her for confirmation.

"I tried a cartwheel, and it hurt my back."

"I think I really did it." The moment was now a memory. But he was sure, sure that for a moment, just a moment, nothing but air held him.

"I told you. I knew you could do it. You're just like your mom."

He watched her for a moment, not knowing if he believed any of this. But she did, and then he did too.

For a moment, frozen in time, he had flown. He would never doubt that moment after this day, always believing in its truth. Eddie thought he might spend the rest of his life trying to recapture that one instance of flight.

He'd never stop trying.

READING GROUP GUIDE AVAILABLE AT

www.westbowpress.com